BENJAMIN FRANKLIN

Also by Esmond Wright

George Washington and the American Revolution

Fabric of Freedom: 1763–1800

Benjamin Franklin and American Independence

American Profiles

Causes and Consequences of the American Revolution (Editor)

American Themes (Editor)

Benjamin Franklin
A PROFILE

EDITED BY
ESMOND WRIGHT

AMERICAN PROFILES

General Editor: Aïda DiPace Donald

HILL AND **WANG** : NEW YORK

Contents

v

Introduction

To his contemporaries, American and European, Benjamin Franklin was the greatest figure America had yet produced. He was publisher and printer, essayist and author, successful businessman and successful "General," internationally known scientist and philologist, politician and diplomat, Fellow of the Royal Society because of his contributions to the fluid theory of electricity, Doctor of Laws of Oxford and St. Andrews, moralist and sage. Yet in all the parts he played, in a long and active career that ran from Cotton Mather's Boston to Washington's Presidency, he remained very much himself: insatiably curious, always the racy writer with an ear for the forceful phrase, earthy, detached, and free from illusion—even when in the end he became fascinated by the cultivation of the image of himself as a "natural man." "There are three things extremely hard," said Poor Richard, "steel, a diamond and to know thyself."

In his origins, his range, and above all in his success, Franklin seemed to be the living answer to Hector St. John de Crèvecoeur's famous question in 1784, "What then *is* the American, this new man?" David Hume thought Franklin "the first philosopher, and

Originally published in *History Today*, Vol. VI (February 1956), pp. 439–447, and printed here by permission of the editors. Some revisions have been added.

indeed the first great man of letters for whom we are beholden to America." Goethe in his youth was fascinated by Franklin and his *"tiefe Einsicht, freie Übersicht."* Lord Kames described him as "a man who makes a great figure in the learned world: and who would make a greater figure for benevolence and candour, were virtue as much regarded in this declining age as knowledge." Some of his own compatriots bracketed him with Washington.

It was not by any means a unanimous view. Honest and splenetic, John Adams wrote to Benjamin Rush,

> The history of our Revolution will be one continued lie from one end to the other. The essence of the whole will be that Dr. Franklin's electrical rod smote the earth and out sprang General Washington. That Franklin electrified him with his rod, and thenceforward these two conducted all the policy, negotiations, legislatures, and war.

Adams admitted that Franklin's genius was original, sagacious, and inventive, but he could not see where his excellence lay as legislator or politician or negotiator. "From day to day he sat in silence at the Continental Congress," he said, "a great part of his time fast asleep in his chair," and in France he was too self-indulgent to attend regularly to the business of the embassy. The view for long prevailed. Despite Parson Weems's pieties and embroideries—his *Life of Franklin* had "many choice anecdotes and admirable sayings of this great man"—many even in Weems's America accepted Adams's strictures. Cobbett, at the time a bitter Federalist pamphleteer in Philadelphia, could refer to Franklin seven years after his death as "a crafty and lecherous old hypocrite . . . whose very statue seems to gloat on the wenches as they walk the State House yard." Joseph Dennie, the Federalist writer and editor of *The Port Folio,* was equally searing.

> The fact is, that "our Benjamin" was no more distinguished for the *originality* of his conceptions, than for the purity of his life, or the soundness of his religious doctrine. . . . He was the founder of the Grubstreet sect, who have professedly attempted to degrade literature to the level of vulgar capacities. . . . He was one of our first jacobins, the first to lay his head in the lap of French harlotry; and prostrate the

Christianity and honour of his country to the deism and democracies of Paris. Above all he was the author of that pitiful system of Economics, the adoption of which has degraded our national character.

Mark Twain poured scorn on Franklin's "stove, and his military inspirations, his unseemly endeavor to make himself conspicuous when he entered Philadelphia, and his flying his kite and fooling away his time in all sorts of such ways when he ought to have been foraging for soap-fat, or constructing candles." D. H. Lawrence's view of him is well known.

Old Daddy Franklin will tell you. He'll rig him up for you, the pattern American. . . . One can just imagine Socrates and Alcibiades roaring in their cups over Philadelphian Benjamin, and Jesus looking at him a little puzzled, and murmuring: "Aren't you wise in your own conceit, Ben?" Middle-sized, sturdy, snuff-coloured Doctor Franklin, one of the soundest citizens that ever trod or "used venery."

Charles Angoff added a Franklinian touch of acid to the portrait— he was, he said, "a cheap and shabby soul."

. . . Franklin represented the least praiseworthy qualities of the inhabitants of the New World: miserliness, fanatical practicality, and lack of interest in what are usually known as spiritual things. Babbittry was not a new thing in America, but he made a religion of it, and by his tremendous success with it he grafted it upon the American people so securely that the national genius is still suffering from it. He extolled the virtues of honesty, industry, chastity, cleanliness, and temperance— all excellent things. But it never occurred to him that with these alone life is not worth a fool's second thought. Philosophy, poetry, and the arts spring from different sources. . . . Not a word about nobility, not a word about honor, not a word about grandeur of soul, not a word about charity of mind! Carlyle called Franklin the father of all the Yankees. That was a libel against the tribe, for the Yankees have produced Thoreau, Hawthorne, and Emily Dickinson. It would be more accurate to call Franklin the father of all the Kiwanians.

Later biographers have described Franklin in more kindly terms and in a variety of ways—*Franklin, the Apostle of Modern Times,* Father of American Democracy, the Many-Sided Franklin, Socrates at the Printing Press, Father of American Ingenuity, the first high priest of the religion of efficiency, or even *Franklin, the First Civilized American*. For Franklin's success was striking. Born with no advantages, he helped to unite his newly independent country, and to manufacture an alliance with France that greatly contributed to American victory in 1783; he became a lion in the literary world of Paris; and he acted as conciliator-at-large and Founding Father Extraordinary in the debates over the Constitution at Philadelphia in 1787. Yet, despite services almost as great as Washington's, references to him in academic circles in the United States were greeted until recently at least with a denigrating smile and a raised eyebrow. Where then does Franklin's reputation stand today?

Franklin's very versatility is suspect in our own more specialist age. In the eighteenth century it was still possible for a man to take all learning to be his province: easier in America than in Europe, and easier there to earn the reputation, like Jefferson, of being a man of parts. Today this catholic range is discredited; Franklin's scientific experiments, his identification of electricity and lightning, his study of solar heat, of ocean currents, of the causes of storms, his interest in population studies and statistics, are dismissed as the amateur dabblings of a superficial scientist.

There is more abundant cause for the raising of eyebrows. Franklin was born, unsuitably as it proved, in Puritan Boston, the tenth son and fifteenth child of a tallow chandler and soap boiler who had emigrated from Northampton; he was baptized in Boston's Old South Church. Despite this favorable beginning, his youthful character was not all that it might have been. He was apprenticed to an older brother, a printer, but relations were never harmonious; he became as egotistical as he was precocious—as an old man looking back on the past he told his son, "I do not remember when I could not read." He ran away to distant Philadelphia; he embezzled money; he had an illegitimate son, William, born in the same year as the father was attempting a literary work called *The Art of Virtue,* a son of whom he was very fond but who later became, through Bute's influence, Governor of New Jersey and a royalist, and later still, himself the father of an illegitimate son. Franklin never lost his interest in women. If never vain, he was certainly not untouched by flattery, in Philadelphia or France. He remained a racy and roguish figure to the end, and rarely chose to hide his indiscretions. It is not a picture to everyone's taste, and the distaste is increased by Franklin's sententiousness, his proneness to give advice—much sought, especially when, over seventy, he was the most popular man in Paris. La Rochefoucauld's maxim of a century before—"Old men are fond of giving good advice, because they are no longer in a position to set bad examples"—applies all too aptly.

Perhaps what is at the root of this distaste is the difficulty our own century finds in understanding the preoccupation of the eighteenth century with personal success and reputation, and in understanding the eighteenth-century American view of character and behavior. In our own day, living in crowded cities and faced with the menace of routine and mechanical processes, we have put an emphasis on spontaneity, on a man's native gifts for life, on untrammeled self-expression. Eighteenth-century Americans would have regarded this as naïve, for they had no illusions about the need for discipline or about the motives that drove men to seek success and influence. Indeed what the colonial frontier taught was that either you learn to discipline yourself, or you die. To lose patience with the elements in a rough sea off Cape Cod or with Indians on the forest trails of the Alleghenies was to lose your life. America bred political freedom, but in practical matters it bred caution and patience, judgment and discretion, tolerance and finesse, and it was on these qualities that successful careers were built. Americans then strove as much for self-restraint and self-mastery as for self-government. Witness the career of Washington on the one hand and his concern with what he called his "honor"; witness the observations of Paine and Jefferson on the other. However divided on matters of political interpretation they might be, all would have shared a common respect for the qualities of discipline and balance; all recognized in their own natures how their instincts had to be curbed by reason. Reputations were made the hard way by deliberate character-training. Witness again Washington's laborious Rules of Civility, the hundred or more rules by which social success might be achieved. There are obvious parallels here with Boswell and Rousseau and Lord Chesterfield.

When Benjamin Franklin devised Poor Richard and used him as a vehicle of exhortation and advice—and when from time to time he revealed how hard self-control was for himself—his fellows knew what he meant. He was a practical man, writing in his annual periodical, *Poor Richard's Almanac,* for other practical men. Frankly recognized natural instincts should, indeed must, be harnessed if a reputation was to be made and merited. And this, the self-reliance that originated as a frontier gospel, became the key doctrine of American transcendentalism. Franklin's disciple is Emerson, as Carlyle saw; if Emerson rejected Franklin's man because "he savoured of nothing heroic," Poor Richard still lives on, with sanctity added to sanctimoniousness, in the pages of *The Journals.* In the *Almanac* Franklin printed common sense observations and wise saws, culled mainly from Rabelais and Swift and Sterne—and he did not pretend to originality. He made it, in fact, the first great syndicated column in American journalism. He wrote with unerring skill and great charm for the colonial equivalent of the man in the street, in this case the man on the farm and on the frontier. He wrote easily on half a hundred topics—*Dissertation on Liberty and Necessity, Pleasure and Pain, The Way to Wealth, On the Causes and Cure of Smoky Chimneys.* He became a folk philosopher, sharper than Confucius, more ruminative than Dale Carnegie. The middle-class morality that Shaw and D. H. Lawrence pilloried but that is still at the vital roots of American prosperity and is reflected in its industry, its native shrewdness, its frugality, its practicality, can be said to find its first prophet in Benjamin Franklin, though no one would have enjoyed Shaw's criticisms or Lawrence's virility more than Franklin. He confessed with gusto that he practiced the frugality he preached just as long as poverty forced him to—and not a moment longer.

Poor Richard has been regarded by many as the mentor of early American capitalism. His advice is certainly keyed to the two notes: work hard and count your pennies: "The sleeping Fox catches no Poultry"; "Then plough deep, while Sluggards sleep, and you shall have Corn to sell and to keep"; "What maintains one Vice, would bring up two Children";

> Many Estates are spent on the Getting
> Since Women for Tea forsook Spinning and Knitting
> And Men for Punch forsook Hewing and Splitting.

Not that all Poor Richard's moralities were exhortations to enterprise. Some were of an earthier sort: a single man is like the odd half of a pair of scissors; he that takes a wife takes care; keep your eyes wide open before marriage, half shut afterwards; you cannot pluck roses without fear of thorns, nor enjoy a fair wife without danger of horns. But in nothing is Franklin more typical of his century and of his country than in his insistence that self-reliance and hard work are basic to liberty. He believed in free speech, free goods, and free men. He opposed the efforts of all exploiters, whether merchants in England, Scotch factors in America, landowners or priests, to restrain man's natural freedoms. And freedom, he argued, paid. Printers, he said, in his characteristically deflated way,

are educated in the Belief, that when Men differ in Opinion, both sides ought equally to have the advantage of being heard by the Publick; and that when Truth and Error have Fair Play, the former is always an overmatch for the latter: Hence they chearfully serve all contending Writers that pay them well, without regarding on which side they are of the Question in Dispute. . . .

Certainly his *Almanac* sold: ten thousand copies a year before long. "I grew in a little time," he said, "expert at selling." And though he did not mention it, expert at buying. He set up eighteen paper mills, purchased rags for them, and took the paper they made, either using it himself or selling it to other printing houses. As Professor Bridenbaugh has shown in his study *The Colonial Craftsman,* "it is extremely doubtful if any Englishman was as large a paper dealer as Poor Richard in these years." And he quickly realized that one source of the successful salesmanship was his own reputation.

In order to secure my credit and character as a tradesman, I took
care not only to be in *reality* industrious and frugal, but to avoid all
appearances of the contrary. I dressed plain and was seen at no places
of idle diversion. I never went out a fishing or shooting; a book, indeed,
sometimes debauched me from my work, but that was seldom, snug
and gave no scandal. . . . Thus being esteemed an industrious, thriving young man, and paying duly for what I bought . . . I went on
swimmingly.

If this sounds like the wiliness of Mr. Pepys in the language of Mr.
Pooter, it could be paralleled by similar, if less frank, reflections in
the papers of many a contemporary, George Washington included.
In a sense all the Revolutionaries were self-made men, and some of
them in making their reputations made a Revolution. The Yankee
virtues triumphed not at Appomattox but at Yorktown.

It is true that there were contemporaries too who were not attracted by Franklin's sentiments. His views never won much approval in the American South, with its open-handed ways, its code
of the gentleman, its aversion to trade; and they were anathema to
many in Boston. But to Carlyle and many since his day, Ben
Franklin has become "the Father of all the Yankees." To many
even outside the Southern states, Yankee is an opprobrious term, a
badge of trade and a badge of infamy; yet it was these Yankee
values that were transforming the eighteenth-century world. Both
Boston and Virginia, in their different ways, were aristocratic:
names and connections counted. Franklin lived by trade, prospered
by it, and was acclaimed across the world. He was completely and
avowedly bourgeois, happy in the company of men, and women
too, efficient in keeping a contract, adept at conciliation and in the
affairs of towns. Virginian Jefferson was afraid of towns as threats
to the rural democracy he worked for; Franklin, though he presented himself to the French as a backwoodsman, was only at ease
when he was in them. He transformed Philadelphia. To him it owed
the fact that it had a city police, the paved and lighted streets that
were the surprise of Virginians and New Englanders. To him too it
owed the American Philosophical Society and the University of
Pennsylvania and the first circulating library in America. To him

the country—before it had yet been born—owed the efficiency of its postal service, and its first project of a federation. His Junto might be called the first collection of Rotarians in history, "seeking the promotion of our interests in business by more extensive recommendation." Versatile, businesslike, complaisant by disposition, Franklin strikes a modern note, the first of the joiners and boosters and glad-handers. Well might William Green call him the Patron Saint of Labor, in his practice and preaching of diligence, thrift, caution, his faith that good causes could be linked to self-advancement, that sweet reasonableness did not prevent a good conceit of oneself. But this doctrine too is out of favor. Hard work and thrift are no longer held to be unquestioned guarantees of success either in Britain or in America. As *The New York Times* put it as long ago as 1938, "Poor Richard appeals now only to vulgar minds. . . . Why count the pennies when millions of dollars are pouring out from the inexhaustible Federal Horn of Plenty?" It was easier in Franklin's day than ours to make a case for his Industrious Apprentice.

History, then, has not been very sympathetic to his reputation or to his doctrine. Nor has it dealt very kindly with his political services to the American Revolution. It has become very clear that in his days as a colonial agent in London he was working not for the independence of the colonies but for a form of federal union. He disapproved of the Boston Tea Party, and until his return to America in 1775 his journalism was much less influential than that of Sam Adams. He admired England, he enjoyed London society, he deprecated violence. And even his services in France are open to question. If one argues that the French alliance was vital to American success in the Revolution, one must admit Franklin's services: yet French troops, money, arms, and commercial privileges were coming through, thanks to Beaumarchais, in secret but abundantly, long before the treaty was signed. It was perhaps the quick loss of New York that checked French intervention as early as 1776. The signing of the alliance after Saratoga suggests that Vergennes was influenced less by emissaries in Paris than by events in America. And too the picture of the homespun patriot at the bar of the Commons in 1766, and that of the fur-capped philosopher at Versailles, the toast of French society, is one that makes little appeal to an age suspicious of histrionics.

Yet this is to deny his diplomatic services—and they were not confined to his years abroad. If as a colonial agent he worked for compromise, he worked for it all his life. Standing at the bar of the House, he told the Commons in 1766 that "every assembly on the American continent, and every member in every assembly" had denied Parliament's authority to pass the Stamp Act. As Deputy Postmaster General of North America he was himself an example of emerging colonial unity. As plain Ben Franklin, large, broadshouldered, with his big head and square deft hands, self-taught and practical, he was the embodiment of the colonial protest, "the ultimate Whig." In the France of 1776 these qualities were held in still higher regard: to Vergennes he was an instrument of French imperial revenge on Britain, to the Encyclopedists and Physiocrats a natural man from a republican wilderness, to bluestockings a rustic philosopher with civilized tastes, an approving eye for the ladies, and a neat democratic wit. In Paris and in Passy he was surrounded by an admiring court. His French, no more than passable, seemed charming. His portrait appeared on medallions, rings, and snuffboxes. To all, Franklin was a proof of republican simplicity and virtue; he was "the American, this new man." The fur cap was worn to hide his eczema; it was mistaken for a badge of the frontier. Since he was cast in the role of wise and simple philosopher, he played the part. He could be Solon and Silenus, gallant and Gallic, to suit all tastes, and not least his own.

During his years in France he showed an uncanny diplomatic skill. He used the same facility in his last great work at the federal Convention in 1787. In his *Autobiography* he has left a description of diplomatic technique around the conference table from which we can still learn.

I made it a rule to forbear all direct contradiction to the sentiments of others and all positive assertion of my own. I even forbade myself . . . the use of every word or expression in the language that imported a fixed opinion such as "certainly," "undoubtedly," etc.; and I adopted instead of them "I conceive," "I apprehend" or "I imagine" a thing to be so or so, or "It so appears to me at present." When another asserted something that I thought an error, I denied myself the pleasure of contradicting him abruptly and of showing immediately some absurdity in his proposition; and in answering I began by observing that in certain cases or circumstances his opinion would be right, but that in the present case there "appeared" or "seemed to me" some difference, etc. I soon found the advantage of this change. . . .

And if he fought for colonial rights and understanding in London in 1766, he was still fighting for tolerance and the other point of view in 1787. The speech that James Wilson delivered for him on the last day of the Convention—he was too old and too infirm to stand—was the product of long experience and expressed that reasonableness that the twentieth century as well as the eighteenth might regard as the closest approximation that finite man can make to wisdom. He appealed to his colleagues among the Founding Fathers who opposed the Constitution to doubt with himself a little of their own infallibility. I confess, he said, that

I do not entirely approve of this Constitution at present, but Sir, I am not sure I shall never approve it: For having lived long, I have experienced many instances of being obliged, by better information or fuller consideration to change opinion even on important subjects, which I once thought right, but found to be otherwise. It is therefore that the older I grow the more apt I am to doubt my own judgment, and to pay more respect to the judgment of others. . . . I consent, Sir, to this Constitution, because I expect no better, and because I am not sure that it is not the best. The opinions I have had of its errors I sacrifice to the public good. I have never whisper'd a syllable of them abroad. Within these walls they were born, and here they shall die.

One can understand the doubts that have over the last century attached to Franklin's reputation, both personal and political. He was not, like Washington or Jefferson, a Virginian landowner devoting himself to public affairs, and he has been harder to fit into a nationalist mythology. When in 1788 he drew up his will, he began "I, Benjamin Franklin, of Philadelphia, printer, late Minister Plenipotentiary from the United States of America to the Court of France, now President of the State of Pennsylvania." There is a ring of triumph about it, but it is a bourgeois triumph; the success is not sublime but smug. And the sentiments would be repeated, indeed from 1828 would become part of the American political creed. In 1840:

> Old Tip he wears a homespun coat
> He has no ruffled shirt, wirt, wirt,
> If Mat has all the golden plate
> He is a little squirt, wirt, wirt.

In 1861, "From log cabin to White House"; in 1940, "I came up the hard way." Dixon Wecter once likened Franklin to a Sancho Panza, "rejoicing in homely wisdom, thinking of belly and pocketbook as he ambles by the side of the greater idealist, the godlike Washington." The fact was that Franklin was infinitely more symbolic, infinitely more dangerous, infinitely more modern-minded, than Washington. And in the contemporary assessments of him there is not a little fear. He was so adept, riches seemed to come his way so smoothly, he left his grandson a fortune of five hundred thousand dollars, he won the plaudits of foreigners. John Adams, always jealous of the affection of the French for Franklin, seemed to think he had caused the French Revolution. "The best talents in France were blind disciples of Franklin and Turgot, and led the blind to destruction."

Of the fathers of his country, Franklin, whatever the years might have done to his reputation, is perhaps the most significant, the most cosmopolitan, the most prescient for the future, the new man. The printer had made himself the first specimen Yankee. He was a successful tradesman in an age of reason; his *Autobiography* is the first American self-revelation of a self-made man. By his *Almanac* and by his career he preached the American faith: reliance on oneself and on one's own efforts, prudence, good sense, and the respect of one's neighbors. Like Jefferson he saw no limits to the capacity of free men as citizens, as workers, or as liberal inquirers after truth in many fields. Like Jefferson again, he was a deist. During his years in England he undertook along with Sir Francis Dashwood a revision of the Prayer Book, and of the Catechism he retained only two questions: "What is your duty to God?" and "What is your duty to your neighbor?" Franklin's faith in political freedom was linked to a faith in economic freedom, and to a faith in scientific freedom too. He ranged widely and he ranged easily: there is no sense of superiority, rather the reverse, but there is certainly an effortlessness that comes not from Balliol or Boston but from a confidence in the capacity of what he called "the middling people." Franklin learned by reading and by observation, and what he learned he sought to apply. The test was empirical, and the tests were endless. Human, gregarious, worldly, unpompous, inquiring yet unspeculative, restless yet equable in temper, a preacher of moralities who honored them as much in the breach as in the observance, a counselor of prudence who was always ready to take a chance, a plain man who liked the graces and the comforts of life, a master of slogans who never deceived himself by them, skeptic and idealist and lover of children, he has left his mark conspicuously on the American character. He was father of all the Yankees, perhaps—for did not Poor Richard say "The cat in gloves catches no mice"?—but ambassador also to two great kingdoms. His worldly wisdom was suited to the philosophes in Paris and in Edinburgh; it was suited too to the old wives in the chimney corner, summing up a lifetime of neighborly experience. He was at home in France. In England, he said, he was thought of as too much of an American, and in America was deemed too much an Englishman. He was rightly thought of as a citizen of the world, and this too is part of his legacy to Americans. He wrote his own epitaph, perhaps the most famous of all American epitaphs: "The Body of B. Franklin, Printer, (Like the Cover of an old Book, Its Contents torn out and Stript of its Lettering and Gilding) Lies here, food for Worms. But the Work shall not be lost; For it will, (as he believed) appear once more, in a new and more elegant Edition, Revised and Corrected, by the Author."

In printing some dozen articles it is impossible to do more than catch the flavor of the man. But some themes do emerge in any study of Franklin. The first and in many ways the most paradoxical is that this most secular and at times Rabelaisian of men was in the line of descent from the Puritans. There is more in common between Franklin and Cotton Mather than a taste for moral precepts and an addiction to sermonizing. There is the same interest in reform and self-improvement, the perennial taste for chastisement, of others and of himself, the foreknowledge that sin would keep breaking out, the morbid streak of self-analysis. The editor in Franklin seemed often to be speaking from a lay pulpit, even if he preached most of the time a witty and worldly sermon. Whitney Griswold, late Professor of History and President of Yale, sees in Franklin one who applied Cotton Mather's ideas to a later generation and a secular world and found in them, if not a guide to conduct, certainly to self-advertisement and self-advancement.

But the young apprentice was rapidly made to feel at home in the City of Brotherly Love. And Frederick B. Tolles of Swarthmore demonstrates how easily the Quaker gospel endorsed the precepts he brought with him from Boston. It was important to be prudent and to be honest. It was even more important to be seen being so. And it was possible, as Carl Van Doren's warm pages on the Junto demonstrate, to gather a group of like-minded, industrious, and companionable folk about one also. Not the least of Franklin's good fortune was that he grew up in the ranks of the middling people in a city recognizably urban and needing improvements by collective action, but small enough for a man to know and trust his neighbors. The Junto has become the model of a host of successors, those lunch-and-talk clubs devoted to gossip, good works, and an atmosphere of camaraderie and companionship that mark the mores of the American male. Anti-Franklin men have made much of this streak in him. It has bred Babbitts; but some of them are the salt of the local earth.

The second theme that emerges is the novelty of Franklin's own ladder of success: the newspaper. In the older society of Europe, it was rare in his day to climb up the social tree at all, except by way of the Church or by a sufficient success in trade to make it possible to buy a place in land and society. Money talked in Europe—as in any society—however it was made; but it did not, of itself, ennoble. But to make money quickly and permanently—and Franklin did so—by the sale of news was a novelty. And not the least interesting aspect of the Franklin saga is the study of how he did it: the polishing of old saws so that they became modern instances, as J. F. Ross shows, the open and genial plagiarizing of other almanacs and readers to produce Richard Saunders, and the skill in bringing this very human figure to life. Indeed, as David Levin demonstrates, Franklin himself is his own creation. Here is a man—the first in American letters—who talks to us apparently frankly about himself but is his own creation, so that at intervals we do not know what—and who—is fact, and what—and who —is fiction. And all is told in a limpid, deceptively simple prose— and we are even told how the style is achieved. Here is a career built at once, and often contradictorily, on moral precepts and on endless self-revelation. It is done always with a twinkle, with a sunny humor—and always, behind all the chat, with a touch of reserve.

Since in letters, as later in dress and portraits, he wore a host of disguises, he also paid a price. Who behind the poses was the real Franklin? He could stoop low, and talk to Mather; he was a General on the Frontier, but he could push a wheelbarrow in Philadelphia; he could sell everything from needles to slaves; he could walk and talk with kings and flirt with the ladies of the salons; this was a natural man who was infinitely malleable. But the real man? What did he really think of the Great Game? Was it all an act put on by a total cynic, and was the easy, chatty prose just designed to sell his readable columns? There is here a mystery no one has yet probed: though in the pages of Van Doren one feels one gets close to the real man. At least J. F. Ross and David Levin reveal how both "Poor Richard" and "B. Franklin" were each conceived and contrived.

A third note is of course the obvious one, the infinite curiosity, the asking of questions, the wish to experiment. If Franklin was

the first great American editor, he was first known in Europe as
scientist and inventor and experimentalist. He was a Fellow of the
Royal Society on merit and before he was an ambassador. For
America, as later for France, this was the Enlightenment made
personal and human.

Yet if Franklin was clubbable, he was also curiously solitary. He
was, for one who lived by selling his own legends, remarkably self-
contained. If you must keep a secret, Poor Richard should have
said, keep it. We will never know who was the mother of his son,
who got the Hutchinson letters for him, what his real feelings were
for his all but illiterate wife. These were qualities that made him a
superb, utterly reliable diplomat and agent. He could keep secrets;
and when he did not, who knew what truth there was in what he
revealed? The whole of his seven years as diplomat in France
shows this skill repeatedly. And R. B. Morris does a brilliant job
in *The Peacemakers* of evoking the atmosphere of Paris in these
years and Franklin's role in it. His best chapter, "The Ball at
Dr. Franklin's Foot," is indeed too long to reprint here, and is
worthy of close study: the playing off of one British emissary,
Thomas Grenville, against another, Richard Oswald, in an embassy
where every secretary was in everybody else's pocket. Neither Jay
nor Adams trusted Franklin. Nor did Vergennes, his ally. Paradoxically again the one to whom he was closest was his chief
enemy-negotiator, that ugly one-eyed tradesman Richard Oswald
from Galloway; between him and Franklin there grew up a curious
love-hate relationship. In such situations presumably only your
major opponent is the man whose motives at least are plain.

If Franklin's qualities were at their best in Paris, they were at
their least effective in the turbulent politics of Pennsylvania in the
1750's. His opposition to the Proprietary party brought him unpopularity. He did not succeed in manufacturing a binding opposition group. Nor did his friendships of these years prove enduring.
But from 1757, and even earlier, he was now the traveler, first
the postal officer, then the frontier general, then the colonial agent
in London. And what does emerge in the years of his London so-
journ, from 1757 to 1774, is his remarkable foresight of the

American empire that might have been had wisdom prevailed at Westminster and Whitehall, and his uncanny modern-minded insight into the future of the New World. Paul Conner is highly perceptive on this. And Verner Crane reveals how, under the challenge of the campaign to repeal the Stamp Act, Franklin began—perhaps for the first time—to question the tenets to which, as politician, he had long held as to a rock, of the permanence of the Old England connection. There emerges after 1767 a firm, tough, unyielding streak. The agent of four colonies, yes; but now Mr. America also. When the break came, in the Cockpit, it would be for him quite final and unbridgeable. Britain had managed to manufacture an enemy who now on the issue of independence would yield no more. On this at least there was no need for poses.

In the final section, Gerald Stourzh and Clinton Rossiter attempt the impossible, to reduce Franklin's political ideas to system and order. They fail, as in my view does Dr. Conner. But they all fail with distinction. Dr. Stourzh sees how small a way where morals are concerned does reason go. Power and pride are stronger forces. There is much in Franklin that he can label as both democratic and conservative. Professor Rossiter disentangles a number of threads in the Franklin tapestry, and concludes that liberty was the central theme. The ideal he sought was a world in which men of philosophic temper would feel free in all countries.

Perhaps one of them should have added that what makes Franklin so compelling to study and so original is his almost total freedom from the limits of his own environment. He made the whole Western World his own parish. Born poor in colonial Boston, he was at ease in Quaker Philadelphia, in royal London, and in Paris, as much at home at St. Andrews or in Passy, or in Bethlehem and Easton on the Pennsylvania wilderness frontier. The reason is clear. He was far in advance of his time, not merely as editor-turned-scientist-turned-statesman, or from the prescience of so much of his writing, but because one is aware of his own awareness of challenges, aware of the immense potential of the human mind when left free to speculate, to question, and to experiment. One is always in a state of delight with Franklin's prose because of his skill in communicating his own enjoyment of the world when a lively mind is let loose in it. So, though nobly done by in his biographies, not least by Carl Van Doren, he has been even more nobly treated by his editors, especially Leonard Labaree. In this sense, the last word ought to rest with the shrewdest, best informed, and most polished writer of them all, himself. All that a collection of secondary commentaries can do is so to excite and interest the reader that he or she is driven to read Franklin himself.

ESMOND WRIGHT

Benjamin Franklin, 1706–1790

Benjamin Franklin was born in Boston on January 17, 1706, the tenth son and fifteenth child of Josiah and Abiah Franklin. He was apprenticed as a printer to his brother James, but in 1723 left Boston to seek his fortune, first unsuccessfully in New York, then in Philadelphia, which became his home and with which he—and his reputation—became identified. After a short and unsuccessful visit to London, he returned to Philadelphia, opened his own printing shop, and founded the Junto, part club, part fraternity, part pressure-group. He began the publication of the *Pennsylvania Gazette* in 1729; and in 1730 he married Deborah Read. From 1732 to 1757 he published *Poor Richard's Almanac* and became prosperous as printer, publisher, dealer in paper and print, and, after 1736, man of affairs. If he was in early days "looking for copy," he became as a result widely read and widely informed; words and news were his trade and profession, and on them he built his career. By 1748 he was wealthy enough to retire, leaving his working business to his partner David Hall. He saw himself as scientist, inventing the lightning rod and carrying out his experiments with electricity. As inventor and practical scientist he became even better known abroad than he was at home; he was in 1753 awarded the Copley Medal of the Royal Society and became in 1756 a Fellow of the Royal Society; the same year he was appointed Deputy Postmaster General for continental North America. In 1754 as one of the Pennsylvania delegation he was present at Albany and helped to draft the Plan of Union. Thirty years before independence was won, he was advocating the federal union of the colonies, but he was ahead of both British and colonial opinion in doing so. After a stormy interlude as an anti-Proprietary leader in Pennsylvania politics, he moved to London in 1757 to present the Pennsylvania case against the Penn family. Apart from a short interval (1762–1764) he was to remain in London for seventeen years, to become colonial agent for Pennsylvania and later for Georgia, New Jersey, and Massachusetts also, to present in the House of Commons the case against the Stamp Act in 1766, and to serve in fact, though never officially, as the delegate of the New World to the Old, the voice of colonial America. He traveled in Britain and in France, where he was held in high esteem as a scientist. When by unknown means he acquired the Hutchinson letters and allowed these frank criticisms to be printed and circulated, he was bitterly attacked in London, and despite Chatham's efforts he sailed for home in 1775. He served as a delegate to the Second Continental Congress; he tried to win Canadian support in 1775; he helped to draft the Declaration of Independence.

In 1776 he was sent to France as one of three commissioners, in the end to become the ambassador of a free and friendly country. For he negotiated the treaty of alliance of 1778, which helped to ensure American independence in 1783. He had a difficult time with his colleagues, Silas Deane and Arthur Lee, John Jay and John Adams. But despite the aid of his fellow commissioners, it was largely to him that the treaty with France of 1778, the treaty with Britain of 1783, and the final recognition of American independence were due. He was immensely popular in France as *le bonhomme Richard,* the good Quaker, the idealized natural man of revolutionary imaginings. He enjoyed the *réclame.* He sailed for home in 1785, the hero of two worlds. On his return he was elected President of Pennsylvania, and in 1787 he attended the Constitutional Convention as delegate: saying little, for he was now eighty-one and he moved with difficulty, but in himself the symbol of the forces that had led to the separation of the New World from the Old. By 1787 he was the least vocal but the most revered and one of the most significant of all the Founding Fathers. He died in Philadelphia on April 17, 1790.

E.W.

✪

A Puritan on Prosperity

don't use

One day in 1724 Cotton Mather received a young caller at his home in Boston. It was a sober youth of eighteen years who presented himself. Benjamin Franklin had returned from Philadelphia for a brief visit to his native town, and had stopped to pay his respects to the great Puritan, whom he much admired. Franklin's later account of the visit indicates that it made some impression on him. Mather

. . . received me in his library [he wrote] and on my taking leave showed me a shorter way out of the house, through a narrow passage, which was crossed by a beam overhead. We were talking as I withdrew, he accompanying me behind, and I turned partly towards him, when he said hastily, *"Stoop, stoop!"* I did not understand him till I felt my head hit against the beam. He was a man that never missed any occasion of giving instruction, and upon this he said to me: *"You are young, and have the world before you; STOOP as you go through it, and you will miss many hard thumps."* This advice, thus beat into my head, has frequently been of use to me, and I often think of it when I see pride mortified and misfortunes brought upon people by carrying their heads too high.[1]

Reprinted from "Three Puritans on Prosperity," *The New England Quarterly,* Vol. VII (September 1934), pp. 483–488.

1. John Bigelow, ed., *The Complete Works of Benjamin Franklin,* 10 vols. (New York, 1887–1888), VIII, 484–485.

Was this all that Mather had to offer his visitor; or was there a real spiritual bond between the two?

The God in which Franklin consistently professed belief was far more genial than Cotton Mather's stern Jehovah. Out of a vast "Chorus of Worlds" He was merely "that particular Wise and good God, who is the author and owner of our System."[2] His greatest gift to man was reason, by which man might discover his true function in the scheme of things. So glaring are the inconsistencies in Franklin's life that we take whatever he said with many grains of salt. We should not, for example, attach too much importance to the "Articles of Faith and Acts of Religion" which he drew up, with solemn precocity at the age of twenty-two. His life proclaims him too palpable a *citoyen du monde* to warrant much attention to his theology. Yet by virtue of this fact, it is all the more intriguing that he should have subscribed to a system of ethics identical to Cotton Mather's. In his life Franklin was a deist, if not an out-and-out agnostic; in his writings, he was the soul of Puritanism. Why was this?

To be sure, Franklin had been born a Puritan in Puritan society. In childhood he heard his father admonish him over and over again on the inestimable value of all the Puritan virtues. But neither heredity nor environment can wholly account for Dr. Franklin. Was there some spiritual kinship, then, some intellectual contact with Puritan philosophers? Franklin himself says there was. The books which he precociously read numbered among them *Pilgrim's Progress,* Plutarch, and the works of Daniel Defoe. But it was from none of these that the spark of Franklin's Puritanism flashed. If we are to take him at his word, we must consider rather a small volume entitled *Essays to Do Good* by the Reverend Cotton Mather. This, he says in the *Autobiography,* "perhaps gave me such a turn of thinking that had an influence on some of the principle future events of my life."[3] And in 1784, from the terminus of his great career, he wrote Cotton Mather's son renewing the acknowledg-

2. Franklin, *Works,* I, 308.
3. Franklin, *Works,* I, 44 (this was written in 1771).

ment. The *Essays* had given him "such a turn of thinking, as to have an influence on my conduct through life, for I have always set a greater value on the character of a *doer of good,* than on any other kind of reputation; and if I have been, as you seem to think, a useful citizen, the public owes the advantage of it to that book."[4]

Before rejecting Franklin's compliments as insincere, let us see what Mather had to say to him. Let us pause, for a moment, over the strange intellectual kinship of the author of *The Wonders of the Invisible World,* and the man who "discovered" electricity. The central theme of the *Essays to Do Good* is that of the sermons: personal salvation achieved through good works. The two callings receive lengthy treatment; and there is a categorical exposition of methods of doing good. Ministers, schoolteachers, lawyers, physicians, all have their specific functions. But the greatest opportunity awaits persons of wealth. To them Mather has something special to say:

Sirs, you cannot but acknowledge that it is the sovereign God who has bestowed upon you the riches which distinguish you. A devil himself, when he saw a rich man, could not but make this acknowledgment to the God of heaven: "Thou hast blessed the work of his hands, and his substance is increased in the land."[5]

But the divine esteem enjoyed by the man of property does not diminish his obligations to society. The Lord has made him His "steward." He has charged him with a sacred trust, charity. Moreover, God in His infinite wisdom has made charity an attractive sacrifice, for if we are to believe Cotton Mather, the charitable

. . . very frequently . . . have been rewarded with remarkable success in their affairs, and increase of their property; and even in this world have seen the fulfillment of those promises: "Cast thy bread upon the waters"—thy grain into the moist ground—"and thou shalt find it after many days." "Honor the Lord with thy substance; so shall

4. Franklin, *Works,* VIII, 484.
5. Cotton Mather, *Essays to Do Good* (Boston: American Tract Society, 1710), pp. 86–87.

thy barns be filled with plenty." History has given us many delightful examples of those who have had their *decimations* followed and rewarded by a surprising prosperity of their affairs. Obscure mechanics and husbandmen have risen to estates, of which once they had not the most distant expectation.[6]

So spoke the Reverend Cotton Mather to young Ben Franklin. His words are at once corroborative and prophetic. They are further evidence of his belief in the piety of individual prosperity, and they whisper of the future when thousands of "obscure mechanics and husbandmen" would rise (as millions would aspire) "to estates of which they had not the most distant expectation."

It would be interesting to lay the texts of Mather's *Essays* and Franklin's *Autobiography* side by side, so much is the former reflected in the latter. The purpose in recording his own rise "from the poverty and obscurity in which I was born and bred, to a state of affluence and some degree of reputation in the world,"[7] Franklin declares, is to allow others to profit by his example. He himself thought it "fit to be imitated" and therefore he would write a book about it. But first he desired "with all humility to acknowledge that I owe the mentioned happiness of my past life to [God's] kind providence, which led me to the means I used and gave them success."[8] How like a Puritan to attribute to the Lord "a state of affluence and some degree of reputation in the world." The *Autobiography* is filled with similar professions of humility and piety. To the uncritical reader, the sermon it preached must have seemed even more convincing than Mather's, for it had received from its author the pragmatic sanction of successful practice. So he declared, at any rate. He had found it helpful as a young printer's apprentice to draw up a chart of the virtues necessary for complete moral perfection, and then to score himself daily on progress made —or not made. Mather himself could not have improved the list. It included temperance, silence, order, resolution, frugality, indus-

6. Mather, *Essays to Do Good*, 89–90.
7. Franklin, *Works,* I, 29.
8. Franklin, *Works,* I, 30–31.

nalist and publisher by trade. *Poor Richard's Almanac,* like most of his other publications, was distinctly a money-making venture. Its shrewd author knew his trade; and what was more, he knew his public. Any publisher knows that catering to a public's taste is profitable, and that is precisely what Franklin did. He understood Puritanism well enough to realize that it offered assurances of material prosperity to all who followed its code of morals. Piety was inexpensive, and so although he himself was worlds apart from orthodoxy, he preached Puritan ethics as good as Mather's. From an unmoral point of view he perceived that the Puritan virtues had immense utilitarian value. And, skeptic though he was, he doubtless thought it wise to be on the safe side, to propitiate whatever God there might be. However that may be, he knew his public would think so.

The popularity of his writings bears witness to Franklin's shrewdness. The *Autobiography* became a famous American success story. Let its author be accused of hypocrisy in affecting the moral austerity of Puritanism. His public must have been delighted to find that he, a scientist, a patriot, a man who had in actuality risen to "a state of affluence and some degree of reputation in the world," endorsed the same democratic virtues as their ministers. It must have relieved them to have such a man turn thumbs down on chance, as it rejoiced them to hear him reaffirm the sanctity of individual prosperity. Benjamin Franklin not only commended prosperity; he dramatized it. . . .

try, sincerity, justice, moderation, cleanliness, tranquillity, chasti
and humility. Of these, industry was most important. "Lose 1
time," he said to himself, "be always employed in something use
ful; cut off all unnecessary actions."[9]

But it is Poor Richard who sings the loudest praise of industry.
Luck, says he, is of no account. Americans need only work hard
and never trouble themselves about luck, for *"Diligence is the
Mother of good luck, and God gives all things to industry."* Poor
Richard likewise knows all about the calling: *"He that hath a
trade hath an estate, and he that hath a calling hath an office of
profit and honor."*[10] In fact the way to wealth was, in his own
words, "as plain as the way to market" to Benjamin Franklin.

It depends chiefly on two words, *industry* and *frugality*—that is, waste
neither *time* nor *money,* but make the best use of both. Without industry and frugality nothing will do, and with them everything. He that
gets all he can and saves all he can . . . will certainly become rich, if
that Being who governs the world, to whom all should look for a blessing on their honest endeavors, doth not, in his wise providence, otherwise determine.[11]

Did Franklin learn all this from Cotton Mather? It is authentic
Puritanism. Mather had, at times, stooped low enough to com-
mend charity as a profitable business venture. Franklin certainly
knew Mather and read his works. Yet the man who paraphrased
classic aphorisms for simple Americans feared no Puritan God.
The thunderbolt which was the angry voice of Jehovah to Mather
trickled harmlessly off a wet kite-string into Franklin's Leyden jar.
Poor Richard's wisdom is savory with business acumen. Whence,
therefore, the piety? Was it an afterthought?

It makes little difference where Franklin got his Puritanism.
Very likely Mather made substantial contributions. Yet the piety,
in all probability, was no afterthought. It was put there with deliberate intent. Let us not forget that Benjamin Franklin was a jour-

9. Franklin, *Works,* I, 176.
10. Franklin, *Works,* I, 444.
11. Franklin, *Works,* II, 120–121.

FREDERICK B. TOLLES

✪

Quaker Business Mentors: The Philadelphia Merchants

Among the figures which people the pages of Benjamin Franklin's account of his early years in Philadelphia, one of the most shadowy is the benevolent Quaker merchant Thomas Denham, who came to Franklin's rescue in London in 1726 and gave him employment in his store after their return to Philadelphia. Little is known of Denham beyond the few sentences which Franklin devoted to him in his *Autobiography*.[1] Yet the economic philosophy of the man who gave Franklin his first training in business should not pass unnoticed in any account of the Boston-born Philadelphian in whom sociologists have seen the classic embodiment of the spirit of modern capitalism.[2] Although we cannot identify the actual eco-

---

This selection was originally published under the title "Benjamin Franklin's Business Mentors: The Philadelphia Quaker Merchants" in *William and Mary Quarterly*, Vol. IV, No. 1 (January 1947), pp. 60–69. Reprinted by permission of the author.

1. A. H. Smyth, ed., *The Writings of Benjamin Franklin* (New York, 1905–1907), I, 274–276, 285–286, 289. An account book of Thomas Denham's is in the Historical Society of Pennsylvania, but it throws little light on his life.

2. See Max Weber, *The Protestant Ethic and the Spirit of Capitalism*, trans. Talcott Parsons (New York, 1930), pp. 48 ff. The only writer who to my knowledge has attached due importance to the fact that Franklin's first business mentor was a Quaker is Richard B. Schlatter, *The Social Ideas of Religious Leaders, 1660–1688* (London, 1940), p. 239. Ernst Troeltsch, how-

nomic ideas of Thomas Denham, we can reconstruct the pattern of economic thinking which was characteristic of the eighteenth-century mercantile Quakers as a group. The purpose of this paper is therefore to outline the salient features of the Quaker economic philosophy under whose influence Franklin became the prototype of the modern American businessman.

I

The popular conception of the Quaker as a shrewd businessman has a long history. Early in the course of Quakerism, George Fox, the founder of the Society of Friends, observed that "Friends had more trade than any of their neighbours, and if there was any trading, they had a great part of it."[3] Opponents of the Quakers delighted in making derogatory comments on their acquisitive talents. The following character of the Quakers, for example, appeared in an enormously popular book first published in England in 1684:

As to these modern Seducers, they are not Men of *Arms* but a herd of silly insignificant People, aiming rather to heap up Riches in Obscurity, than to acquire a Fame by an heroick Undertaking. They are generally Merchants and Mechanicks, and are observed to be very punctual in their Dealings, Men of few Words in a Bargain, modest and compos'd in their Deportment, temperate in their Lives and using great Frugality in all Things. In a Word, they are singularly Industrious, sparing no Labour or Pains to increase their Wealth; and so subtle and inventive, that they would, if possible, extract Gold out of Ashes.[4]

---

ever, makes the significant blunder of calling Franklin a Quaker. *The Social Teaching of the Christian Churches,* trans. Olive Wyon (New York, 1931), II, 783. And the poet John Keats referred to Franklin as "a philosophical Quaker full of mean and thrifty maxims." See M. B. Forman, ed., *The Letters of John Keats* (New York, 1935), p. 235.

3. *The Journal of George Fox,* Bi-Centenary Edition (London, 1891), I, 186.

4. [Giovanni Paolo Marana] *Letters Writ by a Turkish Spy,* 10th ed. (London, 1734), VI, 17.

The reputation for business sagacity followed the Quakers to America, where an anonymous Irishman described them appreciatively as "a God-fearing, money-making people." The strongest proof that this reputation was justified can be found in the Philadelphia tax list for 1769. At this period the Quakers constituted no more than one-seventh of Philadelphia's population,[5] but they accounted for more than half of those who paid taxes in excess of a hundred pounds. Even more striking, perhaps, is the fact that of the seventeen wealthiest individuals in Philadelphia (defining the wealthiest as those who paid a tax of more than five hundred pounds) eight were Quakers in good standing and four were men who had been reared as Friends. Only five were non-Quakers, and one of these—William Shippen—owed the basis of his fortune to his Quaker grandfather.[6]

This striking circumstance cannot be explained on the simple basis of the Quakers' having been "in on the ground floor" by virtue of their early arrival on the Philadelphia scene, for such an explanation is totally inapplicable to the situation of the English Friends, who achieved equal economic success in spite of the persecutions which placed them at a real disadvantage in relation to businessmen of other persuasions.[7] The argument has frequently been advanced that since Friends were excluded by statute or conscientious scruple from government office and from all the professions except medicine, their best talents were channeled perforce

5. Robert Proud, *History of Pennsylvania* (Philadelphia, 1797), II, 339.
6. The Proprietary tax list for 1769 is printed in *Pennsylvania Archives,* 3rd Series, XIV, 151–220.
7. The statement of an English anti-Quaker writer at the end of the seventeenth century that Gracechurch Street Meeting in London was composed of "the *Richest* Trading Men in London" is simply a statement of historical fact. See Charles Leslie, *The Snake in the Grass* (London, 1698), p. 362. The list of attenders at this meeting, situated in the heart of London's trading and financial district, reads like a beadroll of the most famous banking and commercial families of England; it includes the Barclays, Gurneys, Hanburys, Lloyds, Osgoods, Hoares, Dimsdales, and Christys, to name only the most important. For a fuller list see William Beck and T. Frederick Ball, *The London Friends Meetings* (London, 1869), p. 150.

into trade and commerce.[8] Though not without considerable validity, this argument, in contrast to the first, applies with peculiar force to the English Quakers, but is subject to a number of significant exceptions when applied to Friends in Pennsylvania. In both the mother country and the colonies, of course, the professional ministry, the Army, and the Navy were closed to Friends by reason of specific Quaker testimonies. In Penn's commonwealth, however, no oath of allegiance was required for office-holding, and for three-quarters of a century most of the important posts in the provincial government were actually occupied by Quaker merchants. Although there was among the Pennsylvania Quakers some residual prejudice against lawyers and law courts akin to that which led George Fox to cry out feelingly, "away with those lawyers, twenty shilling Councellors, thirty shilling Sergeants, ten groat Attourneys, that will throw men into Prison for a thing of nought,"[9] nevertheless, there were a number of outstanding Quaker lawyers in colonial Pennsylvania like John Kinsey and Nicholas Waln; and furthermore, two Quakers—David Lloyd and James Logan— served as Chief Justices of the provincial Supreme Court. It is well known that several of the greatest English physicians of the eighteenth century were Friends, notably Drs. Fothergill, Lettsom, and Dimsdale, while in Pennsylvania Dr. Thomas Cadwalader, Dr. Lloyd Zachary, and Drs. Thomas and Phineas Bond all came from Quaker backgrounds. Thus the theory that Friends turned to business because every avenue of professional life was closed to them hardly stands scrutiny.

It becomes apparent, therefore, that the fundamental reason for Quaker success in business must be sought in something common to Friends on both sides of the Atlantic. Where shall we find it but in the religious ethic of Quakerism itself? It is a commonplace of recent historical writing that an intimate relationship existed be-

8. See, for example, Werner Sombart, *The Quintessence of Capitalism,* trans. M. Epstein (London, 1915), p. 287; and Amelia Mott Gummere, *The Quaker in the Forum* (Philadelphia, 1910), p. 41.

9. *To the Parliament of the Common-wealth of England* (London, 1659), p. 5.

tween certain of the distinctive ideas of Protestantism and the rise of modern capitalism.[10] Discussion of this problem has been carried on primarily with reference to the Calvinist wing of Protestantism. It would seem desirable to determine how far this line of investigation can be followed with respect to Quakerism.

II

One may begin with the generalization that Quakerism, arising in the middle of the seventeenth century, was one of the many variant expressions of the dominant and all-pervasive Puritanism of the age. Atypical in many respects, it yet shared with Puritanism a common substratum of religious and social ideas and mental habits, some of which were not wholly compatible with the peculiar doctrines which differentiated Quakerism from Puritan orthodoxy. Although Friends believed that the substance of their ethical ideas was the product in each instance of immediate revelation, it is undeniable that in many respects the form and framework in which the ideas were expressed were those of Puritanism. In other words, as a recent writer puts it, "puritans who turned Quaker did not shed their puritanism."[11]

With the Puritans, Friends looked upon the material world of daily toil and daily bread as God's world in which men were called to do His will. There are few more vigorous expressions of the Protestant attitude toward monastic rejection of the world than William Penn's attack upon the "Religious Bedlams" in which

10. Fortunately it is unnecessary here to venture into the disputed realm of priority and to take a position on the moot question of whether the Protestant ethic in some way generated the capitalist spirit or merely rationalized it. It is sufficient to admit with Troeltsch that "both possessed a certain affinity for each other, that [the] Calvinistic ethic of the 'calling' and of work, which declares that the earning of money with certain precautions is allowable, was able to give [capitalism] an intellectual and ethical backbone, and that, therefore, thus organized and inwardly supported, it vigorously developed, even though within the limits of anti-mammon." *Social Teaching of the Christian Churches,* II, 915.

11. Schlatter, *Social Ideas of Religious Leaders,* p. 235.

monks practiced what he called "a *lazy, rusty, unprofitable Self-Denial,* burdensome to others to feed their Idleness."

The Christian Convent and Monastery [he insisted] are within, where the Soul is encloistered from Sin. And this Religious House the True Followers of Christ carry about with them, who exempt not themselves from the Conversation of the World, though they keep themselves from the Evil of the World in their Conversation. . . . True Godliness don't turn Men out of the World, but enables them to live better in it, and excites their Endeavours to mend it.[12]

God's will, in other words, could be carried out as faithfully on the wharves and in the warehouses and counting rooms of Philadelphia as anywhere else. Friends were adjured to remember, however, that this world was transitory and that their hearts should not be set upon its evanescent goods but upon eternal treasures. "So every one strive to be rich in the life, and in the kingdom and things of the world that hath no end . . ." wrote George Fox to the merchants in 1661; "And therefore, let him that buys, or sells, or possesses, or uses this world, be as if he did not."[13] This was, of course, no other than the doctrine of loving the world with "weaned affections" which, we are told, was "a staple moral of Puritan discourse."[14]

This *innerweltliche Askese* was an integral part of the way of life which the Quakers brought over to Philadelphia. Israel Pemberton, so-called "King of the Quakers," writing in 1749 about a severe financial loss occasioned by the sinking of one of his ships,

12. *No Cross No Crown,* in *A Collection of the Works of William Penn* (London, 1726), I, 295–296.

13. "The Line of Righteousness and Justice Stretched Forth over All Merchants, &c.," *The Works of George Fox* (Philadelphia, 1831), VII, 197. William Penn was no less insistent on this theme: "Have a care of cumber, and the love and care of the world . . .," he wrote to Friends in Pennsylvania in 1684; "truly blessed is that man and woman who, in the invisible power, rule their affections about the visible things, and who use the world as true travellers and pilgrims, whose home is not here below." See Samuel M. Janney, *The Life of William Penn* (Philadelphia, 1852), p. 255.

14. Perry Miller, *The New England Mind* (New York, 1939), p. 42.

summed up this aspect of the economic ethic of the Quaker merchants in classic form. Experiences of this sort, he declared,

tend to wean the Mind from delighting in transitories and if rightly improv'd dispose us to look after Enjoyments more certain and permanent. . . . I am sensible there's a Satisfaction and I believe Something of a duty, in doing for ourselves: The Principle of True Religion being Active and never disposes the Mind to Indolence and Sloth, but it likewise Leads us to Consider, I may say often reminds us of the End and Purpose of our Views and Pursuits, and Reproves us for them, if not Consistent with the one Point to which they ought Solely to tend, the Honour of God and Good of Mankind.[15]

Here are the "weaned affections," the "active principle" of true religion, the "duty" of economic activity, and the end thereof conceived in terms of "the Honour of God." Neither Richard Baxter nor John Cotton could have quarreled with any of the sentiments of this pious Quaker except that embodied in his final phrase, "[the] Good of Mankind." No Puritan would have written those words; the Quaker humanitarian strain was foreign to Puritanism. For the Quaker, on the other hand, the "Good of Mankind" was not a bit of pious or sentimental cant; it represented a positive claim upon his worldly goods, and no doubt the prospect of being able to help those in need actually operated as an incentive to further acquisition. There was thus a whole side of the Quaker economic ethic which stressed the doctrine of stewardship and the social responsibility of the man of wealth; this aspect of the economic ethic was taken seriously by the Quakers, as their humanitarian services in colonial Philadelphia show. In the hands of men like Anthony Benezet and John Woolman, it could provide ammunition for sharp attacks upon the acquisitive spirit. We are here concerned, however, with those elements in the Quaker philosophy

15. Israel Pemberton to John Pemberton, 4th month 7, 1749, Pemberton Papers (Historical Society of Pennsylvania), V, 107. This and other manuscript materials from the collections of the Historical Society of Pennsylvania are quoted with the Society's permission.

which promoted the opposite tendency towards economic individualism.

The Puritan concept of the "calling" as the task in life to which each individual was summoned by God was taken for granted by the Quakers.

All Friends [wrote George Fox] in the wisdom of God train up your children in the fear of God . . . and as they are capable, they may be instructed and kept employed in some lawful calling, that they may be diligent, serving the Lord in the things that are good; that none may live idle, and be destroyers of the creation. . . .[16]

No lawful occupation was too gross or too menial to be included among those appointed by God for His service: "the Perfection of Christian Life," declared William Penn, "extends to every honest Labour or Traffick used among Men."[17] We owe to Thomas Chalkley, Quaker minister, sea captain, and merchant, our most representative Quaker rationale of the calling:

We have Liberty from God, and his dear Son lawfully, and for Accommodation's Sake, to work or seek for Food or Raiment; tho' that ought to be a Work of Indifferency, compar'd to the great Work of Salvation. Our Saviour saith, *Labour not for the Meat which perisheth, but for that which endureth for ever, or to eternal Life:* By which we do not understand, that Christians must neglect their necessary Occasions and their outward Trades and Callings; but that their chief Labour, and greatest Concern ought to be for their future Well-being in his glorious Kingdom; else why did our Lord say to his Disciples, *Children, have you any Meat?* They answered, *No;* and he bid them *cast their Nets into the Sea, and they drew to Land a Net full of great Fishes;* and Fishing being their Trade, no doubt they sold them, for it was not likely they could eat 'em all themselves. . . . By this, and much more, which might be noted, it appears that we not only have Liberty to labour in Moderation, but we are given to understand, that it is our Duty so to do. The Farmer, the Tradesman, and the Merchant, do not understand by our Lord's Doctrine, that they must neglect their

16. *Works,* VII, 345.
17. *No Cross No Crown, Works,* I, 295.

Calling, or grow idle in their Business, but must certainly work, and be industrious in their Callings.[18]

If one kept one's inner eye single to the Lord, and labored diligently in one's calling, one could expect that God would show His favor by adding His blessing in the form of material prosperity. And conversely, business success could be regarded as a visible sign that one was indeed living "in the Light." Chalkley's *Journal* contains many entries like the following: "After these several Journeys were over . . . I was some Time at Home, and followed my Business with Diligence and Industry, and throve in the Things of the World, the Lord adding a Blessing to my Labour."[19] Thus by God's blessing the faithful and diligent Friend, living plainly in accordance with "the simplicity of Truth," almost inevitably accumulated wealth "for the Honour of God and Good of Mankind." James Logan, Penn's erstwhile secretary and a great dealer in furs and skins, confided to an English correspondent that he looked upon it as a particular Providence in his favor that he had been led into the Indian trade; "should I with open eyes," he added, "give away those advantages that by God's Blessing my own Industry and management have . . . thrown on me to others who have had no part in that Management . . . I could never account for it to my Self and family."[20]

III

The virtues of industry and frugality were, of course, held in high repute among Friends. Idleness was looked upon with such horror as the breeder of vice and a vain conversation that Friends regarded diligence in a warrantable calling as a religious duty. Thomas Chalkley, our seagoing Quaker, quoted earlier, linked the

18. *A Journal, or Historical Account of the Life, Travels, and Christian Experiences, of that Antient, Faithful Servant of Jesus Christ, Thomas Chalkley*, in *A Collection of the Works of Thomas Chalkley* (Philadelphia, 1749), pp. 97–98.

19. *Ibid.*, p. 52.

20. James Logan to John Askew, 5th month 9, 1717, Logan Letter Books, Logan Papers (Historical Society of Pennsylvania), IV, 37.

religious closely with the secular life and associated the virtue of diligence with both: "I followed my Calling; and kept to Meetings diligently; for I was not easy to be idle; either in my spiritual or temporal Callings."[21] Frugality was most often recommended on religious grounds as being essential to that austere simplicity of life which "Truth" demanded. Occasionally, however, it was justified on more practical grounds, as tending to increase one's capital and credit. Isaac Norris, a great Quaker merchant in early colonial Philadelphia, revealed something of this motivation when he advised his son, just starting out on his first business trip to London: "thou must remember that the more frugall thou art the more will be thy Stock. . . . Come back plain. This will be a reputation to thee and recommend thee to the best and most Sensible people."[22] One remembers Benjamin Franklin's explanation of the methods by which he had established his reputation just after leaving Thomas Denham's employ: "In order to secure my credit and character as a tradesman," he wrote, "I took care not only to be in *reality* industrious and frugal, but to avoid all appearances to the contrary. I drest plainly. . . ."[23]

Prudence, honesty, and a strong sense of order were the other virtues which contributed to Quaker business success. Friends were known for extreme caution in their business undertakings. Their book of discipline contained a standing advice against buying, bargaining, or contracting beyond one's abilities, and in their meetings for discipline Friends were constantly warned against imprudent ventures by the query: "Are Friends careful to live within the Bounds of their Circumstances, and to avoid launching into Trade

21. *Journal, Works,* p. 37.

22. Isaac Norris to Joseph Norris, 2nd month, 1719, Norris Letter Book, 1716–1730, Norris Papers (Historical Society of Pennsylvania), pp. 183–184.

23. *Autobiography, Writings,* I, 307. It will be remembered that many years later, as commissioner to the court of Louis XVI, Franklin, bowing to the popular legend which identified him with the idealized figure of the "good Quaker," rather ostentatiously affected the plain dress of Friends. See Bernard Faÿ, *Franklin, The Apostle of Modern Times* (Boston, 1929), pp. 411, 437; Edith Philips, *The Good Quaker in French Legend* (Philadelphia, 1932), p. 92.

or Business beyond their ability to manage?"[24] If a Friend were so imprudent as to find himself forced into bankruptcy, he stood in danger of disownment by the meeting. Thus prudence had its spiritual as well as its temporal sanctions.

Because Quaker businessmen were known to be scrupulously honest, people were glad to deal with them. From almost the very beginning, as George Fox records, "when people came to have experience of Friends' honesty and faithfulness, and found that their yea was yea and their nay was nay, that they kept to a word in their dealings, and that they would not cozen and cheat them, customers flocked to do business with them."[25] Paradoxically, it was probably an aspect of this very virtue of strict truthfulness that gave Friends the opposite reputation for slyness and dishonesty. Cherishing such a respect for the truth in its stark simplicity, Quakers were characteristically men of few words: "they recommended *Silence* by their Example," reported William Penn, "having few Words upon all Occasions."[26] It is not difficult to understand how the uncommunicative Quaker could come to seem secretive and subtle, and consequently how the suspicion of slyness and dishonesty could be built into the legend of the Quaker businessman.

A sympathetic French visitor to Philadelphia shortly after the American Revolution was to call attention to "the order which

24. "The Book of Discipline as Revised by the Yearly Meeting for Pennsylvania and New Jersey in the Year 1719" (Ms. copy in Friends Historical Library of Swarthmore College), pp. 15, 76.

25. *Journal,* I, 186.

26. *The Rise and Progress of the People Called Quakers, Works,* I, 869. The advice of Friend John Reynell to his apprentice is revealing in this connection: "In doing business be a little on the Reserve, and Observe well the Person thou has to do with. . . . Keep thy Business to thy self, and don't let it be known, who thou dost Business for, or what Sorts of Goods thou Ships off. Some will want to know both, perhaps with a Design to Circumvent thee. Endeavour to know what Prices other People give for Goods, but say nothing of what thou givest thy self, or where thou buys. . . . If thou finds out a Place where they Sell cheap, keep it to thy Self, for if thou Ships off Goods cheaper than others, it will increase Business." John Reynell to Elias Bland, 4th month 22, 1743, Reynell Letter Book, 1741–1744, Coates-Reynell Papers (Historical Society of Pennsylvania).

the Quakers are accustomed from childhood to apply to the distribution of their tasks, their thoughts, and every moment of their lives. They carry this spirit of order everywhere," he continued; "it economizes time, activity and money."[27] This virtue was essential for success in a modern "rationalized" capitalist economy in which the pursuit of gain was regarded as a more or less continuous intensive activity, based upon the expectation of regular production, markets, and profits. Again one cannot help recalling Benjamin Franklin, who gave "order" third place in his catalogue of virtues, adding this appropriate precept: "Let all your things have their places; let each part of your business have its time."[28]

Some years after the Revolution, the unfinished manuscript of Franklin's autobiography happened to fall into the hands of one Abel James, a Philadelphia Quaker merchant and son-in-law of our maritime Friend Thomas Chalkley. Recognizing at once how consummately it inculcated virtues which Friends held in high regard, he urged Franklin to complete and publish it, adding, "the influence writings under that class have on the minds of youth is very great, and has nowhere appeared to me so plain as in our public friends [i.e. Quaker ministers'] journals." He concluded with a eulogy of Franklin which showed how thoroughly he was in sympathy with the formula for business success worked out by the erstwhile protégé of Friend Thomas Denham: "I know of no character living," wrote the good Quaker, ". . . who has so much in his power as thyself to promote a greater spirit of industry and early attention to business, frugality, and temperance with the American youth."[29]

27. Jean Pierre Brissot de Warville, *Nouveau voyage dans les Etats-unis de l'Amérique septentrionale* (Paris, 1791), II, 187. Brissot adds that this habit is quite the reverse of the training and customs usual in Catholic France. For William Penn's views on the importance of order, see *Advice to His Children* in *Works,* I, 899.

28. *Autobiography, Writings,* I, 328.

29. Abel James to Benjamin Franklin, *ibid.,* I, 313–314.

✪

The Junto

No single thread of narrative can give a true account of Franklin's life during the years 1726–1732, for he was leading three lives and—most of the time—something of a stealthy fourth, each distinct enough to call for a separate record and yet all of them closely involved in his total nature. There was his public life, beginning with his friendships in the club he organized in 1727, and continuing with larger and larger affairs as long as he lived. There was his inner life, which was at first much taken up with reflections on his own behavior, and, after he had more or less settled that in his mind and habit, grew to an embracing curiosity about the whole moral and physical world. There was his life as workman . . . and businessman, which greatly occupied him and was to occupy him until, after twenty years in Philadelphia, he was able to retire from an activity he had never valued for itself. In time all three were to be fused in the spacious character of a sage in action, but in 1726–1732 they were still distinct if not discrepant.

In business Franklin was extremely alert to the main chance, adaptable, resolute, crafty though not petty, and ruthless on occasion. But he had too ranging a mind to be taken up with his private concerns alone, and he genuinely desired the public welfare. Having neither wealth nor influence, he began where he could, using

From *Benjamin Franklin* by Carl Van Doren (Viking, 1938), pp. 73–80. Copyright 1938, copyright © renewed 1966 by Anne Van Doren Ross. Reprinted by permission of The Viking Press, Inc.

the tools he had. In the fall of 1727, about the time of his trouble
with Keimer, he brought together the group called the Junto.
Three besides Franklin—Hugh Meredith, Stephen Potts, and
George Webb—were from Keimer's shop. Meredith was

a Welsh Pennsylvanian, thirty years of age, bred to country work;
honest, sensible, had a great deal of solid observation, was something
of a reader but given to drink. . . . Potts, a young countryman of
full age, bred to the same, of uncommon natural parts, and great wit
and humour, but a little idle. . . . Webb, an Oxford scholar . . .
lively, witty, good-natured, and a pleasant companion, but idle, thought-
less, and imprudent to the last degree.

ı   With these were joined:

Joseph Breintnal, a copier of deeds for the scriveners, a good-natured,
friendly, middle-aged man, a great lover of poetry, reading all he could
meet with and writing some that was tolerable; very ingenious in many
little knick-knackeries and of sensible conversation. Thomas Godfrey,
a self-taught mathematician, great in his way, and afterward inventor of
what is now called Hadley's quadrant. But he knew little out of his way,
and was not a pleasing companion; as, like most great mathematicians
I have met with, he expected universal precision in everything said, and
was for ever denying or distinguishing upon trifles, to the disturbance
of all conversation. He soon left us. Nicholas Scull, a surveyor, afterwards surveyor-general, who loved books and sometimes made a few
verses. William Parsons, bred a shoemaker, but, loving reading, had
acquired a considerable share of mathematics, which he first studied
with a view to astrology, but he afterwards laughed at it. He also became a surveyor-general. William Maugridge, a joiner, a most exquisite
mechanic, and a solid, sensible man. . . . Robert Grace, a young
gentleman of some fortune, generous, lively, and witty; a lover of
punning and of his friends. And William Coleman, then a merchant's
clerk, about my age, who had the coolest, clearest head, the best heart,
and the exactest morals of almost any man I ever met with. He became
afterwards a merchant of great note, and one of our provincial judges.

These solid, sensible, good-natured, ingenious—and inconspicu-
ous—men were friends with whom Franklin already liked to talk,
and it was a kind of economy to meet with them all at once at a

tavern every Friday evening. There can be no doubt whose club it was. Franklin gave it form and direction. Many of the topics discussed were raised by him. The Junto was his benevolent lobby for the benefit of Philadelphia, and now and then for the advantage of Benjamin Franklin.

Somewhat unexpectedly, he seems to have borrowed the scheme of the Junto in part from Cotton Mather, who in Boston had originated neighborhood benefit societies, one for every church, and had belonged to twenty of them. Mather had drawn up a set of ten questions to be read at each meeting, "with due pauses," as a guide to discussion. Franklin, in his Rules for the Junto adopted in 1728, followed Mather. Some of the questions were much the same. Mather had asked: "Is there any matter to be humbly moved unto the legislative power, to be enacted into a law for public benefit?" Franklin asked: "Have you lately observed any defect in the laws of your country of which it would be proper to move the legislature for an amendment? Or do you know of any beneficial law that is wanting?" Mather: "Is there any particular person whose disorderly behaviour may be so scandalous and so notorious that we may do well to send unto the said person our charitable admonitions?" Franklin: "Do you know of a fellow-citizen who has lately done a worthy action, deserving praise or imitation; or who has lately committed an error proper for us to be warned against and avoid?" Mather: "Does there appear any instance of oppression or fraudulence in the dealings of any sort of people that may call for our essays to get it rectified?" Franklin: "Have you lately observed any encroachment on the just liberties of the people?" But Franklin has nothing like Mather's: "Can any further methods be devised that ignorance and wickedness may be chased from our people in general, and that household piety in particular may flourish among them?" And Mather has nothing like most of Franklin's twenty-four humane, secular, practical inquiries:

1. Have you met with anything in the author you last read, remarkable or suitable to be communicated to the Junto, particularly in his-

tory, morality, poetry, physic, travels, mechanic arts, or other parts of knowledge? 2. What new story have you lately heard agreeable for telling in conversation? 3. Hath any citizen in your knowledge failed in his business lately, and what have you heard of the cause? 4. Have you lately heard of any citizen's thriving well, and by what means? . . . 7. What unhappy effects of intemperance have you lately observed or heard; of imprudence, of passion, or of any other vice or folly? 8. What happy effects of temperance, of prudence, of moderation, or of any other virtue? 9. Have you or any of your acquaintance been lately sick or wounded? If so, what remedies were used, and what were their effects? 10. Whom do you know that are shortly going voyages or journeys, if one should have occasion to send by them? . . . 12. Hath any deserving stranger arrived in town since last meeting that you have heard of? And what have you heard or observed of his character or merits? And whether, think you, it lies in the power of the Junto to oblige him, or encourage him as he deserves? 13. Do you know of any deserving young beginner lately set up, whom it lies in the power of the Junto any way to encourage? . . . 16. Hath anybody attacked your reputation lately? And what can the Junto do towards securing it? 17. Is there any man whose friendship you want, and which the Junto, or any of them, can procure for you? 18. Have you lately heard any member's character attacked, and how have you defended it? 19. Hath any man injured you, from whom it is in the power of the Junto to procure redress? 20. In what manner can the Junto, or any of them, assist you in any of your honourable designs? . . .

These questions were the Junto's weekly ritual. The members met first at a tavern, later in a room hired in a house belonging to Grace. Between questions there were, as in Boston, due pauses— in Philadelphia long enough to drink a glass of wine. The rules further required that "every member, in his turn, should produce one or more queries on any point of morals, politics, or natural philosophy, to be discussed by the company; and once in three months produce and read an essay of his own writing, on any subject he pleased. Our debates were to be under the direction of a president, and to be conducted in the sincere spirit of inquiry after truth, without fondness for dispute or desire of victory; and, to prevent warmth, all expressions of positiveness in opinions, or direct contradiction, were after some time made contraband, and prohibited under small pecuniary penalties."

Franklin in his own queries asked the Junto things he was asking himself. "How shall we judge of the goodness of a writing? Or what qualities should a writing have to be good and perfect in its kind?" (He wrote out his own answer, and summed up: "It should be smooth, clear, and short.") "Can a man arrive at perfection in this life, as some believe; or is it impossible, as others believe?" "Wherein consists the happiness of a rational creature?" "What is wisdom?" ("The knowledge of what will be best for us on all occasions, and the best ways of attaining it.") "Is any man wise at all times and in all things?" ("No, but some are more frequently wise than others.") "Whether those meats and drinks are not the best that contain nothing in their natural taste, nor have anything added by art, so pleasing as to induce us to eat or drink when we are not thirsty or hungry, or after thirst and hunger are satisfied; water, for instance, for drink, and bread or the like for meat?" "Is there any difference between knowledge and prudence? If there is any, which of the two is most eligible?" "Is it justifiable to put private men to death, for the sake of public safety or tranquillity, who have committed no crime? As, in the case of the plague, to stop infection; or as in the case of the Welshmen here executed?" "If the sovereign power attempts to deprive a subject of his right (or, which is the same thing, of what he thinks his right), is it justifiable in him to resist, if he is able?" "Which is best: to make a friend of a wise and good man that is poor or of a rich man that is neither wise nor good?" "Does it not, in a general way, require great study and intense application for a poor man to become rich and powerful, if he would do it without the forfeiture of honesty?" "Does it not require as much pains, study, and application to become truly wise and strictly virtuous as to become rich?" "Whence comes the dew that stands on the outside of a tankard that has cold water in it in the summer time?"

Many young men have organized clubs for talk and friendship, but only Franklin ever kept one alive for thirty years. He did not lose interest as most young men do, or tire of leadership. The

Junto was his life enlarged and extended. It was convivial as well
as philosophical. Once a month in the pleasant seasons the debaters
met across the river for outdoor exercise. Once a year they had an
anniversary dinner, with songs and healths. The Junto was practical as well as convivial. Perhaps, in the long run, the help the
members gave each other had as much to do as anything with
making it last. It was a secret brotherhood. New members had to
stand up with their hands on their breasts and say they loved mankind in general and truth for truth's sake. But in the ritual questions many of the issues were more immediate. Strangers in
Philadelphia were to be welcomed if they deserved it, young be-
ginners in trade or business encouraged, reputations defended,
friendships furthered, grievances redressed, useful information ex-
changed. Franklin himself was benefited. Breintnal brought the
new printing house its first large order. Grace and Coleman lent
Franklin money to buy Meredith out. The Junto, commonly known
at first as the Leather Apron, became the club of young, poor,
enterprising men, as distinguished from the Merchants' Every
Night, which was for the respectable and established, and the
Bachelors, who were gay and suspected of being wicked. (Grace
was a member of the Bachelors, and Webb, who wrote a poem
called *Batchelors-Hall,* which Franklin published.)

In time the Junto had so many applications for membership that
it was at a loss to know how to limit itself to the twelve originally
planned. Franklin, who preferred the convenient apostolic number,
suggested that the Junto be kept as it was and that each member
organize a subordinate club, "with the same rules respecting
queries, etc., and without informing them of the connexion with
the Junto. The advantages proposed were the improvement of so
many more young citizens by the use of our institutions; our better acquaintance with the general sentiments of the inhabitants
on any occasion, as the Junto member might propose what queries
we should desire, and was to report to the Junto what passed in
his separate club; the promotion of our particular interests in
business by more extensive recommendation, and the increase
of our influence in public affairs, and our power of doing good

by spreading through the several clubs the sentiments of the Junto." Only five or six of these subordinate clubs were founded.

The benevolent imperialism of the Junto did not go beyond these little clubs of artisans and tradesmen in Philadelphia, but Franklin for a few enthusiastic months had world-wide schemes. On May 19, 1731, about the time he became a Mason, he set down in the library of the Junto, which was also the room where the club held its meetings, his observations on his reading of history. The affairs of the world, he had observed, are carried on by parties. These parties act in their own interest or what they think their interest. Their different interests cause natural confusion. Within each party each man has his own private interest. As soon as a party has gained its general point, each man puts forth his special claim, and the party comes to confusion within itself. Few men act for the good of their country except when they can believe that their country's good is also theirs. Fewer men still act for the good of mankind. Consequently: "There seems to me at present to be great occasion for raising a United Party for Virtue, by forming the virtuous and good men of all nations into a regular body, to be governed by suitable good and wise rules, which good and wise men may probably be more unanimous in their obedience to, than common people are to common laws."

The new sect was, much like the Junto, to be begun and spread by young single men joined in a secret society, each of whom should find other worthy members.

The members should engage to afford their advice, support, and assistance to each other in promoting one another's interests, business, and advancement in life. . . . For distinction, we should be called the Society of the Free and Easy: free, as being, by the general habit and practice of the virtues, free from the dominion of vice; and particularly, by the practice of industry and frugality, free from debt, which exposes a man to confinement and a species of slavery to his creditors.

Franklin was himself to write a kind of gospel for these free and easy saints, a book to be called *The Art of Virtue* which would not merely exhort to goodness but would show the precise means

of achieving it. Almost thirty years later he was still hoping to
write the book, which he told Lord Kames would be "adapted for
universal use." About his sect he did nothing but propose it to two
young men who felt his enthusiasm. Then pressing matters inter-
vened, and the Party for Virtue had to wait. Yet at eighty-two
Franklin could say:

I am still of opinion that it was a practicable scheme, and might
have been very useful, by forming a great number of good citizens;
and I was not discouraged by the seeming magnitude of the undertaking, as I have always thought that one man of tolerable abilities may
work great changes and accomplish great affairs among mankind, if he
first forms a good plan and . . . makes the execution of that same
plan his sole study and business.

JOHN F. ROSS

✪

The Character of Poor Richard:
Its Source and Alteration

Despite the considerable and valuable critical discussion of Franklin's Poor Richard, certain important points have been too briefly considered, or have been wholly overlooked. In particular, it has not been recognized (1) how extensively Franklin was indebted to Jonathan Swift in his hoaxing of Titan Leeds, the rival almanac-maker; (2) that the source for the characters Richard and Bridget Saunders was almost certainly Swift's Bickerstaff papers; and (3) that there are *two* Poor Richards—the original comic philomath of 1733 and the final American archetype, the fountainhead of shrewd prudential wisdom. Thus the student of Anglo-American literary relations has been unaware of Swift's part in making a great American figure; and the students of Poor Richard, on the whole regarding him as a static rather than changing character, have been led to make misleading, conflicting, or confused statements concerning him.

The few and incomplete references to the connection between Swift's hoax and Franklin's[1] suggest no more than that Franklin

---

Reprinted by permission of the Modern Language Association of America from John F. Ross, "The Character of Poor Richard: Its Source and Alteration," *PMLA*, Vol. LV, No. 3 (September 1940), pp. 785–794.
1. Early students of Franklin devoted considerable attention to Franklin's hoax without even mentioning Swift—some even praising Franklin for the

was indebted to Swift for the basic idea of a false prophecy. Even
Bernard Faÿ, though he devotes considerable space to Poor
Richard, goes no further.[2] Such references are sound enough, as far
as they go; but they reduce Franklin's debt to a not very important
borrowing. Actually, Franklin followed Swift's hoax in considerable
and definite detail.

There are, first, the basic parallels. Both Bickerstaff and Poor
Richard introduce themselves as astrologers. Both forecast, for
specified days, the deaths of brother astrologers. And, though both
victims are real philomaths engaged in forecasting and almanac-
making, both Bickerstaff and Poor Richard are fictional characters
invented for the occasion. At appropriate times after the prophecies, both hoaxers give accounts of the deaths as forecast. The

---

originality of the idea. Cf. James Parton, *Life and Times of Benjamin Franklin* (New York, 1864), I, 227 ff.; J. B. McMaster, *Benjamin Franklin as a
Man of Letters* (Boston, 1882), Chap. 4; John Bigelow, *Life of Benjamin
Franklin*, 4th ed. (Phila., 1902), Pt. II, Chap. 7; P. L. Ford, *Many-Sided
Franklin* (New York, 1889), Chap. 10; P. L. Ford, Introduction to *Sayings
of Poor Richard* (New York, 1889). In "Was Benjamin Franklin a Plagiar-
ist?" (*Bookman,* IV, 24–30), Kate Stephen raises the question of Franklin's
debt, quotes at length but without analysis, and concludes that Franklin
"might not have known of 'Squire Bickerstaff's jocularity" and that his hoax
has the "vraisemblance of an original conception." Paul Elmer More asserted
the connection between Swift and Franklin, but left the point undeveloped,
in *Shelburne Essays* (New York, 1906), p. 143. Bernard Faÿ is quoted in the
note immediately following, and Carl Van Doren, in his recent *Benjamin
Franklin* (New York, 1938), mentions the connection in a sentence (p. 107).
   2. "Franklin . . . amused himself in his first almanac by continuing a
witticism Swift had employed in his 'Predictions for 1708 by Isaac Bickerstaff, Esquire,' who had violently and quaintly denounced the makers of
almanacs by predicting the death of one of them, a man named Partridge.
. . . [This] did not escape Franklin's notice. So he announced boldly and
with suavity (the element he added to Swift, who was more rough-shod in
his attack) the death of his friend and colleague, Titan Leeds. The stars had
made it known to him beyond a doubt, and Titan Leeds knew it very well
too. This was the reason why Richard, who was not rich and had to make
his living, had taken up the pen. Leeds was furious at this gruesome maneu-
ver. He answered, stirring up a fine battle, to the great joy of Franklin, who
needed just this advertisement to launch his book successfully. The quarrel
lasted eight years, and ended by the clear triumph of Poor Richard, as Titan
Leeds really died." Bernard Faÿ, *Franklin, the Apostle of Modern Times*
(Boston, 1929), pp. 161–162.

victims in each case having protested, Richard, like Bickerstaff, sets forth reasons why his rival *must* be dead.[3]

It is here, after the presumed death of Leeds, that the parallels become more significant. Neither Bickerstaff nor Poor Richard is an eyewitness of his victim's death. Bickerstaff, it is true, has independent testimony in the "Account of the Death of Mr. Partridge"; but it is of some importance that Bickerstaff was not the witness himself. It enables him to stress the bodily death of Partridge less than the reasons why Partridge must be dead. Poor Richard follows suit. Thus Franklin, like Swift before him, is interested less in actual deception, or even a crude joke, than in the comic fantasy of the pseudological demonstrations of death.

In the preface to the second *Poor Richard,* Richard says that the appearance of an almanac under Leeds's name does not argue that Leeds is alive: "that Pamphlet may be only a Contrivance of somebody or other, who hopes perhaps to sell two or three Year's Almanacks still, by the sole Force and Virtue of Mr. *Leeds's* Name."[4] It is the same point urged by Bickerstaff in meeting the objection that Partridge must be alive, since he continues to write almanacs:

Gadbury, Poor Robin, Dove, Wing, and several others, do yearly publish their Almanacks, tho' several of them have been dead since before the Revolution. . . . I have heard the Booksellers affirm, That they have desired Mr. Partridge to spare himself further Trouble, and only lend them his Name.[5]

In *Poor Richard* for 1735, answering Leeds's second protest, Franklin again has recourse to Swift. Here the parallels are so close as to suggest that Franklin actually read over the "Vindication" of Bickerstaff before writing his preface. Bickerstaff assumes an air of

3. All quotations from Franklin, except where otherwise noted, are from A. H. Smyth, ed., *Writings of Benjamin Franklin,* 10 vols. (New York, 1905–1907). All quotations from Swift are from W. A. Eddy, ed., *Satires and Personal Writings* (London, 1932). Temple Scott's edition of Swift's *Prose Works* lacks "Squire Bickerstaff Detected" and "An Account of the Proceedings of Isaac Bickerstaff, Esq."

4. Franklin, *Writings,* II, 202.

5. Swift, *Satires,* pp. 190–191.

pain and surprise at the rough treatment given him in Partridge's almanac—it is "improper," he feels, "for a Person of his Education." Bickerstaff next appeals to the learned world, laments the "Scurrility and Passion, in a Controversy among Scholars," and sorrowfully adds, "I wish Mr. Partridge knew the Thoughts which Foreign Universities have conceived of his ungenerous Proceeding with me; but I am too tender of his Reputation to publish them to the World."[6] Poor Richard is briefer, lacking some of the outward flourishes of Bickerstaff; but his mood is the same—sorrow, surprise, lamentation over scholarly wrangling:

'Tis certain there is no Harmony among the Stargazers. . . . I had resolved to keep the Peace on my own part, and affront none of them; . . . But having receiv'd much Abuse from *Titan Leeds* deceas'd . . . I cannot help saying, that tho' I take it patiently, I take it very unkindly.

Thereupon Richard, like Bickerstaff before him, proceeds to his invincible demonstration that, "whatever he may pretend, 'tis undoubtedly true that he is really defunct and dead."[7] Since Franklin was no mere copyist, and had a good deal of humor of his own, he did not follow Swift slavishly; but for all that there were several of Bickerstaff's proofs too good not to use. Bickerstaff writes:

I will plainly prove him to be dead, out of his own Almanack for this Year. . . . He there says, he is not only now alive, but was also alive upon that very 29th of March, which I foretold he should die on: By this, he declares his Opinion, That a man may be alive now, who was not alive a Twelvemonth ago. And indeed, there lies the Sophistry of his Argument. He dares not assert he was alive but since that 29th of March, but he is now alive, and was so on that day.[8]

Poor Richard writes:

I convince him in his own Words, that he is dead . . . for in his Preface to his Almanack for 1734, he says, *"Saunders adds . . . that by my own Calculation I shall survive until the 26th of the said Month*

6. *Ibid.*, p. 185.
7. Franklin, *Writings*, II, 203–204.
8. Swift, *Satires*, p. 189.

October 1733, which is as untrue as the former." Now if it be, as Leeds says, *untrue* and a *gross Falshood* that he surviv'd till the 26th of October 1733, then it is certainly *true* that he died *before* that Time, . . . anything he may say to the contrary notwithstanding.[9]

Both victims, though presumed to be dead, are gravely addressed; both are "convinced" by their own words, and by an identical technique of seizing upon ambiguities of their words or sentence structure. Again, Bickerstaff writes: "Above a Thousand Gentlemen having bought his Almanack . . . at every Line they read, they would . . . cry out, betwixt Rage and Laughter, They were sure no Man alive ever writ such damn'd Stuff as this."[10] Poor Richard repeats the quip: after remarking that the only smart thing in Leeds's almanac was an extract from *Hudibras,* he adds, "and no Man *living* would or could write such Stuff as the rest."[11] Finally, there is the curious state of existence to which both victims are logically reduced. Though their deaths have been invincibly demonstrated, both Bickerstaff and Richard admit a certain zombilike locomotion in the "deceas'd." The earlier version: "Therefore if an uninformed Carcass walks still about, and is pleased to call itself Partridge, Mr. Bickerstaff does not think himself any way answerable for that."[12] Richard's version: "But if some People will walk and be troublesome after Death, it may perhaps be born with a little."[13]

Further borrowing from the Swiftian hoax could be shown,[14] but

9. Franklin, *Writings,* II, 204–205.
10. Swift, *Satires,* p. 188.
11. Franklin, *Writings,* II, 204.
12. Swift, *Satires,* p. 188.
13. Franklin, *Writings,* II, 205.
14. Thus Franklin reverted to the old hoax in 1739, when Leeds really did die. *Poor Richard* for 1740 prints a complimentary letter to Richard from the ghost of Leeds, who, for good measure, adds three prophecies, one of which forecasts that "J. J—n, *Philomat,* shall be openly reconciled to the church of Rome" (*Writings,* II, 223). Here is another prophecy at the expense of a brother philomath, and here again an echo from Swift, who enlivened his account of Partridge's death by saying that the astrologer "declar'd himself a Nonconformist, and had a Fanatick Preacher" (*Satires,* p. 174). The religion had to be changed to suit the Philadelphia climate, but the basic libel was the same.

is unnecessary here. Franklin's treatment of Leeds in the first three prefaces conclusively shows his thorough familiarity with the Bickerstaff papers, and his habit of utilizing them in some detail.

But there is more than the hoax on Leeds in the early prefaces: there is the emergence of two characters, Richard and Bridget Saunders. Where did they come from? did Franklin create them? or did he help himself to more in the Bickerstaff papers than the mere matter of the hoax?

That the *names* "Richard Saunders" and "Poor Richard" came from two English sources has been often enough pointed out;[15] and that the "hint" for his character "probably came from the characters in the *Spectator*" has been suggested.[16] Ordinarily Franklin is given implicit or explicit credit for creating Poor Richard. We read, "Robin and Richard left all their foreign baggage behind them when they crossed the Atlantic,"[17] or, "Combining the first words of these two titles, he created his own 'Poor Richard' . . . [who] was a distinct and concrete creation of Franklin's brain."[18] But it is dangerous to forget that, when Swift's hoax crossed the Atlantic, the characters of that hoax came too. For, as Sir Walter Scott pointed out, Swift was not only a satirist, but an admirable creator of character. Nor should one forget Franklin's efficiency: he would have been unlikely to borrow the hoax *only,* if he saw as well anything else to his purpose. And it would seem he found the basis for Richard and Bridget Saunders.

Richard's character, though he has the Bickerstaffian role in the hoax, is not primarily based on Bickerstaff. Since Swift's aim is to ridicule prognosticating philomaths, his work uses comedy toward the end of satire. Franklin has no basic satiric intent, but the immediately practical aim of selling his almanac. Hence the necessary

15. McMaster, *Benjamin Franklin,* p. 101; Ford's Introduction to *Sayings,* p. 9; Carl Van Doren's Introduction to *Franklin and Edwards* (New York, 1920), p. xx.
16. W. B. Cairns, *American Literature,* rev. ed. (New York, 1930), p. 95.
17. Van Doren, p. xx.
18. Faÿ, pp. 160, 168.

differences between Bickerstaff and Poor Richard: Bickerstaff is a man of science, with a European reputation—far superior to the rabble of almanac-makers, and contemptuous of them. His purpose is to show "the gross Abuse of Astrology," and his fortune has placed him "above the little regards of Scribbling for a few pence."[19] Despite the masque of learned astrologer, Swift's actual attitude is here revealed, and it is an attitude of no use to Franklin. Swift writes against the usual philomath; Franklin is one himself. Swift makes fun for satire; Franklin makes fun for money. Poor Richard has to drum up trade for this and next year's almanac; he is friendly and ingratiating; he tells frankly how welcome the "fi-pences" are. Thus the superior Bickerstaff can hardly influence the general character of Richard.

Much more to the point are the Partridges. From the "Account of the Death," we learn that Partridge began to droop and languish and was finally confined to his bed. We are given a convincing account of the deathbed conversation, and of Partridge's confession: that he never meddled with the weather, but left that to the printer, and that "the rest was my own Invention, to make my Almanack Sell, having a Wife to Maintain, and no other Way to get my Bread, for mending Old Shoes is a Poor Livelihood."[20] The following paper—Partridge's presumed account of the affair—is made up almost wholly of realistic comic narrative. Partridge is prevailed on by his wife to take medicines and go to bed; his rest is interrupted by the tolling of the death-bell in his honor; his wife falls into a "disorder"; and in the midst of all, the undertaker's man comes to measure the apartment for mourning, in the face of Partridge's protests. Partridge warns the intruder that he hears his wife's voice, "which, by the by, is pretty distinguishable" and that, if she finds out the business at issue, she will employ her stout cudgel "very much to the Detriment" of the intruder's person. The narrative develops further vicissitudes, and presents its absurd situations vigorously and concretely.

19. Swift, *Satires,* pp. 161, 171.
20. *Ibid.,* p. 174.

Franklin's use of the Partridges does not show such borrowings of specific detail as does his use of Bickerstaff's prophecy and subsequent proofs of death. But the similarity of Franklin's technique to that of Swift, and the basic parallels between the Partridges and the Saunderses can hardly be put down to coincidence.

Both Swift and Franklin sketch in the characters by a few lively details rather than by elaborate accounts. Both use a natural, homely, comic realism, effectively suggesting the domestic life of the philomath, the everyday human beings behind the title pages of almanacs. Just as our imaginations are set to work by the implied efficiency of Mrs. Partridge with the cudgel, so are they set to work by Bridget's determined threat "to burn all my Books and Rattling Traps (as she calls my Instruments) if I do not make some profitable Use of them."[21] Franklin's use of the Swiftian technique can be realized more fully if one calls to mind how much it differs from the leisurely and urbane characterization found in the *Spectator,* or the too copious, literal detail of Defoe.

In addition, Richard and Partridge have much in common. Both are poor, needy men, frankly preparing their almanacs not so much for the honor of the stars as for their livelihoods. Both reveal entertaining glimpses of the practical problems of the craft. Both are favored with wives who must be supported; and the wives themselves are of much the same type—Bridget's practicality, talkativeness, vigor, and determination are decidedly reminiscent of Mrs. Partridge's "pretty distinguishable voice" and handiness with the cudgel, and both wives seem to be more practically energetic and forceful than their husbands.

It is clear, it seems to me, that the Partridges supplied the basis for the Saunderses. Nor is the conclusion surprising. Franklin made no bones over borrowing for what was primarily an ephemeral commercial venture: he borrowed the name Richard Saunders, he borrowed maxims and proverbs, he extracted from poems, he borrowed verbatim from Rabelais, and he borrowed Swift's hoax. The Partridges lay in his way, and he found them.

21. Franklin, *Writings,* II, 196.

But Poor Richard is always Partridge's superior. In the hoax on Leeds, Richard has the position of Bickerstaff, and Leeds is the victim. And as philomath Richard represents himself as an expert astrologer (again a touch of Bickerstaff), whereas Partridge confesses he knows nothing of such affairs. Richard arises from the ashes of Partridge, an improved and American phoenix, and with an additional comic irony of which Swift might have been proud. That is, Richard is represented as an intimate and admiring friend of Titan Leeds. Such a presumed friendship might have interfered with Swift's satiric purpose; but Franklin (with the practical necessities of his own almanac business in mind) can hardly afford to make fun of philomaths. Thus, as long as Franklin is more comic than satiric, he can have his cake and eat it; he can extract comic elements from Swift, hoax Leeds to his own advantage, develop the estimable Saunders from the feckless Partridge, add further comedy of his own, and turn all to profitable publishing. Bernard Faÿ has pointed out that Franklin adds "suavity" to Swift's hoax; but it is worth stressing that the careful manipulation and change of Swift's satiric material into nonsatiric, comic entertainment is an urbanity largely conditioned by business reasons. Yet the added comedy remains, as an evidence of Franklin's own rich vein, and of his habit of making as much laughter as he could, within prudential limits.

This entertaining philomath of the early prefaces would scarcely seem destined to become an American archetype—the apotheosis of the shrewd, the thrifty, the utilitarian; yet this destiny has been his.

The first step of this change was the coalescing of what were originally two independent elements in *Poor Richard*. Franklin himself, in the *Autobiography*, said that he had designed the almanac to be "both entertaining and useful."[22] Obviously the original concept of Richard and the hoax are merely entertaining and

22. *Ibid.*, I, 342.

not—in Franklin's sense—useful. All we know of Richard and Bridget as people we find in the early prefaces; and (a point that has not been sufficiently recognized) in those prefaces there is no suggestion or implication that Richard is a storehouse of proverbs —he is the engaging stargazer supporting himself by making almanacs. As late as the sixth preface, which was concocted by Bridget, he is still only the Richard of the first preface, having left his manuscript with his wife and set out "for *Powtowmack,* to visit an old Stargazer of his Acquaintance."[23] For six years Franklin has merely presented the entertaining figure developed out of Partridge.

The "useful" part of the almanac was confined to that which followed the preface. And here Franklin from the first had "filled all the little spaces that occurr'd . . . with proverbial sentences."[24] On the one hand were the Saunderses, fictional characters presented for sheer entertainment; on the other, was B. Franklin, printer, who inserted useful proverbs into vacant spaces. And it was naturally the latter whom Franklin remembered years later, forgetting the hoax and the comic astrologer. Even yet it is too often ignored how distinct the original Richard was from Franklin, though Franklin himself made a careful differentiation. Thus Richard mentions his relations with his printer (*i.e.,* Franklin himself) several times, and insists on their separate identity.[25] Though Franklin had his tongue in his cheek in such passages, it was a very real distinction, and one not to be obscured by the later development of Richard. In fact, from first to last, the material in the *body* of the almanacs is impersonal, or reflective of genuine interests of Franklin. Thus the suggestions concerning lightning rods in the almanac for 1753 emanate from Franklin, the modern scientist, writing with no thought of Richard, the astrologer. Briefly, in the early years when Richard and Bridget are presented as people, the

23. *Ibid.,* II, 213.
24. *Ibid.,* I, 342.
25. Cf. prefaces for 1733, 1737, 1739, 1750.

proverbial sayings are confined to the body of the almanac, with no particular reference to Richard;[26] whereas the character is confined to the prefaces, with no indication of his proverbial wisdom.

Quotable maxims, however, would naturally be attributed to the genial Richard, who had appeared so like a real person in the prefaces. As a result, a new and discrete element was added to Richard's character. This thoroughly adventitious development Franklin accepted as easily as his readers; yet, even so, we do not find the new note until the seventh preface, where Richard writes, "Besides the usual Things expected in an Almack, I hope the profess'd Teachers of Mankind will excuse my scattering here and there some instructive Hints in matters of Morality and Religion."[27]

In this preface Richard is still the astrologer-philomath; but once Franklin has definitely added the didactic element, the original character begins to fade. Regrettably, Bridget drops out of sight, and there is less and less of Richard as character.[28] The verse preface for 1746 shows clearly how far Franklin has abandoned his original Richard. Purporting to answer the question, "Who is *Poor Richard?*" the writer promises some "slight slight sketches of my Dame and me"; but what he does is to draw an edifying and abstract picture of a good, simple life—in a set of verses almost as

26. In the body of the almanac for the first six years, I find only one touch suggestive of Richard, the character: the verses for December, 1734, are said to be "by Mrs. Bridget Saunders, my Dutchess, in answer to the December verses of last year." But both sets of verses (Ford, *Sayings of Poor Richard,* pp. 31–32, 43) are impersonal: six lines each on a bad wife and a bad husband, neither identifiable as Richard or Bridget. The name Richard, or Dick, occurs in such impersonal lines as

Take this remark from Richard, poor and lame,
Whate'er's begun in anger, ends in shame. [*Sayings,* p. 38]

wherein *lame* is scarcely to be regarded as additional information about Richard Saunders, but as a rhyme-word. More than this, the names, even, appear rarely in the body of the almanac (for these six years)—Bridget's once, and Richard's four or five times.

27. Franklin, *Writings,* II, 217.

28. See also the Preface for 1743 (impersonal directions for making wine) and that for 1748 (largely made up of extracts concerning the winter season in the Hudson's Bay country).

impersonal and general as the *Essay on Man*.[29] This preface may be taken as symptomatic of the second phase of Richard's development—the instructive Richard has replaced the entertaining Richard.

It is easy to see why Franklin let the original character go, and made no attempt to relate the maxims to the character of his stargazer. He was interested in getting an almanac to press every fall, not in the depiction of character or the maintenance of literary consistency. Furthermore, the early Richard was a fiction, whereas the later Richard expressed a strong part of Franklin's real character. "Keep your shop and your shop will keep you" and "He that riseth late, must trot all Day, and shall scarce overtake his Business at night" are business maxims suited to B. Franklin, printer. "Early to bed, and early to rise" might make a businessman healthy, wealthy, and wise—but it would be ruinous for a stargazer. Nor need we assume that Franklin or his readers would be at all concerned at the blurring of the originally clear comic character, and its final replacement by the "useful" Richard. Twenty-six years was enough for an unconscious and painless effacement of the old stargazer.

This change in Richard is the first example in American literature of a tendency common much later—the blurring of a popular comic character through identification with its creator. Writing of the "literary comedians" of the last half of the nineteenth century, Professor Blair has pointed out how the original concept of Artemus Ward as a fat, genial, illiterate showman took on more and more the character of his creator, Browne; and Professor Blair has

29. Thanks to kind Readers and a careful Wife
    With plenty bless'd, I lead an easy Life;
    My business Writing; less to drain the Mead,
    Or crown the barren Hill with useful Shade; . . .
    Some Books we read, tho' few there are that hit
    The happy Point where Wisdom joins with Wit; . . .
    The Friend sincere, and honest Man, with Joy
    Treating or treated oft our Time employ.
    Our Table next, Meals temperate; and our Door
    Op'ning spontaneous to the bashful Poor. . . . [*Writings,* II, 294–295.]

rightly generalized, "This sort of identification happened frequently. . . . This meant . . . a significant contrast between earlier and later humorous characters [in that] the characters became blurred."[30] It would appear, however, that this was not a sudden appearance of the late nineteenth century, but a trait of American humor present or latent since the time of Poor Richard, eldest of the line.

The early Richard was finally submerged by the famous farewell Preface of 1758, wherein a shadowy Richard appears, only to introduce the speech of a wise old man, Father Abraham, who quotes maxim after maxim from the body of the almanacs. It may be noted that Father Abraham quotes *only* the shrewd, prudential maxims, that his speech is a highly specialized culling from the almanac. The pungency of "Fish and visitors smell after three days," and the cynical wisdom of "The first mistake in public business is the going into it," are not present. Thus Father Abraham's speech is not representative even of Franklin's maxims, much less of the original Poor Richard. But the popularity of this preface, and its frequent reprinting as "The Way to Wealth," definitely fixed Richard in the minds of readers as—above all—the fountainhead of prudential wisdom.

Since 1758, this final speech has apparently been taken as the starting point for Richard, rather than as a final phase of development. Thus it can be written, "Shadowy figure though he was, Poor Richard embodied the Yankee characteristics of thrift, industry and godliness,"[31] wherein the character is regarded as static and based on the final Richard. Or, "It is perhaps because he is so like Franklin himself that he and his wife Bridget 'are quite as real as any characters in the whole domain of fiction,' "[32] wherein no distinction is made between the earliest and latest Richard. Again, as a distinguished recent biographer of Franklin puts it:

30. Walter Blair, *Native American Humor* (New York, 1937), pp. 113–115.
31. *Ibid.,* p. 18.
32. Cairns, p. 95.

[Poor Richard] was a distinct and concrete creation of Franklin's brain, expressing, like a character in a play, all the feelings, ideas and instincts which Franklin could not express in public himself. . . . He so pervaded the life of Benjamin Franklin that he imposed not only an attitude on Franklin, but finally forced him to play a role. . . . People ended by seeing Franklin through Saunders, and thought they were one and the same person.[33]

Now, in so far as a character was created, it was the poor astrologer, the philomath with his wife, Bridget. He did not embody Yankee characteristics, he was not at all like Franklin himself. Nor did this character impose an attitude on Franklin. Rather, Richard had an aspect of Franklin imposed upon him . . . the distinct and concrete creation was brushed aside to make way for the author of useful sayings—that is, Franklin forced Richard to play a role. And, if people "ended" by seeing Franklin through Saunders, they had some justification—it was the original Richard who was distinct from Franklin; the final Richard speaks with the same voice which produced the *Autobiography*. (This is not to say, of course, that the *Autobiography* by any means expresses all the important aspects of Franklin.) That writers ordinarily thorough and perspicuous should fall into confusion through oversimplifying the character of Richard sufficiently indicates the need of seeing Richard as he was—a changing figure, not a static one.

Swift, with his contempt for any nation of shopkeepers, would have been the first to satirize this ultimate Richard—to whose initial vitality he had contributed much. As for Franklin, he was quite content to take just what he wanted, manipulate it efficiently for his own American ends, and then, unconsciously, to let the figure transmute itself into something wholly his.

33. Faÿ, p. 162.

DAVID LEVIN

✪

The Autobiography of Benjamin Franklin: The Puritan Experimenter in Life and Art

It would be difficult to find a book that seems more widely understood, as a model of plain exposition of character, than *The Autobiography of Benjamin Franklin*. Everyone knows that this is the life of a self-made, self-educated man and that *Poor Richard's Almanac* was a best seller. Everyone knows that the penniless sixteen-year-old boy who first walked down the streets of Philadelphia with his pockets bulging with shirts and stockings, and with two great puffy rolls under his arms, worked so diligently at his calling that for him the promise of Scripture was fulfilled, and he one day stood before kings. (He "stood before five," he wrote later, with characteristic precision, and sat down to dine with one.) We all know, too, that the Franklin stove and bifocals and the electrical experiments bear witness to Franklin's belief in lifelong education, and that it was because of his ability to explain clearly and persuade painlessly—even delightfully—that his international reputation soared higher than his famous kite.

Too often, however, we forget a few simple truths about this great man and his greatest works. We forget the chief purposes for which he wrote his autobiography, and the social system that led

Reprinted from David Levin, "The Autobiography of Benjamin Franklin: The Puritan Experimenter in Life and Art," *The Yale Review*, Vol. LIII (December 1963), pp. 258–275. Copyright © 1963 by Yale University.

him to conceive such aims. Remembering his plainness, his clarity, we overlook the subtlety of his expression, his humor, and his qualifying statements. Above all, we forget that he was a writer, that he had a habit of creating characters. And so he takes us in. Some of us forget that Poor Richard is just as clearly Franklin's creation as is Mrs. Silence Dogood, the fictitious character through whom young Benjamin had published in his brother's newspaper in Boston; many of us forget that *The Way to Wealth,* Franklin's brilliantly successful collection of economic proverbs, is a humorous *tale* narrated by Poor Richard, who at first makes fun of himself and then reports the long speech made by another fictitious character named Father Abraham; and most of us overlook the crucial distinction, especially in the first half of Franklin's autobiography, between the *writer* of the book and the chief *character* he portrays.

Please understand that I do not mean to call Franklin's autobiography a work of fiction. I must insist, however, that we refuse to let its general fidelity to historical fact blind us to the author's function in creating the character who appears in the book. Franklin's first entry into Philadelphia may serve as an example. We are apt to consider the picture of that boy as a natural fact of history, as if no conceivable biographer could have omitted it. It merges in our experience with the myth that Horatio Alger exploited a century later, and with dozens of other pictures of successful men at the beginning of their careers: the country boy walking into the big city, the immigrant lad getting off the boat and stepping forth in search of his fortune. So grandly representative is this human experience that our current critical fashion would call it archetypal. But it was Franklin the writer who elected to describe this picture, and who made it memorable. He was not obliged to include it. He *chose* to make it represent an important moment in his life, and he chose to depict his young former self in particular detail. His dirty clothes, his bulging pockets, and the huge rolls constitute nearly the only details respecting his personal appearance in the entire book. He might have omitted them, and he might have ignored the whole incident.

If we try to imagine what our view of Franklin might have been had he not written his autobiography, we will recognize that the author's conception of himself has considerably more literary significance than one can find in a single descriptive passage. Though the honest autobiographer refuses to invent fictitious incidents, he *actually creates himself as a character.* He selects incidents and qualities for emphasis, and discards or suppresses others. He portrays himself in relation to some other character (whom he also "creates" in this book), but refrains from portraying himself in relation to some others whom he once knew. He decides on the meaning of his life and the purpose of his book, and he selects traits, incidents, and characters accordingly. Obviously he cannot record everything that happened unless he spews forth every feeling, impulse, twitch, that ever entered his mind or affected his senses. Indeed, the very conception of a happening requires some selection, some ordering of experience, and a point of view from which to perceive that order. D. H. Lawrence did not understand Franklin's autobiography, but he saw that it recognized a kind of order, and a view of the self, which imposed a planned control on natural feelings. "The ideal self!" he cried scornfully in his critique of Franklin.

Oh, but I have a strange and fugitive self shut out and howling like a wolf or a coyote under the ideal windows. See his red eyes in the dark? This is the self who is coming into his own.

The perfectibility of man, dear God! When every man as long as he remains alive is in himself a multitude of conflicting men. Which of these do you choose to perfect, at the expense of every other?

Old Daddy Franklin will tell you. He'll rig him up for you, the pattern American. Oh, Franklin was the first downright American.

As we shall see later on, this gross caricature of "the sharp little man" reflects some imperfections in Franklin's ability to communicate with ages beyond his own, and as we shall see even sooner, it reflects an inability or unwillingness in Lawrence and many others to read carefully. For the moment, however, let us content ourselves with two observations in support of Lawrence's limited perception. First, Franklin's autobiography represents that kind of art in which the author tries to understand himself, to evaluate himself, to see himself, in a sense, from outside; it is a *portrayal* of the self rather than simply an *expression* of current feeling or an outpouring of those multiple selves that Lawrence celebrates. Old Daddy Franklin did indeed know what he was about. But the second observation must limit the praise in the first. The very terms in which Franklin expresses his admirable self-awareness limit his communication in a way that obscures the identity of the author. The technique of humor, and the disarming candor about techniques of influence and persuasion—these occasionally make us wonder which of several selves Benjamin Franklin is.

Franklin's art is deceptive. At first there may seem to be none at all. The book, written at four different times from 1771 to 1790, the year Franklin died, is loosely constructed; it is almost conversational in manner. It begins, indeed, as a letter to Franklin's son. It is episodic, anecdotal. Clearly, however, its narrative order includes two major divisions: the first half of the book describes his education, as he strives for a secure position in the world and for a firm character; the second half concentrates on his career of *public* service, though the account breaks off well before the American Revolution.

That simple pattern itself illustrates the most important fact about Franklin's autobiography. He not only creates an attractive image of himself but uses himself as a prototype of his age and his country. There are three essential ways in which he establishes this story of the self-made man securely in the broadest experience of his time. If we examine them with some care, we may understand his purposes and his achievement more clearly.

The first context is that of Puritanism, represented here by Franklin's admiration for John Bunyan's *Pilgrim's Progress* and Cotton Mather's *Essays To Do Good*. Although Franklin says that he was converted to deism by some antideistic tracts in his Presbyterian father's library, we cannot overestimate the importance of his Puritan heritage, and his own account gives it due credit. (I refer, of course, not to the gross distortion suggested by the word "puritanical," the joy-killing and fanatical, but to that firm tradition that required every Christian to venture into this world as a pilgrim, doing right for the glory of God.) It is to this tradition that we owe Franklin's great proverb "Leisure is time for doing something useful," his emphasis on diligence in one's calling, the moral preoccupation that colors his view of ordinary experience. We see the Puritan influence in his insistence on frugality, simplicity, and utility as standards of value; and we see it just as clearly in his acceptance of public duty, his constant effort to improve the community, his willingness at last to serve the local and international community without pay. When we remember that the Protestant ethic combines the profit motive with religious duty, we should remember that in Franklin's day (as in John Winthrop's before him) it also obliged one to use one's fortune, and one's own person, in public service.

The Puritan tradition, indeed, gave Franklin a more purely literary kind of model. By the time he was growing up there existed in both old and New England a fairly large body of personal literature that emphasized objective self-examination and the need to keep an objective record of divine Providence as it affected an individual life. One recorded one's daily life in order to evaluate one's conduct and also to find evidence of God's will in the pattern of events. It was the Puritan custom, moreover, to improve every opportunity to find moral instruction and signs of universal meaning in particular experience. Franklin himself describes and exemplifies this custom in an anecdote (not in the *Autobiography*, but in a letter) of a visit that he made in 1724 to the old Puritan minister Cotton Mather. As Franklin was leaving, he wrote later, Mather

showed me a shorter way out of the house, through a narrow passage, which was crossed by a beam overhead. We were talking as I withdrew, he accompanying me behind, and I turning partly towards him when he said hastily, "STOOP, STOOP!" I did not understand him till I felt my head against the beam. He was a man that never missed any occasion of giving instruction, and upon this he said to me: "You are young, and have the world before you; STOOP as you go through it, and you will miss many hard thumps." This advice, thus beat into my head, has frequently been of use to me, and I often think of it when I

see pride mortified and misfortunes brought upon people by carrying
their heads too high.

One of the most successful devices that Franklin uses in his autobiography is this kind of symbolic anecdote, or parable; what brings
Franklin's practice closer to Puritan preaching than to the parables
in the Bible is his careful addition of a conclusion that drives home
the point—the application or use—for those who might otherwise
misunderstand it.

Before turning from Puritanism to a second quality of eighteenth-
century experience, we should pause for another minute over the
name of John Bunyan. For the first half of Franklin's autobiography, as Charles Sanford has said, represents a kind of pilgrim's
progress. As his pious contemporaries Jonathan Edwards and John
Woolman published accounts of their growth in Christian grace,
so Franklin, acknowledging the aid of Providence, narrates the
progress of a chosen, or at least fortunate, and often undeserving
young man through a series of perils (including the valley of the
shadow of death) to a relatively safe moral haven, if not to the
Heavenly City. Others, we must remember, do not fare so well.
A number of his early associates fall into one pit or another, and
although Franklin tries to show what he did to save himself, so that
others might profit by his example, he makes it perfectly clear that
on several occasions he was so foolish that he too would have gone
down had he not been preserved by Providence—or plain good
luck.

It is this sense of the perils facing a young man in the free
society of the new capitalism that brings me to the second of my
three kinds of representativeness. Whether he was a Puritan or not,
the young indentured servant, the young apprentice, the young
artisan or farmer of Franklin's time had to walk a perilous way in
the world. And if, like a great many Americans, he was leaving
his childhood community as well as the restraints and comforts of
his childhood religious faith, when he came forth to make his way
in the world, he faced those dangers with very little help from outside himself. He had precious little help in the experience of others,

for often his experience was new for the entire society. The mistakes he made did not entitle him to the protection of bankruptcy laws or of the less grand comforts of our welfare state. They sent him to a debtor's prison, or subjected him to the permanent authority of a creditor. Franklin described plain economic fact as well as moral truth when he said, "It is hard for an empty sack to stand upright."

Thus one of Franklin's major purposes in the *Autobiography* was to instruct the young, not only by good example but by warning. Especially in his account of his youth, he presents himself repeatedly as the relatively innocent or ignorant young man in conflict with those who would take advantage of him. Much of the sharp dealing that annoys D. H. Lawrence and others occurs in this kind of situation. Franklin's older brother, exploiting and sometimes beating the young apprentice, tries to circumvent a court ruling against his newspaper by freeing young Benjamin and making him nominal owner of the paper; Benjamin takes advantage of the opportunity by going off to Philadelphia to strike out on his own. Samuel Keimer uses Franklin to train other printers so that Franklin's services may then be dispensed with; but Franklin plans to set up his own shop, and when he does, he prospers as Keimer fails.

As in the fiction of Daniel Defoe, whom Franklin admired, and Samuel Richardson, whom he was among the first American printers to publish, Franklin's *Autobiography* indicates clearly that the relations between the sexes concealed some of the chief dangers of the young freeman's liberty. Luckily, he concedes, he escaped the worst consequences of occasional encounters with "low women"; but in a society that frankly recognized marriage as an economic contract he was almost entrapped by a clever pair of parents who seem to have counted on hoodwinking the young lad because he had to bargain for himself in a matter that required cooler heads. Franklin's account of the episode is priceless:

Mrs. Godfrey [his landlady] projected a match for me with a relation's daughter, took opportunities of bringing us often together, till a serious courtship on my part ensued, the girl being in herself very deserving. The old folks encouraged me by continued invitations to supper and by leaving us together, till at length it was time to explain. Mrs. Godfrey managed our little treaty. I let her know that I expected as much money with their daughter as would pay off my remaining debt for the printing house, which I believe was not then above a hundred pounds. She brought me word they had no such sum to spare. I said they might mortgage their house in the Loan Office. The answer to this after some days was that they did not approve the match; that on enquiry of Bradford [another printer] they had been informed the printing business was not a profitable one, the types would soon be worn out and more wanted; that Samuel Keimer and D. Harry had failed one after the other, and I should probably soon follow them; and therefore I was forbidden the house, and the daughter shut up. Whether this was a real change of sentiment or only artifice, on a supposition of our being too far engaged in affection to retract and therefore that we should steal a marriage, which would leave them at liberty to give or withhold what they pleased, I know not. But I suspected the motive, resented it, and went no more. Mrs. Godfrey brought me afterwards some more favourable accounts of their disposition and would have drawn me on again, but I declared absolutely my resolution to have nothing more to do with that family.

This anecdote is not among the most popular with modern readers. It should be noticed, however, that people who owned their house outright did not ordinarily leave their daughter alone with a young man until they had some assurance of his economic eligibility for marriage, and that these parents were not worried about Franklin's ability to provide for their daughter until he demanded the usual dowry. We should notice, too, that the young Franklin who is described in this anecdote seems at last to have obeyed his own feelings of resentment rather than the economic interest that might have been served by allowing the girl's parents to reopen negotiations.

But although he always prospers, the innocent young man is not infallibly wise. Although he is never so roguish as Moll Flanders, his confession appears to be remarkably candid. He concedes that he was greatly deceived by the Governor of Pennsylvania,

who sent him as a very young man to England, along with supposed letters of recommendation and letters of credit that never
arrived. (That, by the way, was probably the greatest peril of
Franklin's young life, and he confesses that he walked into it
despite his father's clear warning.) He admits freely to motives
and perceptions that we, along with most of his contemporaries,
prefer to conceal. He thanks heaven for vanity, "along with the
other comforts of life," and admits that it is useful to cultivate
not only the reality but the *appearance* of industry and humility.
It was effective, he says, to carry his own paper stock through the
streets in a wheelbarrow, so that people could see how hard he
was willing to work. A book, he confesses, "sometimes debauch'd
me from my work, but that was seldom, snug, and gave no
scandal."

This apparent honesty leads us to the heart of the book. My
third kind of representativeness, the most important of all, can
be summed up in a single statement that appears near the end of
the *Autobiography*. "This," Franklin wrote, "is an age of experiments." It *was* an age of experiments, an age of empirical enlightenment, when every freeman might, if wary and lucky, learn
by experience and test for himself. Franklin's greatest achievement
in this book is that of characterizing himself repeatedly as a man
of inquiry. He creates for us a convincing image of the inquiring
man, self-educated, testing for himself, in morality, in business,
in religion, in science. On almost every page we see some evidence
of his willingness to learn. He contrives to reveal the vast range
of his interests—from the pure science of electricity, to the effect
of lading on the speed of merchant ships, to street-lighting and
street-cleaning, to the value of learning modern romance languages
before trying to learn Latin—all these he contrives to reveal in
anecdotes of questioning and discovery. And in anecdote after
anecdote, the plain questioning of Benjamin Franklin in action
applies an experimental test to theories and assumptions. As a
young journeyman printer in England, he demonstrates to his
fellow workmen that the customary beer is not necessary to the
maintenance of strength; he drinks water, and carries more type

than they can carry. Young Franklin and a friend agree that the one who dies first will prove the possibility of communicating from beyond the grave by getting in touch with the other who remains alive; but, Old Franklin the narrator reports, "he never fulfilled his promise." As a military commander at the start of the Seven Years' War with France, Franklin hears the zealous Presbyterian chaplain's complaint that the men do not attend religious services; he solves the problem by persuading the chaplain himself to serve out the men's daily rum ration just *after* prayers, ". . . and never," the narrator comments, "were prayers more generally and more punctually attended—so that I thought this method preferable to the punishments inflicted by some military laws for non-attendance on divine service."

Especially in the narrative of the early years, this wide-eyed freshness of perception is perfectly compatible with the young man's shrewdness, and it is nowhere more delightful than in his depiction of some of the other chief characters in the book. One of the most remarkable qualities in the book is the author's almost total lack of rancor. His brother James, Samuel Keimer, Governor Keith, and General Edward Braddock—all these people may be said to have injured him; yet he presents them all with the charitable curiosity of a man who was once interested in learning from his experience with them something about human nature. I refer here not to the kind of curiosity that can be so easily caricatured, the ingenious Yankee's humor that leads him to tell us how he measured reports of the distance at which the revivalist George Whitefield's voice might be heard. What I mean to admire is the humorous *discovery* of another person's strange faults. Consider the economy of this portrayal of Samuel Keimer, whose faults are balanced against those of the young Franklin:

Keimer and I lived on a pretty good familiar footing and agreed tolerably well, for he suspected nothing of my setting up [for myself]. He retained a great deal of his old enthusiasm and loved argumentation. We therefore had many disputations. I used to work him so with my Socratic method and had trappaned him [that is, tricked him] so often by questions apparently so distant from any point we had in hand, and yet by degrees leading to the point and bringing him into difficulties and contradictions, that at last he grew ridiculously cautious and would hardly answer the most common question without asking first, "What do you intend to infer by that?" However, it gave him so high an opinion of my abilities in the confuting way that he seriously proposed my being his colleague in a project he had of setting up a new sect. He was to preach the doctrines, and I was to confound all opponents. When he came to explain with me upon the doctrines, I found several conundrums which I objected to, unless I might have my way a little, too, and introduce some of mine. Keimer wore his beard at full length, because somewhere in the Mosaic Law it is said, "Thou shalt not mar the corners of thy beard." He likewise kept the seventh day Sabbath, and these two points were essentials with him. I disliked both but agreed to admit them upon condition of his adopting the doctrine of not using animal food. "I doubt," says he, "my constitution will bear it." I assured him it would and that he would be the better for it. He was usually a great glutton, and I wished to give myself some diversion in half-starving him. He consented to try the practice if I would keep him company; I did so, and we held it for three months. Our provisions were purchased, cooked, and brought to us regularly by a woman in the neighbourhood who had from me a list of forty dishes to be prepared for us at different times, in which there entered neither fish, flesh, nor fowl. This whim suited me better at this time from the cheapness of it, not costing us above eighteen pence sterling each per week. I have since kept several Lents most strictly, leaving the common diet for that, and that for common, without the least inconvenience, so that I think there is little in the advice of making those changes by easy gradations. I went on pleasantly, but poor Keimer suffered grievously, tired of the project, longed for the flesh pots of Egypt, and ordered a roast pig. He invited me and two women friends to dine with him, but it being brought too soon upon table, he could not resist the temptation and ate it all up before we came.

Franklin's acute awareness that Keimer is a ridiculously pretentious, affected character does not prevent him from expressing some unsentimental sympathy for his former victim, or from hinting broadly that he himself now disapproves of giving himself diversion at the expense of others—although he might relish

the chance to repeat the same experiment. We must remember, in
reading this anecdote, that Franklin has previously told us of his
decision some years later to abandon the Socratic method, because
it had sometimes won him victories that neither he nor his cause
deserved. And we must notice that his rational skepticism, his
testing by experience, extends even to reason itself.

In an age of reason Franklin was not afraid to admit the limits
of reason, nor did he hesitate in his autobiography to illustrate
those limits by recounting an experience in which young Franklin himself is the only target of his humor. He used this device
on several occasions, but one of them is astonishing in its brilliance,
for it not only establishes the author's attitude toward himself
but phrases the issue in the key terms of eighteenth-century psychology. The battle in young Franklin is a battle between principle
and inclination. The anecdote appears immediately before the
vegetarian experiment with Keimer. During a calm on his voyage
back from Boston to Philadelphia, Franklin says,

our crew employed themselves catching cod, and hauled up a great
number. Till then I had stuck to my resolution to eat nothing that had
had life; and on this occasion I considered . . . the taking every fish
as a kind of unprovoked murder, since none of them had or ever could
do us any injury that might justify this massacre. All this seemed very
reasonable. But I had formerly been a great lover of fish, and when
this came hot out of the frying pan, it smelled admirably well. I balanced some time between principle and inclination, till I recollected
that when the fish were opened, I saw smaller fish taken out of their
stomachs. "Then," thought I, "if you eat one another, I don't see why
we mayn't eat you." So I dined upon cod very heartily and have since
continued to eat as other people, returning only now and then occasionally to a vegetable diet. So convenient a thing it is to be a
reasonable creature, since it enables one to find or make a reason for
everything one has a mind to do.

Franklin gives us, then, the picture of a relatively innocent,
unsophisticated, sometimes foolish young man who confounds
or at least survives more sophisticated rivals. Consistently, the
young man starts at the level of testing, and he often stumbles

onto an important truth. We see his folly and his discoveries through the ironically humorous detachment of a candid old man, whose criticism of the young character's rivals is tempered by the same kind of affectionate tolerance that allows him to see the humor of his own mistakes. The wise old writer expects people to act selfishly, but retains his affection for them. He leads us always to consider major questions in terms of simple practical experience, as when he tells us that he soon gave up converting people to belief in deism because the result seemed often to be that they thus became less virtuous than before. Deism, he said, might be true, but it did not seem to be very useful. Because he assumed that at best people will usually act according to their conception of their own true interest, because all his experience seemed to confirm this hypothesis, and because metaphysical reasoning often turned out to be erroneous, he concentrated on demonstrating the usefulness of virtue.

It is right here, just at the heart of his most impressive achievement as an autobiographer, that Franklin seems to have made his one great error in communication. Many people, first of all, simply misunderstand him; he did not take sufficient account of the carelessness of readers. Many are completely taken in by the deceptive picture. So effective has Franklin been in demonstrating the usefulness of virtue through repeated anecdotes from his own educational experience, so insistent on effectiveness as a test of what is good in his own life, that many readers simply believe he has no other basis for deciding what is good. They simply conclude that the man who would say "Honesty is the best *policy*" will be *dis*honest if ever dishonesty becomes the best policy. Readers wonder what the man who tells them candidly that he profited by *appearing* to be humble hopes to gain by *appearing* to be candid.

If I were to follow Franklin and judge chiefly by the results, I would give up trying to clarify the misunderstanding, for I am sure that many readers will refuse to follow me beyond this point. Yet it seems to me important to understand Franklin's intention as clearly as possible, if only to measure properly the degree of his miscalculation or his inadequacy. Let us examine one other brief passage from the *Autobiography,* a statement describing Franklin's own effort to propagate a new set of religious beliefs, to establish a new sect which he proposed, characteristically, to call the Society of the Free and Easy. "In this piece [a book to be called *The Art of Virtue*] it was my design to explain and enforce this doctrine: That vicious actions are not hurtful because they are forbidden, but forbidden because they are hurtful, *the nature of man alone considered;* that it was therefore everyone's interest to be virtuous who wished to be happy *even in this world."*

I have stressed the qualifying phrases in this statement in order to emphasize the nature of Franklin's faith: *the nature of man alone considered;* everyone who wished to be happy *even in this world.* This doctrine of enlightened self-interest represents an important reversal—almost an exact reversal—of a sentence written by a sixteenth-century English Puritan named William Perkins, who in propounding the absolute sovereignty of God had declared: "A thing is not first of all reasonable and just, and then afterwards willed by God; it is first of all willed by God, and thereupon becomes reasonable and just." Yet Franklin's reversal does *not* say that discovering what is apparently to our interest is the only way of *defining* virtue. He, every bit as much as the Calvinist, believes that virtues must be defined by some absolute standard. Vicious actions, he says, *are forbidden*—by the benevolent authority of a wise God and by the universal assent, as he understood it, of wise men throughout history. But some actions *are* inherently vicious, whether or not they seem profitable.

Franklin's faith, then, professes that a true understanding of one's interest even in this world will lead one to virtue. Since the obvious existence of viciousness and folly in every society demonstrates that men do not yet practice the virtues on which most philosophers *have* agreed, finding a way to increase the practice of virtue—the number of virtuous actions—is a sufficiently valuable task to need no elaborate justification. And so the same Franklin who in the year of his death refused to dogmatize on the question of Jesus Christ's divinity because he expected soon to "have an opportunity of knowing the truth with less trouble" contented himself with questions of moral practice. His faith told him that the best way to serve God was to do good to one's fellow men, and he reasoned that just as all wise men preferred benevolent acts to flattery, so the infinitely wise God would not care very much to be flattered, but would prefer to have men *act* benevolently. He denied, however, that any man could ever *deserve* a heavenly, infinite reward for finite actions. He knew perfectly well the implications of his faith, but he saw no reason to worry very much about whether it was absolutely correct. For all his experience indicated that whether or not virtue and interest do coincide, no other argument but that of self-interest will persuade men to act virtuously, and even that argument will not always persuade them.

It is in this context that we must read Franklin's account of the thirteen-week course he gave himself in the Art of Virtue. D. H. Lawrence and other critics have overlooked the humorous self-criticism with which Franklin introduces the account. "It was about this time," Franklin says, "that I conceived the bold and arduous project of arriving at moral perfection. As I knew, or thought I knew, what was right and wrong, I did not see why I might not *always* do the one and avoid the other. But I soon found I had undertaken a task of more difficulty than I had imagined. While my attention was taken up and care employed against one fault, I was often surprised by another." Franklin, you will remember, listed the chief instrumental virtues under thirteen headings and at first devoted a week to concentrating especially on the habit of practicing one of the thirteen virtues. He made himself a chart, and in the daily period that he allotted to meditating the question "What good have I done today?" he entered a black mark for each action that could be considered a violation of the precepts. He worked to achieve a clear page. At thirteen weeks for each completed "course," he was able, he says, to go through four courses in a year. As he was surprised, at first, to find himself so full of faults, so he was pleased to find that he was able to decrease the number of his faulty actions. He endeavors to persuade us by pointing out that this improvement of conduct made him happier and helped him to prosper. But he makes perfectly clear the relative nature of his progress. He compares his method of attacking one problem at a time to weeding a garden, a task that is never really completed. He tells us not only that he later advanced to taking one course each year (with four weeks for each virtue), but also that he bought a book with ivory pages, so that he could erase the black marks at the end of one term and begin the course anew. The task was endless. Wondering about D. H. Lawrence's reading of Franklin, we may echo his own uncomprehending words: the perfectibility of man, indeed!

In trying to clarify Franklin's beliefs, I have not meant to absolve him of all responsibility for the widespread misunderstanding of his work. As I have already suggested, he invites difficulty by deliberately appearing to be more simple than he is, by choosing the role of the inquisitive, experimental freeman. By daring to reduce metaphysical questions to the terms of practical experience, he sometimes seems to dismiss them entirely, and he draws our attention away from the books that he has read. Thus, although he alludes to the most influential philosophical and psychological treatises of his age, and although he certainly read widely in every kind of learning that attracted his remarkably curious mind, he does not give this theoretical groundwork any important place in the narrative of his life. He mentions that he read John Locke at a certain point, and the Earl of Shaftesbury, and he says that this sort of education is extremely valuable. But in the narrative itself he is plain Benjamin Franklin, asking questions prompted by the situation. Even as he recounts, much later in the book, his successful correspondence with some of the leading scientists of England and the Continent, he underemphasizes his learning and portrays himself as a fortunate and plain, if skillful and talented, amateur.

This effect is reinforced by another quality of Franklin's literary skill, the device of humorous understatement. I have already cited one or two examples, as in his statement about answering the question of the divinity of Jesus. Similarly, he refers to the discovery that an effective preacher was plagiarizing famous English sermons as "an unlucky occurrence," and he says that he preferred good sermons by others to bad ones of the minister's own manufacture. He repeatedly notices ridiculous incongruity by putting an apt word in a startlingly subordinate place and thus shocking us into a fresh, irreverent look at a subject that we may well have regarded in a conventional way. So he says that for some time he had been regularly absent from Presbyterian church services, "Sunday being my studying day"; and he remarks that enormous multitudes of people admired and respected the revivalist George Whitefield, "notwithstanding his common abuse of them by assuring them they were naturally 'half beasts and half devils.' " This is the method that Henry Thoreau later used in *Walden* when he declared that the new railroads and highways, which were then called internal improvements, were all external and superficial; it is the method Samuel Clemens employed through his narrator Huckleberry Finn, who says that at mealtime the widow Douglas began by lowering her head and grumbling over the victuals, "though there warn't really anything the matter with them." The device is often delightfully effective in negative argument, in revealing ludicrous inconsistency. But because it depends on an appeal to simple self-reliance, and often to a hardheaded practicality, it is not conducive to the exposition of positive, complex theory. The particular form of Franklin's wit, his decision to portray himself as an inquisitive empiricist, the very success of his effort to exemplify moral values in accounts of practical experience, his doctrine of enlightened self-interest, and the fine simplicity of his exposition—all these combine to make him seem philosophically more naïve, and practically more materialistic, than he is.

Yet this is a great book, and despite the limitations implicit in his pedagogical method, the breadth and richness of Franklin's character do come through to the reasonably careful reader. One chief means, of course, is the urbane yet warm tone of the wise old narrator, who begins by conceding that one of his reasons for writing an autobiographical statement to his son is simply the

desire of an old man to talk about himself. We should also notice
that although his emotional life is clearly beyond the bounds of
his narrative purpose, he expresses an unmistakable affection,
even in retrospect, for his parents, his brother, and his wife. His
judgment is nowhere firmer or more admirable than in his account
of the self-satisfied young Benjamin's return to taunt brother James,
his former master, with the signs of the Philadelphia journeyman's
prosperity. His record of his wife's lifelong usefulness to him is
not in the least incompatible with genuine affection for her. And
in one brief paragraph citing as an argument for smallpox vac-
cination the death of his own son, "a fine boy of four years old,"
he reveals that his serenity could be rippled by the memory of an
old grief.

We must remember, finally, that Franklin was one of the most
beloved men of his time. The first American who was called the
father of his country, he had no reason to feel anxious about the
quality of what our own public relations men would call his
"image." He had retired at the age of forty-two to devote the rest
of his long life to public service and scientific study; he was known
internationally as a faithful patriot who had for decades defended
the popular cause in almost every political controversy; he had
been a great success at the French court, and he was a member
of the Royal Society in England. With these sides of his character
known so well, he had no reason to expect that his instructive
Autobiography would be taken as the complete record of his
character, or of his range as a writer. The polished *Bagatelles* that
he had written in France; the brilliant ironic essays that he had
published in England during the years just before the Revolution;
the state papers that he had written in all seriousness as an agent
of the Congress—all these formed a part of his public character
before he completed his work on the *Autobiography*. He could
not foresee that in a romantic age in which many writers believed
capitalism and practical science were overwhelming the human
spirit, a novelist like D. H. Lawrence would make him a symbol
of acquisitive smugness; nor could he foresee that F. Scott Fitz-
gerald, lamenting in *The Great Gatsby* the betrayal of the great

American dream, would couple Ben Franklin's kind of daily schedule with a Hopalong Cassidy book, and would imply that in the 1920's anyone who followed Franklin's advice would have to be a stock-waterer or a bootlegger.

What Franklin represented in his day, and what we should see in his greatest book, was something much more complex than this stereotype. He was deceptively simple, to be sure; but his life and his character testified to the promise of experience, the value of education, the possibility of uniting fruitful public service with simple self-reliance, the profitable conduct of a useful business enterprise, and the free pursuit of knowledge in both pure and practical science. His book remains an admirable work of art, and its author still speaks truth to us as an admirable representative of the Enlightenment.

❂

The Empirical Temper of
Benjamin Franklin

As an expression of the American character, Franklin spoke with the personality of his own genius, but the particular qualities of the American character that he represented were also the results of the time and place in which he lived. He was a product of the philosophies of the eighteenth century, but he also came out of an American background—in Boston and Philadelphia—that conditioned the way he thought and that gave him a view of man and nature that stamped his contributions to our American way of life with a mark of its own. To define exactly what Franklin was, and to grasp in its full integrity what it is that Franklin stands for, we must pause to examine the wellsprings of that blend of idealism and practicality that he displayed.

It is true, of course, that even when we emulate Franklin, or address ourselves to problems of business, government and society in the Franklinian manner, we do so from a motivation that is apt to be somewhat different from his. Yet, even though two centuries of time and culture intervene between him and us, there are elements in his general approach to the world that have appeared again and again in Americans from his day to ours. Franklin's orientation is most easily discernible in the field of action in which

From I. Bernard Cohen, *Benjamin Franklin* (Bobbs-Merrill, 1953), pp. 48–67. Reprinted by permission of the author.

he made the most original contribution—science—and so we may best see him in his own terms by first exploring the qualities of mind he displayed in studying nature and only then seeing how these qualities illuminate his way through life.

It has become commonplace to say that Benjamin Franklin was a practical man and to imply that his standard of value was always the working usefulness of the end result rather than the means of obtaining it or the motivation. We think of Franklin as having been primarily a practical man because so many of his enterprises were successful and because he had a doctrine of "usefulness" that seems akin to practicality. But in thus limiting Benjamin Franklin, we fail to grasp his full dimensions and may even slight our own national character. For there is a sense in which practicality implies expediency, and its ascription to the American character would rob our history of the lofty ideals and high purposes which have motivated so many of our leaders and our ordinary citizens; it would make a parody of Franklin as a guide through life.

As a man of the eighteenth century and an American, Benjamin Franklin was an empiricist. The America of his day was a young country in which a man's courage, faith, optimism or ability counted for nothing if he could not recognize and face up to the raw facts of life and nature. Franklin was not a product of the frontier in that he was an urban American, spending his boyhood in the city of Boston and his young manhood in the city of Philadelphia; he did not grow up in a log cabin in the wilderness, tilling fields with a flintlock by his side. But the spirit of the frontier certainly made its presence known in Philadelphia: the city itself was rough, unfinished and growing; there were Indian alarms not far away and a threat of pirates; and, in general, a spirit of building and material creation produced an atmosphere of close contact with the real world.

Nature, as Franklin realized, is both man's enemy and friend, providing fertile soil and rain and also plagues of insects and droughts. The only way to master Nature is to understand her laws and to operate within her framework. Shaking a fist at the skies will neither make it rain nor stop the locusts, although in Franklin's day men believed that prayer and fasting might do both. But the men who had braved the wilderness, although placing their reliance on their prayer book and Bible, knew that their faith in God needed to be buttressed by hard work and skill in shooting muskets. The Old World patterns of life, in which man lived like his father and his father's father before him, could not long survive in the New World, where a man had to adapt himself to the realities of the situation in which he found himself, to find a way of life consistent with the data of experience that made up the external environment. It is this last quality which is the primary ingredient of empiricism: a respect for the data of experience and the application of reason to them.

In Benjamin Franklin this strain of empiricism enabled him to become a foremost scientist of that age, and it was a major factor in producing that special view of man, his needs, his rights and his works which has become so precious an element in our American heritage. Franklin stands in the American tradition for the proposition that reflections about society should produce useful institutions for the improvement of the conditions of life; considerations about the estate of man should yield more than eternal principles and noble concepts, and must be fruitful of a system of government and laws to safeguard man's rights; an understanding of the nature and character of man should lead to conduct that respects a man for what he is without regard to color or religion or economic and social origin. Many Americans have acted in accordance with these principles simply because they have become a part of our American pattern of behavior, but in Franklin they were a result of the brand of empiricism that marked his thought and conduct. To see Franklin's particular contribution to America, therefore, we must try to understand how being a good scientist and being a good neighbor, friend and citizen were but different aspects of a single fundamental quality of mind.

Empiricism is a philosophy which is of the eighteenth century and may be studied in Locke, whom Franklin respected, and Hume, whom Franklin knew and admired. One of its major tenets was the theory of how ideas originate in the mind by the action of sensations. Skeptical of any sort of metaphysics, Franklin was not a systematic philosopher, and doctrines of the origin of ideas held no great interest for him. Even so, throughout his writings we find a tendency to regard experience as the grand source of values and doctrines. He was certainly an empiricist in the sense that he considered an experiential test more important in evaluating the worth of concepts than their logical consistency or their mutual relatedness in a system.

Franklin's outlook demanded that concepts be founded on experience, whether that experience was the data of experiment in the laboratory or the observation of man's behavior. Reason, operating on these concepts, discovers laws of nature or rules of conduct, which must meet two important tests. First, these laws or rules or principles must be true—that is, they must be testable against that same experience of the laboratory or the world. But even if such an experiential test reveals the validity of the discovered generalization, the whole effort is not worthwhile unless it is productive of something new. It is this quality of productivity that gives man the final measure of the way in which the initial data and the reasoning process have led to the final conclusions.

Real works are thus, as Bacon put it, the fruits of knowledge, and it is in this sense that he wrote that the roads to knowledge and to power are the same. For in the empiricist philosophy the end product can be no more divorced from real experience than the original concepts. In science, then, an empiricist begins by making experiments with his own hands, then constructing concepts that are related to the actual operations or manipulations he performs; next he applies his reason to generalize what he has observed into ground principles on which a logical theory can be built; then the final result is a new form of experience or at least a new view of some segment of experience.

One result of empirical science is a prediction, such as Newton made, of the tides; the time of tides was observable to anyone, but until the time of Newton no one had understood the attractions of the sun and moon sufficiently well to explain how they might control the seas. Newton's predictions agreed so well with observation that the validity of his theory was assured. Newton's work led to predictions which were testable by experience, and it contributed to an enlarged view of the world that we observe around us, thus being doubly productive. Sometimes the end product of empirical science is a new effect or phenomenon that the scientist can produce with his own hands in the laboratory, but often it is a new instrument or device which is itself the new experience that is the product or fruit of investigation.

As a scientist Franklin knew that the life of ideas in science is always controlled by experiment and observation and that a new theory such as he created is valuable in correlating phenomena that had not been thought related or in predicting new phenomena which, on being discovered, would prove the theory's usefulness. Applying his new concepts of electrical equilibrium and the states of electrification he called "plus" or "positive" and "minus" or "negative," Franklin discovered the first exact law of electricity: the law of conservation of charge. This occurred in the course of his experiments to analyze the charge in a condenser—the Leyden jar, consisting of a glass bottle coated on the outside with metal foil and filled with water or bird shot. Such an instrument, when charged, was capable of giving a noticeable shock to seven hundred men, but Franklin stated that there was no more "electricity" in a charged jar than an uncharged one, and he proved it by the experiment of "electrical convection." He also found that the charge "resided" in the nonconducting glass rather than the metal coat or water. But this led immediately to the production of new experience, because if charge "resides" in glass because glass is a special kind of nonconductor, then a condenser need not have the shape of a bottle, but could be made of glass plates with metal sheets affixed to either side. To the nonscientist this example may appear trivial, but it marked the beginning of condenser design, and the condenser is one of the vital organs of every piece of electronic equipment ever made.

Furthermore, one of Franklin's greatest achievements was to show which electrical properties of bodies depend on their shape and which do not. Franklin never saw any practical use in the condenser, by which I mean that in his day the Leyden jar was never embodied in an instrument to serve man's needs or increase his fortune. Franklin's explanation of the condenser's action, we may note, was considered by his contemporaries to have been one of his major contributions to science; this discovery was useful because it increased man's understanding of nature's operations, and it was productive because it led to new principles or laws of nature.

The distinction between productive usefulness and practicality may best be illustrated by Franklin's research on the lightning discharge. Having discovered that a pointed conductor will "draw off" the charge from an electrified body at a considerable distance, and having at last understood the role of grounding and insulation in electrostatic experiments, Franklin was in a position to make the grand experiment. If clouds are (as he thought) electrified, then an elevated vertical metal rod ending in a point will "draw off" some of the charge from low clouds though they are far away. This original experiment, described by Franklin and performed according to his specifications before he had thought of the kite experiment, established as an empirical fact the phenomenon that clouds are electrically charged and that lightning is therefore an electrical discharge. So the facts of experience and a theory based on correct reasoning had been productive of new experience; nature's artillery had been shown to be only a large-scale instance of a common laboratory phenomenon: the spark discharge. In this case, however, the research was not only productive, it was useful; it revealed the function of electricity in the "economy of nature," and it was applied by Franklin in an attempt to throw light on the whole process of cloud formation and rain.

But Franklin's research had led him to another conclusion, that a long vertical rod of metal, pointed at the top and set deep into the earth, would protect buildings from a stroke of lightning; the empirical test was to construct lightning rods in order to discover whether they would afford such protection (which Franklin, as an empiricist, never doubted), which is only another way of saying that the result of Franklin's research was a predicted new element of experience—a lightning rod—which had to be put to the trial of lightning.

This whole process of empirical science was beautifully described in the seventeenth century by Robert Hooke, who wrote:

So many are the links upon which the true philosophy depends, of which, if any one be loose, or weak, the whole chain is in danger of being dissolved; it is to begin with the hands and eyes, and to proceed on through the memory, to be continued by the reason; nor is it to stop there, but to come about to the hands and eyes again, and so, by a continual passage round from one faculty to another, it is to be maintained in life and strength, as much as the body of man is by the circulation of the blood through the several parts of the body. . . .

This is the sense in which Franklin's scientific research was productive and useful and fruitful. It was productive in that it led to a new theory of electrical action which was the source of a more profound understanding of nature, one which enabled men to predict (and for the first time) what would happen in many of their common electrical experiments in the laboratory, and it also led to many new physical phenomena that had never before been observed. It was useful in that it produced an instrument that enabled men (again for the first time) to protect their homes, barns, churches and ships from destruction by lightning. And the rod itself was fruitful in that it became an instrument that in Franklin's hands and ours has led to a deeper knowledge of the electrification of clouds and of the earth itself and the mechanism of the lightning discharge.

The doctrine of empiricism was always hospitable to the view of Bacon that "fruits and works" are "sponsors and sureties" for the truths of science. But we must keep in mind that Bacon had added that "works themselves are of greater value as pledges of truth than as contributing to the comforts of life." As an empirical scientist Franklin would have agreed, although, being Franklin, he might have questioned the word "greater." The empirical view of the scientist would be satisfied equally by the production of new experience, whether a phenomenon of importance or a device that embodied the newly discovered principles.

Franklin did not pursue the science of electricity because of a particular practical aim; had this been his intent he would hardly have chosen electricity as his major area of inquiry: in his day electricity was not a practical subject. The only supposedly practical application of electricity then was in a kind of medical therapy, but Franklin was convinced that the "cures" arose from the patient's desire to get well rather than from the electric shock. But once Franklin had reached the stage in his investigations where the new knowledge could be put to use in the service of man, he was quick to see an application. I believe that Franklin was convinced that pure science would always produce useful innovations, and here we may see him in the great scientific tradition that has only recently become a major feature of American civilization.

Throughout the nineteenth century, America was noted more for the applications of scientific discoveries that had been made in other lands than for the production of that fundamental scientific knowledge we applied so fruitfully. It is only in the last fifty years or so that America has risen to be a foremost scientific nation of the world. During the nineteenth century Franklin was considered by Americans to be an "applied scientist," the inventor of the lightning rod and the Franklin stove, and his whole contribution to pure science was reduced to the kite experiment. The great laboratory discoveries, the first unitary theory of electrical action— the research in pure science that made his contemporaries call him the Newton of their age—were ignored.

Today we are beginning to recognize that the applications of scientific discovery to the cure of disease, the improvement of our living conditions and the safeguarding of our national existence must depend on fundamental discoveries to apply. We may, therefore, in this new tradition look back on Franklin as our first scientist. We may see him as one of those pioneers who understood that empirical science must *always* produce new experience which enlarges our view of nature and our understanding of the processes going on in the world around us, and that it *sometimes* produces (along the way) practical innovations of inestimable value for our health and our economic security. Characteristically, Franklin's most eloquent defense of that research in science that has no particular practical consequence in view took the form of a witticism. Watching the first balloon ascent in Paris, he overheard the usual question: What good is it? His reply has never been equaled: "What good is a newborn baby?" Discussing the new element chlorine, discovered in 1810, and applied to the bleaching of cloth, Michael Faraday said in 1816:

> Before leaving this substance, chlorine, I will point out its history, as an answer to those who are in the habit of saying to every new fact, "What is its use?" Dr. Franklin says to such, "What is the use of an infant?" The answer of the experimentalist would be, "Endeavor to make it useful." When Scheele discovered this substance it appeared to have no use, it was in its infantine and useless state; but having grown up to maturity, witness its powers, and see what endeavors to make it useful have done.

Franklin's scientific ideas and his conception of the potentialities of science have influenced Americans only indirectly, through the nineteenth-century European masters under whom our scientists studied. But, wholly apart from his personal influence or the effect of his discoveries and theories on the development of science as such, his empirical approach to the world of man produced qualities of concept and action that are embodied in great American institutions and that have become a precious American heritage.

Franklin was not a true philosopher in the sense that Jonathan Edwards was, but he was a natural philosopher—in that larger sense in which scientific learning and a general outlook on God, man, nature and the world were included within a single expression in a day when scientists were not merely physicists or chemists or astronomers or biologists. Franklin may be fairly described as an empirical Newtonian in the realms of science and of human affairs. In both realms, the principles and conclusions of reason applied to experimental data—the facts of nature and the facts of man—had to be embodied in experience or they were meaningless and irrelevant. Franklin's understanding of nature led him to control nature's operations just as his knowledge of men's actions made him a master of men and the affairs of the world. And just as in science his conclusions became elements of experience in new phenomena to be observed or new instruments to be put in use, so in society new elements of experience were created and put to the trial of use: new institutions (a hospital, school and fire company), new rules of conduct, a new form of government, a tax or a simple act of kindness.

It is well known that the original rough draft of the Declaration of Independence contained Jefferson's statement that principles such as that all men are created equal were held to be "sacred and undeniable," and that in the manuscript these words are changed in Franklin's handwriting to make the statement read: "We hold these principles to be self-evident." Now historians usually interpret this alteration simply as a literary improvement, and certainly Franklin's cadence has a wonderful ring to it and is much more effective than Jefferson's. But the difference between the two phrases is much more profound than mere literary quality. Jefferson implied that the principles in question were holy, of divine origin, and were to be respected and guarded with reverence for that reason: to deny them would be sacrilege. But "self-evident" was a technical or scientific term applied to axioms, as John Harris's popular eighteenth-century *Dictionary of Arts and Sciences* defined it, and was exemplified in such propositions as: "That nothing can act where it is not; That a thing cannot be and not be at the same time; That the whole is greater than a part; That where there is no law, there is no transgression; etc." Such an axiom is "a generally received ground principle or rule in any art or science," and "it cannot be made more plain and evident by demonstration, because 'tis its self much better known than any thing that can be brought to prove it." This is the sense in which Franklin's phrase represents the summit of effectiveness.

Axioms or postulates are considered in our contemporary scientific language (mathematics, logic) to be propositions which are assumed without proof solely for the purpose of exploring the consequences or logical deductions which follow from them. But in Newtonian science, consequences were deduced from axioms because the axioms were true, which should imply that if the reasoning process or deduction were correct, the results would be equally true or verifiable in experience. In the *Principia Mathematica* Newton explored the logical or mathematical consequences of certain laws of force, notably the famous three laws of motion and the law of universal gravitation. Now, as Newton explained the matter in 1713, "experimental philosophy" or empirical science "proceeds only from phenomena" or the data provided by experience, and it "deduces general propositions from them only by induction." Thus anyone who wanted to take exception to the *Principia* would have to "draw his objection from some experiment or phenomenon." In this "experimental philosophy," Newton added, the "first principles or axiomes which I call the laws of motion" are "deduced from phenomena and made general by induction: which is the highest evidence that a proposition can have in this philosophy."

In other words, Newton's scientific outlook in the *Principia Mathematica* was that the whole system of dynamics was derived by reason (*i.e.,* mathematics) from self-evident principles, which were "self-evident" because they were based on phenomena or experience; the test of the reasoning process and the correctness of interpretation of the evidence from which these principles were "deduced" (we would rather say "induced") lay in the conformity of the final results with phenomena or further experience.

Franklin's revision of the Declaration of Independence placed the principle that all men are created equal in the category of an axiom, self-evident; like the laws of motion, it was a principle "deduced" from experience. Now the particular experience that Franklin had in mind was probably his own and that of his fellow Americans. The inequalities in men's material circumstances or position that could be observed in Europe must have been a product of the artificial circumstances of society, continued by the system of class structure and hereditary rights. Proof lay in America, where land was plentiful and where a man's fortune was

apt to be determined by his industry, so that the differences between rich and poor tended to be less than in Europe. Franklin
once compared American conditions to those in Ireland and Scotland, observing:

> In those countries a small part of society are landlords, great noble-
> men, and gentlemen, extremely opulent, living in the highest affluence
> and magnificence; the bulk of the people tenants, living in the most
> sordid wretchedness in dirty hovels of mud and straw and clothed only
> in rags. I thought often of the happiness of New England, where every
> man is a freeholder, has a vote in public affairs, lives in a tidy, warm
> house, has plenty of good food and fuel, with whole clothes from head
> to foot, the manufacture perhaps of his own family. Long may they
> continue in this situation!

The absence of great differences between rich and poor in a land
of opportunity, America, surely was empirical justification that
such inequality was not a result of man's innate character. Of
course, some men are better endowed than others, just as some
men are more virtuous than others. As Poor Richard put the
matter in "How to get riches"—"The art of getting riches consists
very much in thrift. All men are not equally qualified for getting
money, but it is in the power of every one alike to practise this
virtue." This led to the conclusion that "Useful attainments in
your minority will procure riches in maturity, of which writing and
accounts are not the meanest." Hence the need for education:
"Learning, whether speculative or practical, is, in popular or mixt
governments, the natural source of wealth and honor."

. . . Franklin was a confirmed abolitionist, but could he
believe that Negroes were in any sense the equal of whites? Experience certainly showed that they were not, because anyone
could observe that "negroes, who are free [and] live among the
white people, . . . are generally improvident and poor." But
experience must always be interpreted by reason, and in this case
reason, said Franklin, tells us that free Negroes are not by nature
"deficient in natural understanding," but simply that Negroes
"have not the advantage of education." Here we may see more

than an example of the application of reason to explain the data of experience, the condition of free Negroes. In considering society, ideas must be just as productive as in the study of nature. Thus Franklin's analysis was fruitful in creating a new form of experience, a trade school for Negroes, and by its means the whole doctrine was put to the test: if Negroes are inferior because they lack education, he said in effect, let us educate them and see whether they will not then be able to do the work of whites.

Franklin was secure in his convictions about the natural equality of men despite their color, and so he had no fear about the outcome of the proposed test in experience. As a matter of fact, Franklin firmly believed that truth could, by his definition, survive every experimental test which falsehood would necessarily fail; so it is very much in keeping with his character of empiricist that he maintained the freedom of the press, the right of the printer to publish all views and to let truth combat error publicly and vanquish her on the field of experience. Over and over we see Franklin embodying his conclusions in acts rather than concepts. It is misleading to think of him as the enemy of the abstract and master of the concrete, however, because this description would rob his empiricism of the role of reason.

Reason produces concepts out of experience, and these concepts are always abstract, like the mutually repelling invisible particles in the electric fluid which he supposed was transferred from one body to another in electrostatic experiments; or abstract generalizations about matter, like its inability to act where it is not, or about man, like equality or rights. But a wide gulf separated Franklin from those who professed equality, for example, but did not practice it universally. He was not necessarily more sincere than they were; he was motivated by a different philosophy which made each abstraction live in its productive effect upon society rather than live a life of its own. This may not be the dominant philosophy in our history, but Americans have often acted as if it were. Like Franklin we have worked to found and support schools, hospitals, orphanages, homes for the aged, and we too have tried to improve our cities and towns and generally to make our habitation on earth pleasanter.

Next to the scientist the businessman is probably the greatest empiricist the world knows. Dealing with facts and with figures, he too contrives theories and applies reason to the facts of experience. A businessman, be he a manufacturer, merchant or shopkeeper, who finds his theories killed by ugly facts will probably be a failure. To make money requires predictions about trends and events which are verified. To earn a fortune demands qualities of initiative, shrewdness, observation and judgment, but also an empirical temper of mind. Franklin's rise to fortune came from his industry and thrift, but also from his ability to see opportunities and to make the most of them and to gauge the public needs and desires.

Franklin's major contribution to political thought was a theory of population growth, based on the data available to him in America. He had observed that "the natural livelyhood of the thin inhabitants of a forest country is hunting; that of a greater number, pasturage; that of a middling population, agriculture; and that of the greatest, manufactures; which last must subsist the bulk of the people in a full country or they must be subsisted by charity, or perish." He claimed that the American population was increasing so as to double every twenty or twenty-five years and would continue to do so (it did up to about 1860), and that cheap and plentiful land, one of the principal causes of American population increase, would maintain high wages in America (as it did for at least a century).

Franklin's essay had two consequences. It influenced Malthus (in the second edition of his work) and it was embodied in action, in accordance with the empiricist philosophy. Franklin's observations on population growth produced his influential pamphlet advocating the annexing of Canada rather than Guadeloupe; America needed room for expansion. Furthermore, it led him to a view based on simple calculation that America would eventually become more populous than Britain. America in the 1750's and 1760's was, he said, "to be considered as the frontier of the British empire," but in 1760 he wrote that he had "long been of opinion that the *foundations of the future grandeur and stability of the British empire lie in America;* and though, like other foundations, they are low and little seen, they are, nevertheless, broad and strong enough to support the greatest political structure human wisdom ever yet erected." Franklin's concern for the empire thus became, in a real sense, the interest of the future major partner. Franklin's political thinking was based always on his study of society—or societies—through history books he had read and firsthand observation.

The empirical scientist may wrestle with the facts revealed by his laboratory experiments, but as an empiricist he cannot deny them. Franklin's theory of electrical action was generally satisfactory even though it could not adequately explain the repulsion between two negatively charged bodies, and yet he could not deny that such repulsion existed—despite his theory. Experience, as every scientist knows, is a hard taskmaster, and it often makes the investigator abandon or alter cherished ideas by presenting an ugly little fact that does not fit. Early in his electrical research, Franklin had such an experience and "observed a phenomenon or two" that he could not account for on the principles he had set forth. "In going on with these experiments," he commented, "how many pretty systems do we build, which we soon find ourselves obliged to destroy! If there is no other use discovered of electricity, this, however, is something considerable, that it may *help to make a vain man humble.*" This facing up to facts, so natural to scientists in their laboratories, was a valuable asset to Franklin in ordinary life. The *Autobiography* shows how easy it was for him to accept the realities of experience and to learn from them how to be effective in achieving his aims.

The inflexible facts of nature constantly remind the experimental scientist that he is human enough to err, and they induce a kind of humility and honesty that are always concomitants of an empiricist outlook on nature, man or society. The successful investigator is familiar with the need of altering his most cherished theories to make them fit the realities of experiment, the only way in which he can save the phenomena without jeopardizing the fundamental axioms of his science. In many ways this quality of integrity and adaptability in the scientist reminds us of the statesman whose code permits him to effect a compromise on matters of detail and mechanism and even degree without sacrifice of his fundamental principles. Whether Franklin's outstanding performance as the representative of America in France during the Revolution arose from such qualities, or whether nothing more was required than a native shrewdness and the bargaining skill of a businessman, he was certainly a master of the conference table. His major contribution to the Constitution was that compromise between the large and small states on the question of representation in the Congress.

Carl Van Doren, Franklin's greatest biographer, has written that this compromise "was Franklin's great victory in the Convention." He was author of "the compromise which held the delegates together at a time when they were ready to break up without forming any new federal agreement. The Constitution was not his document. But without the weight of his prestige and the influence of his temper there might have been no document at all."

One of the features of the Constitution that most appealed to Franklin was the provision for amendment on trial, the possibility for alterations to be made in the light of actual experience. I am convinced that in Franklin's mind the greatest experiment was not the test of the electrification of clouds but the test of whether a democratic form of government could be established in the world and whether it could survive the trials of experience and function as its framers had intended.

PAUL W. CONNER

✪

The Continentalist

THE INCREASE OF OUR KIND

Late Children, early Orphans.
—*Poor Richard* (1742)

If the increase of goods was a delight to Franklin, the increase of people was an inspiration. There was something about human life —especially in quantity—that set him to scholarship and energized his politics. An empty continent was as unthinkable as an empty wineglass. Though his myriad writings have long provided livings for historians of science, government, and literature, the only one of his essays which can be said to qualify as a lasting contribution to social science is a treatise on demography. His major economic essay, *A Modest Inquiry into the Nature and Necessity of a Paper Currency* (1729),[1] was modest indeed, and has been described by a modern economist as "hazy," having no clear idea of depreciation.[2] His socio-economic discussions of the English poor laws,

From *Poor Richard's Politicks: Benjamin Franklin and His New American Order* by Paul W. Conner. Copyright © 1965 by Oxford University Press, Inc. Reprinted by permission.
1. *Papers of Benjamin Franklin* (Yale University Library), I, 139–157.
2. Frank A. Fetter, "The Early History of Political Economy in the United States," *Proceedings of the American Philosophical Society*, LXXXVII (July 14, 1943), 51.

On the Labouring Poor (1768) and *On the Price of Corn and Management of the Poor* (1766),[3] are regarded as more an affront to social science than a contribution.[4] But his *Observations Concerning the Increase of Mankind* (1751)[5] continues to intrigue demographers of this day, as it did Adam Smith and Thomas Malthus.[6] Two of its predictions were uncanny in their accuracy. Franklin's estimate that population in America would double every twenty or twenty-five years held substantially true until 1890, and his theory that English stock in the New World would outnumber

3. A. H. Smyth, ed., *The Writings of Benjamin Franklin,* 10 vols. (New York, 1905–1907), V, 122–127, 534–539. The latter was dated by V. W. Crane in *Benjamin Franklin's Letters to the Press, 1758–1775* (Chapel Hill, N.C., 1950), p. 78.

4. This seems to be the judgment of Howell V. Williams, "Benjamin Franklin and the Poor Laws," *Social Service Review,* XVIII (1944), 79–91.

5. *Papers,* IV, 225–234. Hereafter cited as *Increase.*

6. Smith had two copies in his library, conferred with Franklin while drafting the *Wealth of Nations,* and cited Franklin's hypothesis that the North American population, unchecked by adequate space or sustenance, doubled every quarter century. See Thomas R. Eliot, "The Relation Between Adam Smith and Benjamin Franklin Before 1776," *Political Science Quarterly,* XXXXIX (1924), 67–96.

Malthus, too, used the twenty to twenty-five year calculation, after finding it in Richard Price's *Observations on Revisionary Payments* (1769), as a basis for his theory that food supply would not keep abreast of population growth. To raise the wages of English laborers, therefore, was merely to multiply mouths and misery. *An Essay on the Principle of Population,* reprinted in its original style as *First Essay on Population, 1798* (London: MacMillan, 1926), p. 105.

Although Franklin, also, at times expressed disapproval of raising wages, his motivation was a fear that coddled workers would lose incentive and become less productive. By 1788 he was taking an un-Malthusian stand against letting "half the nation . . . languish in misery . . . to enrich a few merchants," holding that "the low rate of wages . . . is one of the greatest evils of political communities." John Bigelow, ed., *The Complete Works of Benjamin Franklin,* 10 vols. (New York, 1887–1888), X, 48, 51. He realized in theory the possibility of population outrunning food supply, but the American case was apparently to receive Divine exemption. Here, a growth of production would coincide with a growth in population, resulting in the increase not of misery but happiness. Abundance, not privation, might eventually check population, for "The greater the common fashionable expense of any rank of people the more cautious they are of marriage." *Increase,* p. 232.

Englishmen in the old in one hundred years came true on schedule around 1851.[7]

Franklin collected population statistics, published them in his *Almanac,* and obviously believed, with Sir William Petty, Bernard Mandeville, and Daniel Defoe, that people were the riches of a country.[8] It was not logically necessary, however, for Franklin to reason, as he did, from populousness to happiness. That the deduction was not a necessary one was acknowledged by several thinkers before Malthus or even Franklin. In fact, Charles Davenant, Lawrence Braddon, and Jonathan Swift had even argued that numbers could become excessive and burdensome.[9] Franklin's contrasting view sprang from his opinion that filling up the American continent would contribute to the growth of a mercantile empire and the expansion of the Anglo-Saxon race. English mercantilists had stressed the desirability of a dense population in the mother country, since it depressed wages, cheapened manufactures, and raised export levels. William Horsley was to summarize this sentiment in 1753:

Herin [*sic*] consists the Marrow of that Maxim, *that Numbers of People are the Wealth of a Nation:* as where they are plenty, they must

7. See Conrad Zirkle, "Benjamin Franklin, Thomas Malthus, and the United States Census," *Isis,* XLVIII (March 1957), 58–62.

8. Petty, *A Treatise of Taxes and Contributions* (London: R. Brooks, 1662); Mandeville, *The Fable of the Bees* (London: Jay Tonson, 1729); Daniel Defoe, *Giving Alms No Charity* (Booksellers of London and Westminster, 1704).

Franklin was familiar with works by Petty (*Papers,* I, 149), Mandeville (*Autobiography,* p. 54), and Defoe (*Autobiography,* p. 16), but whether he knew their views on the blessings of population is conjectural. The doctrine had been propagated by other writers as well, such as William Petyt in *Britannia languens* (1680), Sir Francis Brewster in *New Essays on Trade* (1702), and Sir Josiah Child in *A New Discourse on Trade* (1698). See Louis A. Landa, "A Modest Proposal and Populousness," *Modern Philology,* XL (1942), 161–170.

9. Davenant, *Essays upon . . . the balance of trade* (London: J. Knapton, 1699); Braddon, *To Pay Old Debts Without New Taxes* (London, 1723); Swift, *Maxians Controlled in Ireland* (1724), *An Answer to the Craftsman,* and *A Modest Proposal* (1729) in Temple Scott, ed., *The Prose Works of Jonathan Swift,* 12 vols. (London: Bell, 1905), III.

work cheap, and so Manufactures are encouraged for a foreign Market, and their Returns is the Wealth of a Nation, which numbers thus procure.[10]

It was Franklin's emphasis, rather, that demographic expansion *in the colonies* could be an additional source of profit, providing a growing market for the products of the metropolis. This thesis, too, was long implicit in mercantilism.[11] Defoe had noted,

It is evident, that by the Increase of our Colonies, the Consumption of our Manufactures has been exceedingly increased; not only experience proves it, but the Nature of the Thing makes it impossible otherwise.[12]

Franklin's originality lay in his belief that the expansion of the colonial population and market, to the greater glory of the British mercantile system, would be facilitated by permitting manufacturing in the colonies, a most unmercantilist notion. His reasoning, admirably ingenious if not convincing to such as the Board of Trade, was that Americans, inundated by British goods and restricted in producing their own, 'were being (1) encouraged to indulge in English luxuries, the expense of which deterred many a young man from assuming the added obligations of marriage and propagation,[13] and (2) deprived of employment in the manufac-

10. Horsley, *The Universal Merchant* (London, 1753), Preface, p. xv.

11. See Philip W. Buck, *The Politics of Mercantilism* (New York: Holt, 1942), pp. 60–62.

12. Daniel Defoe, *An Humble Proposal to the People of England* (London, 1729), p. 43.

13. Franklin's conception of luxury seems puzzling when one contrasts his disdain for "foreign Gegaws" (Franklin to Humphrey Marshall, London, April 22, 1771, *Writings*, I, 316) with his endorsement of the comfortable life. He reconciled these antipodes, perhaps, in the following manner: An inordinate thirst for luxury could lead to avoidance of marriage and, ultimately of work; but the desire for *moderate* luxury would spur incentive and result in expenditures which would filter prosperity downward through the economy. A happy mediocrity in tastes would make the expenses of married life tolerable and thus contribute to generation. A source of confusion is Franklin's failure to define the term "luxury." One suspects it was a "Gegaw" when imported, but a "manufacture" when made at home, where its fabrication provided employment for domestic workers. For an analysis which does away with the theory that *Increase* was a tract against luxury, see Alfred Owen Aldridge, "Franklin as Demographer," *Journal of Economic History,* IX (May, 1949), 25–44.

tory arts, a pursuit which could afford livelihood to many, fostering matrimony and generation. There was no danger of America's becoming an industrial rival of the mother country, Franklin added, because the ample North American hinterlands would draw most men into agriculture and preclude the development of an urban pool of cheap labor. Anyone in the colonial office worth his pension could have seen through the argument in an instant. If lands were so plentiful and alluring in the New World, why should a colonist need or desire the added employments which manufacturing might provide? And if, in the spacious wilds, the population were already doubling every twenty years or so, how could British luxuries be said to have stifled procreation? And why need England stimulate further a rate of increase already phenomenal? Indeed, the prospect was rather alarming. Nor did talk of a Polypus steady British nerves:

. . . A Nation well regulated is like a Polypus; take away a Limb, its Place is soon supply'd; cut it in two, and each deficient Part shall speedily grow out of the Part remaining. Thus if you have Room and Subsistence enough, as you may by dividing, make ten Polypes out of one, you may of one make ten Nations, equally populous and powerful; or, rather, increase a Nation ten fold in Numbers and Strength.

Was it his point that England was the Imperial Polypus or that a new one had shot off from the old and begun its autonomous process of self-generation? Dwell as he might on the "Accession of Power to the British Empire," Franklin was hinting at something ominous and—dare it be said?—revolutionary, when he predicted that the English in America needed only a century to equal numerically the English in Britain.[14]

The whole tenor of his disquisition smacked of a new economic conception—America as a mercantile empire in itself. Such a concept included the development of manufacturing, a growing market and labor force, ships, seamen, commerce, and (it would make a Josiah Child catch his breath) a vast interior to colonize and fur-

14. *Increase, Papers,* IV, 229, 233.

nish raw materials to the Atlantic seaboard, as the latter had served as a plantation for England. The Americocentrism of Franklin's mercantile theory has sometimes been neglected. William Appleman Williams perceptively notes that America revolted against *British* mercantilism, not mercantilism per se, yet he fails to see Franklin's prescient role in this economic revolution. For Williams, Franklin was a British colonial nabob who wanted to "keep the people busy farming and in that way turn them from domestic manufacturing while creating a limitless market for British manufactures." But Franklin anticipated an American future replete with its own manufacturing, which was not at all what one would expect from a nabob. This was the man whose own family manufactured "the best Soap in the World for Shaving or Washing fine Linens," known in its advertisements for "Sweetness of the Flavor and . . . fine Lather."

Perhaps Williams and others have been misled by Franklin's passages on population and manufacturing in *The Interest of Great Britain* (1760). Read out of the larger context of Franklin's vision of the New American Order, the Canada pamphlet, as it is called, could well convince one that the author felt America "must for ages be employed in agriculture chiefly." The English-speaking people's new North American home, with Canada included, would be such a vast space—Franklin explained innocently—as to prevent for centuries a population concentration dense enough to provide the cheap labor and variety of human skills on which profitable manufacturing depended. His aim in writing this pamphlet, however, was not honest social analysis but political propaganda. He wanted to convince Britain that it should snatch Canada from the French, and toward this end Franklin had to exterminate English fears that an expanded American domain would become an economic rival. Even so, the Canada pamphlet granted that Americans might come to engage in some simple forms of manufacturing and predicted that, "with *Canada* in our possession, our people in America will increase amazingly." Four years later, he was relating population growth to the rise of an American textile industry:

. . . [A]s to our being always supply'd [with cloth] by [England], 'tis folly to expect it. Only consider *the rate of our Increase,* and tell me if you can increase your Wooll in that Proportion, and where, in your little Island you can feed the Sheep. Nature has put Bounds to your Abilities, tho' none to your Desires.

America's very numbers would require that it develop an industrial plant equal to increasing demand, whether or not population was as concentrated in the New World as in the old. The latter was simply physically incapable of supplying the American millions with sufficient manufactures.[15]

There was still more in Franklin to suggest the American mercantilist: a belief in government as stimulator of enterprise, a fondness for "Bridges, roads, canals, and other usefull works & institutions, tending to the common felicity"; a concern over monetary outflow, the trade balance, superfluous foreign luxuries, and production; and a zeal for planting colonies in the wilderness.[16] True, Franklin's empire would not countenance trade monopolies, protective tariffs, or the regulation of prices, quality of goods, or wages.[17] A mercantilism without complex internal regulation or ruthless international competition, it was the sort of system one would expect from the advocate of a benign and virtuous order. Living in a world where mercantilism was a fact of life for politi-

15. William Appleman Williams, "The Age of Mercantilism: An Interpretation of the American Political Economy," *William and Mary Quarterly,* Third Series, XV (October 1958), 421; *The Contours of American History* (Cleveland: World, 1961), p. 93. *The Interest of Great Britain,* 1760; Franklin to Peter Collinson, Philadelphia, April 30, 1764, *Writings,* IV, 48–70, 245. I am indebted to Edwin Wolf, II, for reminding me of Franklin's pride in Crown Soap. See *Papers,* I, 348; II, 413; VI, 85; VII, 215; and *Mecom Letters,* pp. 129–132.

16. Franklin to David Hartley, Passy, October 16, 1783, *Writings,* X, 107–108. *Paper Currency, Papers,* I, 141–157.

17. Franklin to Peter Collinson, April 30, 1764, *Writings,* IV, 243–245; "Protective Duties," *Complete Works,* IV, 21; "Argument for Making the Bills of Credit Pay Interest," December 1763, *Jackson Papers,* pp. 127–128; "Remarks on the Plan for Regulating the Indian Affairs," 1766, or before, *Writings,* IV, 469; *On the Labouring Poor,* 1768, *On the Price of Corn and Management of the Poor,* November 29, 1766, *Writings,* V, 122–127, 534–539. Dated by Crane, *Letters to the Press,* p. 78.

cians, and *laissez faire* a seductive formulation of avant-garde intellectuals and a rising bourgeoisie, Franklin—at home in both circles—fashioned a philosophy which combined the structured purposefulness of the one with the humane, enlightened qualities of the other.

A reading of David Hume's *Essay on the Jealousy of Commerce* (1758) prompted him to write the author that free-trade sentiments would have "a good effect in promoting a certain interest, too little thought of by selfish man, and scarcely ever mentioned, so that we hardly have a name for it; I mean the interest of humanity, or common good of mankind."[18] It was the unique mission of America's "free trade mercantilism,"[19] Franklin hoped, to translate this common good into a rising standard of living and international peace. Toward the end of his life, he felt the dawning of American free trade would be hastened by population growth, since increased density of settlement would expedite the collection of direct taxes, freeing the new American government from reliance upon imposts for revenue. This generous spirit toward foreign importations had to be reconciled, of course, with his antagonism toward "foreign Gegaws" and his sympathy for American industry, a feat accomplished by reference to the size of the American market and to industrial division of labor. He seemed to think the American market potentially large enough to absorb the products of both foreign and domestic industry, while at the same time remaining uncorrupted by superfluities; and an international specialization, with each country manufacturing its most appropriate export commodities, would permit both free trade and the development of some distinctive home manufactures.

Free trade and an expanding American population, thought Franklin, would benefit all humanity by reducing the economic

18. Franklin to David Hume, Coventry, September 27, 1760, *Writings,* IV, 83.
19. My phrase, not Franklin's. If he had been a mercantilist early in life and later a free trader, this awkward definition would not be necessary. But from at least 1760, his economic thought was a composite of elements from both doctrines.

causes of international friction and, in addition, raising the living standards of workers everywhere. The logic of the latter benefit worked as follows: the more Americans, the larger the market for European goods; and the more profitable their goods, the less excuse European industrialists would have to depress wages. The conversion of earnings into higher wages was insured by the fact that the necessities of life were cheaper in America, where plentiful, than in Europe, where scarce. European workers would flee, therefore, to the New World paradise unless adequately paid. If they did emigrate in large numbers, the remaining European labor force would contract in size and the cost of labor would rise proportionately. Hence, a growing America would, in a setting of free trade, diffuse prosperity throughout an interdependent and peaceful world. In their highest refinement, Franklin's economic and demographic views were an expression of his ideal of benevolence. The whole plan, of course, depended upon filling up the continent.[20]

But not with just anyone. Orderly and unified development required a high degree of cultural homogeneity. Inching westward, clearing forests, and erecting a New Order were challenge enough without the added trials of interethnic friction. Particularly troublesome were Indians, Negroes, and Germans.

Franklin could not help admiring the proud, simple life of America's native inhabitants. There was a noble quality in the stories, apocryphal or not, which he told of their hospitality and tolerance, their oratory and pride.[21] But was it the Indian himself or the qualities he represented that Franklin appreciated? As a living symbol of simplicity and "happy mediocrity," the Indian could be dramatized as exemplifying essential aspects of the Virtuous Order. Depiction of his healthful, primitive morality could be instructive for transplanted Englishmen, still doting on "foreign Gegaws." "Happiness," Franklin wrote, "is more generally and

20. *Reflections on the Augmentation of Wages Which Will Be Occasioned in Europe by the American Revolution,* 1788, *Complete Works,* X, 46–60.
21. *Remarks Concerning the Savages of North America,* 1784?, *Writings,* X, 97–104. Hereafter cited as *Savages.*

equally diffus'd among Savages than in our civilized Societies."[22] Why, then, did he not incorporate the Indian into his plans for the new society? Exemplars of manly lack of affection, might they not be edifying incarnations of republican simplicity, walking in the midst of the colonials like Watusi among Bahutus?

Unfortunately for the Indian, Franklin also saw in him another set of images. He was not only a simple primitive but a barbarous savage as well—lazy, vain, insolent, and in need of an occasional blow to keep him honest.[23] When Franklin promoted colonial unification by declaring that even Indians had their confederacies, and when he noted that the councils of savages proceeded with better order than the British Parliament, he was not complimenting Indians but criticizing Englishmen.[24] Prolonged association with Indians could be morally enfeebling: captured whites, raised by the savages and recovered by the English, "take the first good Opportunity of escaping again into the Woods" and returning to a life "of freedom from care and labour." Franklin could sympathize with such an attitude. It was quite understandable to him why "No European who has tasted Savage Life, can afterwards bear to live in our Societies."

The Care and Labour of providing for artificial & fashionable Wants, the sight of so many Rich wallowing in superfluous plenty, whereby so many are kept poor and distress'd for Want. The Insolence of Office, . . . the Restraints of Custom, all contribute to disgust them with what we call civil Society.[25]

22. Franklin's marginal note in Matthew Wheelock's *Reflections Moral and Political on Great Britain and Her Colonies* (London: T. Becket, 1770), p. 2. Hereafter cited as *Reflections*.

23. Franklin to William Strahan, Philadelphia, July 4, 1744, *Papers*, II, 411; "Supplement to the Boston *Independent Chronicle*," March 1782, *Writings*, VIII, 437–442; *The Interest of Great Britain Considered with Regard to her Colonies, and the Acquisition of Canada and Guadaloupe*, 1760, *Writings*, IV, 76. Hereafter cited as *Interest*. Franklin to Peter Collinson, Philadelphia, May 9, 1753, *Papers*, IV, 481; Franklin to Richard Jackson, New York, June 27, 1763, *Jackson Papers*, p. 107.

24. Franklin to James Parker, Philadelphia, March 20, 1750–1751, *Papers*, IV, 118–119; *Savages*, p. 99.

25. Franklin's note in Wheelock's *Reflections*, p. 2.

But Franklin was no escapist. Others may have fled from artifice, insolence, and restraint, but not he. His task was to purify society, not abandon it.

The figure of the Indian furnishes a clue for understanding a central problem in Franklin's thought. As he pushed aside the Original American to make way for the Anglo-American, he was tacitly acknowledging that the Evolving Order might render facets of the Virtuous Order obsolete. He could not accept the full implication of this development; he wished to keep the two social concepts in unresolved equilibrium, simultaneously enjoying both while avoiding sudden, destructive changes. Hence his horror at the periodic news of frontier massacres perpetrated by whites on unsuspecting Indians. The frontiersmen were destroying vital repositories of primitive life and, at the same time, revealing themselves to be wholly devoid of the humane, constructive attributes of civilization. How much better to advance the New Order by the more gradual method of inserting clauses in Indian treaties, declaring their lands forfeit should they disregard the terms. Honesty was not an Indian virtue, Franklin must have reasoned, so lands would fall into white hands legally and at regular intervals. Though his plans for increasing mankind did not include Indians, neither did he wish for their summary removal. They had a symbolic value.[26]

Negroes, however, were another matter. As anyone might see, they were the wrong color:

. . . [W]hile we are, as I may call it, *Scouring* our Planet, by clearing America of Woods, and so making this side of our Globe reflect a brighter Light to the Eyes of the Inhabitants in Mars or Venus, why should we in the Sight of Superior Beings, darken its People? why increase the Sons of Africa, by planting them in America, where we have so fair an Opportunity, excluding all Blacks and Tawneys, of Increasing the lovely White and Red?

26. "A Narrative of the Late Massacre in Lancaster County," January 1763, *Writings,* IV, 289–314; Franklin to Richard Jackson, Philadelphia, December 24, 1763, *Jackson Papers,* p. 120.

Moreover, they were slaves, and as such deprived poor whites of employment, thus depressing their income, marriage rate, and rate of propagation. Even masters were not immune to corroding effects; they and their children became accustomed to luxury, disgusted with labor, idle, and unproductive. Above all, Negroes as slaves were a potential fifth column. Franklin, at the opening of the French and Indian War, joined in drafting a protest to Massachusetts Governor William Shirley against the latter's recruiting into his army indentured servants from Pennsylvania who otherwise would "raise Families, add to the Number of our People, and cultivate more Land." The last thing the petitioners wanted to see was

. . . the People driven to the necessity of providing themselves with Negro Slaves. . . . Thus the growth of the Country by Increase of white Inhabitants will be prevented, [and] the Province weakened rather than strengthened (as every Slave may be reckoned a domestick Enemy). . . .[27]

Solicitude for white welfare, then, seems to have been the earliest motive inclining Franklin toward slave-trade abolition and gradual emancipation. For some time his attachment even to this consideration was theoretical rather than practical. White men in general might be economically and morally debilitated by Negro servitude, but not a certain Philadelphia printer. Slave buyers, slave sellers, and writers of antislavery tracts all found their way in and out of Franklin's Market Street shop. When his press was not in use producing the *Gazette* with its slave-sale notices, he was perfectly willing to let Quaker reformers hire it to turn out abolitionist literature. There was Ralph Sandiford's *A Brief Examination of the Practice of the Times* (1729), Benjamin Lay's *All Slave-Keepers that Keep the Innocent in Bondage* (1737), and John Woolman's *Considerations on Keeping Negroes* (1762), all printed with the Franklin name. One suspects this was less a reflection of his devo-

27. *Increase, Papers,* IV, 234, 231. Pennsylvania Assembly, "Address to the Governour," February 11, 1756, *Papers,* VI, 397–398. See also letter to Sir Everard Fawkener, New York, July 27, 1756, *Papers,* VI, 475.

tion to benevolence than to business, since he was himself a keeper of slaves. We know that he rid himself of them in 1751, the reason probably being that they were unprofitable. In *Increase,* published not long before, he drew attention to the expensiveness of slaves—not only because of upkeep, but, in addition, because "almost every Slave [is] by Nature a Thief." Whether this conclusion derived from personal experience and was related to his action, he does not mention. But he did not cavil at acquiring more slaves, he and his son William each taking one to England in 1757. That was the year he inserted in his final testament a kindly provision that his slaves Peter and Jemima be set free *after* his death. While two colored attendants ministered to the Franklins in London, Deborah in 1760 kept a "black boy" at home in Philadelphia.[28]

He continued to keep slaves, probably because he felt them useful despite their disadvantages, and in London he might even have found them to possess an incidental propaganda value. A justification used by the English for taxing America was colonial prosperity, variously described as New England opulence and "Virginia luxury." Britain, by comparison, was portrayed as burdened with debtors and parish poor. American planters and merchants, therefore, not the English gentry—already devoting sizable sums to public and private philanthropy—should be called upon to meet the increasing costs of empire. It was an odd sight: two proud, ambitious, and powerful lands vying in protestations of poverty. Never to be outdone, Franklin could respond, with his London dependents at hand as living illustrations, "Are not the poor Negro Slaves . . . as great a burthen to the Colonists?" Especially when "past their labour, sick or lame," the blacks were every bit as good an excuse for escaping taxes as the English poor. That his line of argument took hold is rather doubtful, for maintaining colored attendants—one of whom, incidentally, ran away

28. Carl Van Doren, *Benjamin Franklin* (New York: The Viking Press, 1938), p. 129. Franklin to Mrs. Abiah Franklin, Philadelphia, April 12, 1750; *Increase;* "Last Will and Testament," April 28, 1757; *Papers,* III, 474; IV, 229; VII, 203. Franklin to Deborah Franklin, London, June 27, 1760, *Writings,* IV, 23–24, 88.

—was not the most convincing demonstration of self-sacrifice. Working with Thomas Bray's Associates, a London philanthropy, to promote Negro education in the colonies was a far better evidence of benevolence.[29]

Franklin finally translated his theoretical aversion to slavery and the slave trade into abolitonist activity in the early 1770's. The Pennsylvania and English Quakers like to think that under their influence the crass Philadelphian replaced his worldly lights with the Inner Light and began emitting humanitarian beams.[30] His arguments against slavery took on a more empathic cast, and he came to portray the institution as a hardship not only for whites but even for Negroes. A change there was, but what caused it? The answer begins to unfold in a series of events starting in 1769 with the publication of a tract by the Englishman Granville Sharp attacking the existence of slavery in his native land. Sharp was a devout Anglican layman who had been smitten with fear that God would destroy England as He had the Philistines if she did not begin at once casting out a few motes, the most conspicuous of which was slavery. Accepting a divine commission, he gathered around him the forces of philanthropy and led forth England's abolitionist host. Since most of England's slaves were located in her American domains, it was inevitable that his path should cross that of Franklin, the colonies' prime spokesman. In 1769 the G. Sharp trumpet was pointed westward and shrilly blown:[31]

29. The English position is developed in [William Jackson?], *The True Constitutional Means for Putting an End to the Disputes Between Great Britain and the American Colonies* (London: T. Becket and P. A. DeHondt, 1769). Franklin answers in his marginal note, p. 26.

30. See, for example, Arthur Stuart Pitt, "Franklin and the Quaker Movement Against Slavery," *Bulletin of Friends Historical Association,* XXXII, No. 1 (Spring 1943), 13–31. For a discussion of his abolitionist activities, see Lewis J. Carey, *Franklin's Economic Views* (New York: Doubleday, Doran, 1928), Chap. 4.

31. The author offers no apologies for the foregoing pun, for Granville himself was both a musician and punster and occasionally signed his name "G♯." See E. C. P. Lascelles, *Granville Sharp and the Freedom of Slaves in England* (London: Humphrey-Milford–Oxford University Press, 1928), cover imprint.

The boasted liberty of our American colonies . . . has so little right
to that sacred name, that it seems to differ from the arbitrary power of
despotic monarchies only in one circumstance; viz. that it is a *many-
headed monster of tyranny,* which entirely subverts our most excellent
constitution; because liberty and slavery are so opposite to each other,
that they cannot subsist in the same community.

Sharp then brandished as specimen of American indecency some
slave sale and runaway slave notices he had spotted in the *New
York Journal*—notices which, one must observe, were not unlike
advertisements a certain Pennsylvanian printed in his *Gazette.*[32]

His walls trembling, Franklin turned out one of the most dis-
pirited defenses of Jericho that the London press had seen. The
"letters to the editor" he wrote in England were often gems of
pro-American propaganda and are usually cited as such, but his
response to Sharp was so dull as to be worth quoting on that score
alone had it not the additional merit of revealing the damage Sharp
had done to Franklin's armor:

ENGLISHMAN.   You Americans make a great Clamour upon every little
   imaginary Infringement of what you take to be your Liberties; and
   yet there are no people upon Earth such Enemies to Liberty, such
   absolute Tyrants, where yours have the Opportunity, as you your-
   selves are.
AMERICAN.   How does that appear?
ENGLISHMAN.   Read Granville Sharpe's [*sic*] Book upon Slavery:
   There it appears with a Witness.
AMERICAN.   I have read it.
ENGLISHMAN.   And pray what do you think of it?
AMERICAN.   To speak my Opinion candidly, I think it is in the Main
   a good Book. I applaud the Author's Zeal for Liberty in general. I
   am pleased with his Humanity. But his *general Reflections* on *all
   Americans,* as having no real Regard for Liberty . . . I cannot ap-
   prove of; nor of the Conclusion he draws, that therefore our Claim
   to the Enjoyment of Liberty for ourselves, is unjust. I think, that in
   all this, he is too severe upon the Americans, and passes over with

32. Sharp, *A Representation of the Injustice and Dangerous Tendency of
Tolerating Slavery in England* (London: Benjamin White, 1769), pp. 82–87.

too partial an Eye the Faults of his own Country. This seems to me not quite fair: and it is particularly *injurious* to us at this Time, to endeavour to render us odious, and to encourage those who would oppress us, by representing us as unworthy of the Liberty we are now contending for.

He tried to rescue his position by reminding his readers that only one family in a hundred in North America owned a slave, that there were multitudes of colonial Sharps, and that Britain's own soldiers and sailors—to say nothing of her Scottish coal miners, white faces darkened with soot—were in a more lamentable condition than the American blacks.[33] But he left the main charge still unrefuted. How could the colonists ask London for a liberty which they themselves would not grant their slaves? Franklin had two choices in rebuttal. If he wanted to recapture the offensive, he could attack either slavery or Sharp. On the one hand, taking on Sharp might be imprudent. He could be a potent enemy, capable of drawing from the side of the colonies a segment of enlightened English opinion with his persuasive pamphleteering and family connections. Grandson of an Archbishop of York, Sharp had friends and relatives in the Church of England, and his brother William was the King's surgeon. Though Franklin took issue with Granville in the foregoing exchange, he did it meekly and with deference to Sharp's humanity and libertarian zeal. On the other hand, Franklin could attack slavery; but an institution which contributed indirectly to his colonial agent fees had to be treated gently too, and Franklin hesitated to set loose on his constituents a people "of a plotting Disposition, dark, sullen, malicious, resentful and cruel in the highest Degree."[34]

Two years passed. Whether Franklin was wrestling with his conscience, suspending his judgment, or had quietly reached a de-

33. "A Conversation between an Englishman, a Scotchman, and an American on the Subject of Slavery," January 30, 1770, *Letters to the Press*, pp. 187–191. Hereafter cited as "A Conversation." See "Benjamin Franklin and American Liberties," *Pennsylvania Magazine of History and Biography*, LXII (1938), 1–11.

34. "A Conversation," p. 189.

cision is difficult to say. But by mid-1772 the new Franklin made
his debut. The slave trade, he announced in the English press, was
"pestilential detestable traffic in the bodies and souls of men."[35]
It has been implied that the Pennsylvania Friend Anthony Benezet
brought him out on the side of the Lord with such pleas as that
found in a letter to Franklin imploring his aid in abolitionism as a
"fellow traveller on a dangerous & heavy road."[36] Indeed, who is
to say Franklin did not give his ear to Benezet, a man who, in the
past, had thrown bits of business to his Philadelphia printshop?[37]

But a more likely cause of his conversion was Lord Chief Justice
Mansfield. Upholding a defense prepared under the eye of Sharp,
Mansfield decreed in June, 1772, that James Sommersett, a Ja-
maican Negro who had the good fortune to accompany his master
on a trip to England, was to be liberated. "The air of England has
long been too pure for a slave," Mansfield decreed, "and every
man is free who breathes it."[38] This was enough for Franklin.
Besides casting aspersions on the quality of American air, the
decision was judicial hypocrisy as long as English galleys were still
scouring the coasts of Africa for unfortunates to drag into bondage.
And why had not London's liberating atmosphere stimulated
Parliamentarians to grant more freedom to the colonies? One
could not apply a charge of hypocrisy with soiled hands, however,
as his 1770 reply to Sharp should have taught him, so the price
of an editorial victory was necessarily personal commitment to
abolition—at least of the slave trade.

The result of Mansfield's glib decision was Franklin's condemna-
tion not only of *"Pharisaical Britain"* but of that "pestilential detestable traffic."[39] Some eight months later, he had progressed far

35. "The Sommersett Case and the Slave Trade," June 20, 1772, *Letters
to the Press*, p. 223. Hereafter cited as "Sommersett Case."
36. Benezet to Franklin, Philadelphia, April 27, 1772, in George S.
Brookes, *Friend Anthony Benezet* (Philadelphia: University of Pennsylvania
Press, 1937), p. 287.
37. Benezet recommended Franklin's shop to a friend in 1752 as a good
place to buy Nathan Bailey's *Dictionary* and in 1760 bought magazines
from David Hall, Franklin's partner. Brookes, pp. 209, 235.
38. 20 *Howell's State Trials* 1–82.
39. "Sommersett Case," *Letters to the Press*, pp. 222–223.

enough down Benezet's "dangerous and heavy road" to report to him, "I have commenced an Acquaintance with Mr. Granville Sharpe [*sic*], and we shall act in Concert in the Affair of Slavery."[40] The collaboration did not entirely deflect the Sharp thrusts ("If I had a child, I had rather see him the humblest scavenger in the streets of *London,* than the loftiest tyrant in *America,* with a thousand slaves at his beck"[41]), but it may have helped separate in his mind the issues of American slavery and American autonomy, so that he could condemn the one and not the other. Up to and during the war, Franklin found Sharp a helpful accomplice, doing far more for the colonies than Franklin seems to have accomplished for abolition. Anglicans and politics, in short, seem to have worked his conversion quite as much as Quakers and ethics.

After the Revolution and back in Philadelphia, the Friends took him up on his professions and, in 1787, made him President of the Pennsylvania Society for Promoting the Abolition of Slavery and the Relief of Free Negroes Unlawfully Held in Bondage. He plunged in enthusiastically enough, addressing the public with fund requests, drawing up a *Plan for Improving the Condition of the Free Blacks,* signing a petition to the United States House of Representatives, and spinning out a final bagatelle to spoof Congressional defenders of the slave trade, Representative James Jackson of Georgia for one.[42] Franklin, thus, finally came to be a "white liberal"; but if modern integrationists count him as a solid early ally, they must overlook the prejudice and expedience that colored his racial position throughout most of his life.

The Germans were more perplexing. Saxons excepted, they were "of what we call a swarthy complexion," a discoloration not quite

40. Franklin to Benezet, London, February 10, 1773, *Writings,* VI, 9.

41. "Extract of a Letter from a Gentleman in Maryland to his Friend in London," Appendix No. 2 to Sharp's *An Essay on Slavery* (Burlington: West Jersey, 1773; reprinted in London, 1776), p. 43.

42. "An Address to the Public," Philadelphia, November 9, 1789; *Plan . . .* (undated); "On the Slave Trade," March 3, 1790. *Writings,* X, 66–68, 127–129, 87–91.

sufficient to suggest moral taint. If only they had been a shade or two darker, Franklin would have felt securer in his judgment; as it was, he was reduced to expletives:

. . . [W]hy should the Palatine Boors be suffered to swarm into our Settlements, and by herding together establish their Language and Manners to the Exclusion of ours? Why should Pennsylvania, founded by the English, become a Colony of *Aliens,* who will shortly be so numerous as to Germanize us instead of our Anglifying them, and will never adopt our Language or Customs, any more than they can acquire our Complexion.[43]

Franklin's principal early patron in Pennsylvania society was James Logan, business agent for the Penns, leader of the conservative Quaker "city party" in the Assembly, and a fur trader—a man whose position made him an advocate of ordered and homogeneous expansion. As early as 1727 Logan was complaining about the habit the Germans—and then the Irish—had of settling on Indian land, stirring up feuds, and embarrassing the proprietor. But the real problem was not that the Germans were too primitive, like the Indians, but too civilized.[44] In colonial Pennsylvania, they were a potential threat far graver than the Negroes—militarily, economically, and culturally.[45] Were they not being talked of as a possible buffer state between the English and the French, as likely to ally with the one nation as the other? Were not some of them Papists, like the French? And were they not imbued with an alien culture, particularly a language which cut them off from participation in the Virtuous Order? It had sometimes been difficult to make onself understood in the colonial Assembly unless one were bilingual, and how many Germans bought *Pennsylvania Gazettes?* Franklin's disposition toward the Germans probably was not sweetened by their boycott of his German-language newspaper,

43. *Increase,* p. 234.
44. Tolles, *Logan,* pp. 159–185; Tolles, *Meeting House,* pp. 15–16.
45. For a treatment of Franklin's suspicion of the Germans on all the foregoing counts, see Glenn Weaver, "Benjamin Franklin and the Pennsylvania Germans," *William and Mary Quarterly,* Third Series, XIV (October 1957), 536–559.

Philadelphische Zeitung. Granted, America was the Land of Labor, but the Germans were *so* organized, industrious, and frugal that "an accumulation arises that makes them all rich." In sum, they were becoming a political power: ". . . I remember when they modestly declined intermeddling in our Elections, but now they come in droves, and carry all before them, except in one or two counties." He would especially remember the election of 1764, when an angry proprietor was to circulate the "Palantine Boors" passage among the boors themselves and thus contribute to Assemblyman Franklin's defeat.[46]

Too powerful to be suppressed and too useful to be excluded, they had to be assimilated and diverted. Reluctantly he admitted, ". . . they have their Virtues, their industry and frugality is exemplary; they are excellent husbandmen and contribute greatly to the improvement of a Country." He chastened Peter Collinson, whom he had stirred up in the first place,[47] for suggesting such extremes as intermarriage and the banning of German books and printing houses.[48] Franklin thought it more seemly to establish English-language schools among them, invalidate public documents written in German, ban from public office those who did not speak English, and close the doors of Pennsylvania to new Teutonic arrivals. This final expedient was especially advisable, since the latest waves had been composed of "all the Refuse Wretches poor and helpless who are burthensome to the old Settlers, or Knaves

46. Franklin to James Parker, Philadelphia, March 20, 1750–1751; Franklin to Collinson, Philadelphia, May 9, 1753; *Papers*, I, 230–231, 233–234, 274; IV, 120, 479, 483. See Weaver, pp. 49–50.

47. In response to a letter from Franklin, May 9, 1753, Collinson prepared "Hints Humbly proposed to Incorporate the Germans more with the English and Check the Increase of their Power," which contained the strategies censured by Franklin along with those he later adopted. From Collinson, August 12, 1753, *Papers*, V, 21.

48. An English printer might find it embarrassing to encourage the latter as an official measure, especially if he were already trying to accomplish the same end privately. Franklin during this period was unsuccessfully engaged in attempts to drive the German printer Christopher Sauer out of business by financing a rival German press. From H. M. Muhlenberg, Providence, August 3, 1754, *Papers*, V, 419.

and Rascals that live by Sharking and Cheating them." Many of
them came "without Change of Raiment, or any other Means of
keeping themselves sweet and clean," and as a consequence were
infecting the country with fever and distemper. "The Stream may
therefore be well enough turned to the other Colonies. . . ."
Franklin, who functioned as a broker in Pennsylvania's Quaker-
proprietor politics up to 1756, could not afford to overly antagonize the German districts, and he noted with pleasure that the
established Germans in the colony shared his antipathy for their
late-arriving *Landsmänner*.[49]

When Franklin spoke of "the increase of mankind," therefore, he
had in mind a preference for the increase of *his* kind. The immigra-
tion of English, Welsh, Scots, and Protestant Irish[50]—providing
they were not felons[51]—had the happy dual effect of spreading
civilization and raising land values. Franklin calculated that if half
the inhabitants of England were transplanted to America, the English-speaking people would multiply in a hundred years as they
could never have done at home in a thousand, and with no danger
to the population level of the mother country. Any deficiency in
England would be soon corrected by "earlier and more prolific
marriages" resulting from greater availability of foodstuffs. British
attempts to restrict emigration, therefore, were quite unnecessary
and obstructed the expansion of the race. Besides, there was an in-
equitable flavor to imprisoning masses of laborers in Britain while

49. Franklin to Collinson, 1753?; Pennsylvania Assembly, "Reply to the
Governor," Philadelphia, May 15, 1755. *Papers,* V, 158–160; VI, 40. See
John Zimmerman, "Benjamin Franklin and the Quaker Party, 1775–6,"
William and Mary Quarterly, Third Series, XVII (July 1960), 291–313.
50. Franklin was also concerned about the Catholic Irish as a potential
source of American disunity. In the Revolutionary period he feared that the
vicar-apostolic of London, who superintended the flock in America, would
try to entice the New World Irish to side with Britain. Franklin to Comte de
Vergennes, Passy, December 15, 1783, *Writings,* IX, 125.
51. Britain was polluting the American continent by sending over not
only Africans but the dregs of English jails. Franklin suggested the colonies
reciprocate by sending back American rattlesnakes. "Felons and Rattlesnakes," May 9, 1751, *Papers,* IV, 130–133.

suffering the "idle and extravagant gentry to travel and reside abroad at their pleasure." The issue called forth one of his few references to natural rights. "The Right of Migration," he declared, "is common to all men, a natural Right." The presumption, of course, was that a migration of the right sort of people, English-speaking whites, would flow in the proper direction, from Great Britain to the New World.[52]

An American quasi-mercantilist empire and the growth of the Anglo-Saxon people—these were the socio-economic manifestations of the Evolving Order. There was a physical manifestation as well: the acquisition of space.

THE INTEREST OF GREATER AMERICA

> Green Hills and Dales, and Cottages embower'd,
> The Scenes of Innocence, and calm Delight.
> —*Poor Richard Improved* (1755)

Franklin's social ideal was anything but static. The New Order existed in a continuous—almost fervid—state of expansion. Especially important were the dynamics of space. The filling of storehouses and cradles was to occur upon an ever-broadening geographic base, in youthful contrast to senescent Europe.

Three currents of Franklin's thought carried him toward territorial expansion. Of paramount concern was the fact that an increasing population demanded room.

The human body and the political differ in this, that the first is limited by nature to a certain stature, which, when attain'd, it cannot, ordinarily, exceed; the other by better government and more prudent policy, as well as by change of manners and other circumstances, often

52. Franklin to Collinson, 1753?; Franklin to James Parker, Philadelphia, March 20, 1750–1751. *Papers,* V, 160; IV, 120. "On a Proposed Act of Parliament for Preventing Emigration," November 1774; Franklin to Henry Royle *et al.,* Passy, January 4, 1782. *Writings,* VI, 291–298; VIII, 354–356. Franklin's note in Wheelock's *Reflections,* p. 54.

takes fresh starts of growth, after being long at a stand; and may add tenfold to the dimensions it had for ages been confined to.

One of the "other circumstances" Franklin was contemplating was the addition of new lands. With a growing domain, there was no upward limit to the growth of an economic and racial empire. "How important an Affair then to Britain," he wrote with his eye on the West, "is the [1748 Aix-la-Chapelle] Treaty for settling the Bounds between her Colonies and the French, and how careful she should be to secure Room enough, since on the Room depends so much the Increase of her People." But the mother country was not careful enough, Franklin believed, of the territorial aspirations of her colonists. Some ten years later, he was urging further acquisitions in *The Interest of Great Britain Considered with Regard to her Colonies* (1760), a piece which might have been more truthfully entitled *The Interest of Greater America Considered with Regard to Britain*. Predicting that the Americans could easily populate as many more colonies beyond the Appalachians as existed already on the Atlantic seaboard, he pleaded for the accession of Canada instead of Guadaloupe—a profitable but small island already filled with the wrong kind of people, Frenchmen and Negroes —as the price of peace with France.

The annual increment alone of our present colonies, without diminishing their numbers, or requiring a man from hence, is sufficient in ten years to fill *Canada* with double the number of *English,* than it now has of French inhabitants.[53]

With foreign policy being made in London, not Philadelphia, he was obliged to justify the retention of French America as politically advantageous to the mother country. He reasoned, therefore, that a consolidated North America would not be too large a parcel for Britain to manage (though he was to smile later at the thought of an old lion checking a young one); that a manufacturing competitor could hardly develop in an area so thinly settled (though he added slyly that if such occurred, it would merely enable the

53. *Interest, Writings,* IV, 55; *Increase, Papers,* IV, 233; *Interest, Writings,* IV, 70, 77–81.

colonists to afford more of Britain's luxury goods—this from an arch-critic of "foreign Gegaws"); and that the colonies might be tempted to assert themselves if a French Canada hovered protectively on the northern horizon as a waiting ally (though he professed horror of the French, who, with their Indian accomplices, had subjected the colonials to "horrid barbarities"). Franklin was clearly more sensitive to the future of the American population than to the interests of the British Empire.[54]

Further territory was necessitated by human quantity, true, but also by Franklin's desire to enrich the quality of social and economic institutions. The increase of land was essential to "happy mediocrity," a cardinal feature of the New Order. If an accelerating population were to saturate the available area, whence would come the land to support new generations of contented yeomen? Contentment required that every yeoman possess relatively equal and adequate lands to furnish the material and psychic gratifications of life. These needs could not be met indefinitely in the East. A trans-Appalachian escape valve from the oppressions of inequality was suggested by Franklin in 1772, when he observed that new settlements would draw off the poor of the middle colonies and settle them with their large families upon land not monopolized by great landholders or crowded with surplus workers.[55]

Then too, real estate was a lucrative pastime. A speculator in land as well as philosophy, Franklin joined with John Sargent and Sir Matthew Featherstone in applying for a Crown grant on the Ohio River and was in touch with others who also wanted to "strike while the iron is hot." When the Ohio iron cooled, Franklin interested himself in the South Carolina claims of Daniel Coxe and solicited the aid of a London lawyer, Richard Jackson (successor to Franklin's first Pennsylvania colonial agency), in searching out

54. *Interest, Writings,* IV, 72–73; "New Fables," January 20, 1770, *Letters to the Press,* pp. 166–167; *Interest, Writings,* IV, 48–49, 61, 69, 51–52, 76. See Albert Weinberg, *Manifest Destiny: A Study of Nationalist Expansionism in American History* (Baltimore: Johns Hopkins Press, 1935), pp. 17–18, 384.
55. "Reply to a Friend of Lord Hillsborough," after September 7, 1772, *Writings,* V, 518.

Coxe's lost title. Not until Jackson reported that he had conducted a search "for many Hours several Successive Days among the Inrollments of Grants" and picked through "Bundles of Warrants . . . out of a Heap covered with dust" did Franklin stop pressing him on the issue. Despite these setbacks, Franklin's personal holdings grew to include a portion of northwestern Pennsylvania equal to four township sections.[56]

Considerations of human quantity, social quality, and personal profits thus combined to lead Franklin to a strategy of continental expansion. The strategy itself was also threefold. America's territorial base, first of all, was to be preserved and guarded; secondly, population pressures would be relentlessly generated until, thirdly, colonizing shafts broke through into the wilderness. That land which America already possessed should be well used and not an inch wasted or relinquished. Cost was no object. In 1748, he unsuccessfully proposed an expensive swamp drainage program to the Philadelphia City Council, and years later in Paris he warned against Spain's being "suffered to encroach on our Bounds," exclaiming—with pre-Jeffersonian overtones of a Louisiana purchase, "I would rather agree with them to buy at a great Price the whole of their Right on the Mississippi than sell a Drop of its Water. A Neighbor might as well ask me to sell my Street Door."[57]

When Franklin turned from thoughts of preserving and improving the domain to expanding it, he could not have helped perceiving the role of a growing population as both impetus and justification. If a crowded people needed breathing room, justice itself would cry out for space; and should the councils of world opinion remain unmoved, the burgeoning horde would at length burst from its confines and legitimize its aspirations with a *fait accompli*. The rela-

56. Franklin to Richard Jackson, November 12, March 29, 1763, *Jackson Papers*, pp. 112, 96. See Alfred P. James, "Benjamin Franklin's Ohio Valley Lands," *Proceedings of the American Philosophical Society*, XCVIII (August 16, 1954), 261.

57. "Report on the Swamp," February 24, 1748, *Papers*, III, 276–279; Franklin to Robert Livingston, Passy, April 12, 1782; Franklin to John Jay, Passy, October 2, 1780; *Writings*, VIII, 144.

tionship between demography and geography in Franklin's thought was not a simple one. The desire for space was not entirely a derivative of population increase, as has been shown above. The very securing of land seemed at times to take priority in his mind, and triggering a population explosion was, one suspects, a means to that end. Why else did Franklin, who of all men was most aware of the astounding New World growth rate, promote an even more rapid increase by encouraging propagation? Nature was doing rather well, doubling the number of Americans every twenty to twenty-five years; but Franklin apparently concluded that, with his help, she could do better. Describing for his readers an imaginary courtroom scene, Franklin introduces "Miss Polly Baker," who is being prosecuted for the fifth time for producing a child indiscreetly. She is made by Franklin to say, "Can it be a Crime (in the Nature of Things I mean) to add to the Number of the King's Subjects, in a new Country that really wants People?" Who better to make such an inquiry than one whose own procreative activities have long eluded definitive treatment?[58]

Though a political adversary once accused him of keeping Negro paramours, and though he showed an aptitude for diplomacy-by-flirtation in London and Paris, he became an advocate of aging mistresses, "Because [among other reasons] there is no hazard of Children, which irregularly produc'd may be attended with much Inconvenience." With respectability came a measure of prudence. In compensation, he touted marriage—the earlier and more prolific the better. Men and women unmarried, he declared, were like separated halves of a scissors, unnatural and useless. He assured his Deborah, left behind in Philadelphia, that the numerous bachelors and expensive women he found in London only served to tighten his attachment to wedlock. To advocate multiplication, it was necessary that he advocate marriage—and this Franklin came

58. "The Speech of Miss Polly Baker," April 15, 1754, *Papers*, III, 124. See Max Hall, *Benjamin Franklin and Polly Baker* (Chapel Hill: University of North Carolina Press, 1960); Paul Leicester Ford, *Who Is the Mother of Franklin's Son? An Historical Conundrum Hitherto Given up—Now Partly Answered* (Brooklyn, 1889).

to do most convincingly, even though his own family was rather small by eighteenth-century standards.[59]

While the generative dynamic was at work on the eastern side of the Appalachians, wedges of settlement were to be driven into the West.

The great country back of the Appalachian mountains on both sides the Ohio, and between that river and the lakes . . . must undoubtedly (perhaps in less than another century) become a populous and powerful dominion. . . .

To prevent this new dominion from becoming a seat of Gallicism, to secure the borders of the existing British colonies, and to provide an outlet for the "many thousands of families that are ready to swarm," the Ohio country had to be opened to English homesteaders. Franklin's Albany Plan was intended to facilitate this process. Far more than a defense scheme, it was the blueprint for a cultural invasion. "A particular colony has scarce strength enough to extend itself by new settlements, at so great a distance from the old," Franklin explained,

. . . but joint force of the union might suddenly establish a new colony or two in those parts, or extend an old colony to particular passes, greatly to the security of our present frontiers, increase of trade and people, breaking off the French communication between Canada and Louisiana, and speedy settlement of the intermediate lands.

With a governor general and grand council supervising the purchase of Indian lands, distributing small tracts to settlers, framing laws for the new communities, and collecting quit-rents to finance operations, the backlands could be opened efficiently and speedily. Order would expedite expansion. Franklin mused in the twilight of life that, had the Albany Plan been enacted, the British Empire might

59. Edward R. Turner, *The Negro in Pennsylvania* (Washington, D. C.: American Historical Association, 1911), p. 31, *n*43; "Old Mistresses Apologue," June 25, 1745, *Papers*, III, 31; Franklin to John Alleyne, Craven Street, August 9, 1768; Franklin to John Sargent, Passy, January 27, 1783; Franklin to Deborah Franklin, London, June 27, 1760. *Writings*, V, 157–158; IX, 14; IV, 24.

have been spared a revolution. The colonials would have been able to provide for their own defense, rendering unnecessary the stationing of British regulars in America and the levying of obnoxious taxes for their support. There was a further reason which Franklin did not mention but which he well knew. Had his countrymen been permitted to manage their own growth, a major source of anti-British friction would have been removed. The colonies, busied in subduing the interior and organizing its resources, could have compensated for the restrictions of British mercantilism in the East by devoting themselves to the development of the West. But Franklin was wise in not adding this possibility, for it carried a latent implication that America, united and expanding under the Albany Plan, might have caused England more trouble before 1776 than it did.[60]

Sooner or later, Franklin's expansionism was bound to bring him into conflict with the colonial policy of the mother country. He was a claustrophobe in fear of American suffocation. "Canada in the hands of *France* has always stinted the growth of our colonies," he complained in 1760, and twenty years later he was apprehensive lest Spain "shut us up within the Appalachian mountains." Well before the Quebec Act of 1774 established a virtual French enclave north of the Ohio, and even before the Proclamation of 1763 restricted white settlement to the Appalachian crest, Franklin had satirically predicted that the English would take delight in enjoining the colony midwives to "stifle at birth every third or fourth child," in order to keep their plantations manageable.[61]

In view of his discomfort over restrictions on American growth, it is remarkable that he mustered sufficient self-control to serve as a go-between in English-American politics as long as he did. His forbearance, as shall be seen, stemmed at least in part from his de-

---

60. "A Plan for Settling Two Western Colonies," 1754; "Reasons and Motives for the *Albany Plan of Union*," July 1754; "Remark," February 9, 1789. *Papers*, V, 457, 462, 411, 417. See John A. Schutz, *Thomas Pownall: British Defender of American Liberty* (Glendale: Arthur N. Clark, 1951), pp. 43–50.

61. *Interest*, pp. 50, 77; Franklin to Robert R. Livingston, Passy, April 12, 1782, *Writings*, VIII, 425.

sire for a Harmonious Order characterized by compromise and discretion. When hostilities began, however, and he returned to an America defiled by British raiders, the propagandist, who had urged the timorous to do battle for Canada in 1760, once again saw no alternative but war. Naturally, he never justified it in terms of American expansionary motives; the colonials had simply been tilling their lands in peaceful content. England, on the other hand, "unquiet, ambitious, avaricious, imprudent, and quarrelsome," was a Gargantua whose territorial lust was insatiable.[62]

The war nearly over, Franklin quietly tried to slip into the peace treaty a clause which would turn Canada and Nova Scotia over to the United States. He might have been remembering his dictum of thirty years earlier: "The Prince . . . that acquires new Territory, if he finds it vacant, or removes the Natives to give his own People Room" may properly be called the father of his nation, for such a man is "the Cause of the Generation of Multitudes. . . ."[63] In an America without princes, Franklin qualified admirably as a symbol of national paternity.

62. Franklin to Joseph Priestly, Philadelphia, July 7, 1775; "Of the Means of Disposing the Enemy to Peace," 1760; "Comparison of Great Britain and the United States . . . ," 1777. *Writings,* VI, 408; IV, 90–95; VIII, 6.
63. "Journal of the Negotiations for Peace with Great Britain," March 21–July 1, 1782, *Writings,* VIII, 469–473; *Increase,* p. 231.

✪

The Stamp Act Crisis

The role of Benjamin Franklin in the Stamp Act crisis and its influence upon the development of his political ideas have not yet been fully explored. The ambiguity which surrounds this chapter in his life was created partly by his own equivocal conduct; partly by the secrecy in which he concealed some of his ideas and employments. To the attacks of political enemies who charged in America that he was himself the plotter with Grenville of the hated measure, he made no direct reply; but he permitted his friends to draw back the curtain a little way upon a scene of activity in which he was engaged in London in the winter of 1765–1766. For the most part, however, he seems to have relied upon his brilliant examination before the House of Commons, followed so soon by repeal, to confute his critics.

As a result, historians and biographers have presented only a series of episodes to link Franklin with the Stamp Act. We glimpse him in the early months of 1765 laboring with his fellow-agents, not too strenuously it would seem, to turn Grenville's mind from his favorite scheme back to the old device of requisitions. We see him, a little later, accepting perhaps too philosophically the *fait accompli:* confused between the claims of patriotism and patronage,

Originally published under the title "Benjamin Franklin and the Stamp Act" in *Proceedings of the Colonial Society of Massachusetts,* Vol. XXXII (February 1934), pp. 56–77. Reprinted by permission of the author.

nominating John Hughes for stamp distributor in Pennsylvania, advising Jared Ingersoll to accept the Connecticut post. And then, after many months of apparently complaisant silence, we discover him, tardily aroused by news of his own unpopularity and the plight of the anti-Proprietary party in Pennsylvania, writing a few essays for the newspapers, lobbying in Parliament, and finally rising to the height of an adroit and persuasive argument on the great occasion of his hearing before the House of Commons.

Not all the gaps in this inadequate narrative can be filled, for in the mass of Franklin papers there are also gaps. It is possible, however, to disclose the secret of Franklin's counterproposals to Grenville prior to the enactment of the stamp tax measure. It is possible also to reveal Franklin as a principal agent in the agitation for reopening the whole American question under the Rockingham ministry. It can be demonstrated, moreover, that the Stamp Act controversy had a decisive influence upon his formulation of theories of the empire and of American rights which, until he espoused independence, he had occasion to modify only in detail.

I

When Franklin returned to England as agent for Pennsylvania at the end of 1764, Grenville's revenue policy had long since been notified to the Americans, the new trade restrictions were in force, and the year of grace for the enactment of the stamp tax would expire the following March. Ten years earlier, in correspondence with William Shirley,[1] Franklin had placed himself strongly on record against taxation of the colonists by Parliament, in terms which anticipated certain of the arguments shortly to be heard against the Stamp Act. The colonists, he had predicted, would assert: "That it is suppos'd an undoubted Right of Englishmen not to be taxed but by their own Consent given thro' their Representa-

1. First published in the *London Chronicle,* February 8, 1766, with an introduction by "A Lover of Britain." See A. H. Smyth, ed., *The Writings of Benjamin Franklin,* 10 vols. (New York, 1905–1907), III, 231; and C. H. Lincoln, ed., *Correspondence of William Shirley,* II, 103–107. The text of the quotations is from the latter, pp. 104, 106–107.

tives." "Secondary taxes," incidental to the regulation of trade, they did not complain of, but direct taxes laid by Parliament

must seem hard Measure to Englishmen, who cannot conceive, that by hazarding their Lives and Fortunes in subduing and settling new Countries, extending the Dominion and encreasing the Commerce of their Mother Nation, they have forfeited the native Rights of Britons, which they think ought rather to have been given them, as due to such Merit, if they had been before in a State of Slavery.

These were views to which Franklin would shortly recur; at the beginning of 1765 they were perhaps somewhat obscured by other considerations. There is no evidence, however, apart from the in-nuendoes of his enemies, to support the view of his latest biog-rapher that among the agents Franklin did less to oppose the law than any other. From such records of their conferences with Gren-ville as have come down it is apparent that the agents pressed upon the minister arguments which can be definitely attributed to Frank-lin; and that it was Franklin who contended for a return to the method of requisitions.

To be sure, it is said that it was this unhappy suggestion which enabled Grenville in his replies to reduce the agents to silence. But Franklin was not entirely silenced. There is definite evidence to show that he met Grenville's challenge that the Americans produce a feasible substitute for the stamp tax. The evidence comes from Franklin himself, it is true, and from a letter written some twenty months later; but it fits neatly into what is known of his ideas at the time, and is consistent with his course on another significant American issue, the currency question. Had the facts been widely known in America, his enemies would not have been appeased, but they would have shifted the ground of their attack. Franklin did not propose the Stamp Act to Grenville, as some malicious men chose to believe; but he did bring forward a scheme for an equivalent American revenue.

The abortive interviews with Grenville occurred in February, 1765. By February 14, Franklin knew that the Stamp Act must pass, but he held out hope to an American correspondent that

Parliament would ease the colonies "in some particulars relating to our commerce, and a scheme is under consideration," he added, "to furnish us with a currency, without which we can neither pay debts nor duties."[2] Here Franklin was sketching the outlines of that coordinated program of economic and financial reform which throughout 1765 and 1766 was the objective of the "friends of America" in England. In the broader view of the American question of those years the movement for the repeal of the Stamp Act becomes an episode, though a major one, in this inclusive reform program. Trade reform, with repeal, was the common ground upon which the agents and the merchants trading to North America could take their stand. But currency reform was Franklin's own peculiar interest. Long after the repeal of the Stamp Act, and after the partial victories of the trade reformers in the spring of 1766, he continued to press it in one form or another upon successive ministers through the channel of the London merchants' committee. In a letter to Joseph Galloway of October 11, 1766, he described the status of the scheme at the time, and in one noteworthy passage revealed in confidence the origin, in 1765, of his currency proposals:

You take notice, that in the London Merchants Letter there is mention made of a Plan for a general Currency in America, being under Consideration of the Ministry;—And you wish it may suit the Temper of the Americans. I will let you into the History of that Plan. When we were opposing the Stamp Act, before it pass'd, Mr. Grenville often threw out to us, that the Colonies had had Notice of it, and knew it would be necessary for Government here to draw some Revenue from them, and they had propos'd nothing that might answer the End and be more agreable to themselves: And then he would say, Can you Gentlemen that are Agents name any Mode of Raising Money for Public Service that the People would have less Objection to, if we should agree to drop this Bill?—This encourag'd me, to present him with a Plan for a General Loan Office in America, nearly like ours, but with some Improvements effectually to prevent Depreciation; to be established by Act of Parliament, appropriating the Interest to the American Service,

2. *Writings,* IV, 362.

&c. This I then thought would be a lighter and more bearable Tax than the Stamps, because those that pay it have an Equivalent in the Use of the Money; and that it would at the same time furnish us with a Currency which we much wanted, and could not obtain under the Restrictions lately laid on us. Mr. Grenville paid little Attention to it, being besotted with his Stamp-Scheme, which he rather chose to carry through.[3]

It thus appears that early in 1765 Franklin was willing to concede an American revenue under an act of Parliament, in a form which he described as a tax, so long as it might be expected to release those springs of abundant currency which, he believed, would revive the flagging prosperity of the colonies. Save for this disclosure, he seems to have kept his proposal a deep secret. Galloway probably counseled him to suppress the story. Indeed, on receiving this communication, Galloway wrote to Franklin's son:

This part of his Letter I shall keep private, as I have heard from many very warm objections against such a Plan, and in the present Temper of Americans, I think it w[d] occasion great Clamours. I have been full in my Sentiments to him on the Subject by the Packet.[4]

3. Ms. William L. Clements Library. In this letter Franklin went on to assert that the plan had later found favor with members of the Rockingham ministry, who conferred frequently with him upon it, "and really strengthened one another and their Friends in the Resolution of Repealing the Stamp Act, on a Supposition that by this Plan of a Loan Office they could raise a greater sum with more satisfaction to the people." The letter is referred to briefly by R. A. Humphreys in the *English Historical Review,* L, 267–268; and also by L. J. Carey in *Franklin's Economic Views* (p. 20). But by the latter the episode is assigned to the year 1766, which obscures the true *raison d'être* of the proposal. I have also been able to identify a portion of Franklin's draft of his scheme in the Franklin Mss. (American Philosophical Society), L, ii, 18. It is clear that this is the project which Pownall inserted in 1768 in his current edition of *The Administration of the Colonies,* and which he described as the joint production of himself and an American friend. But by 1768—indeed by 1767, when it looked for a time as if Parliament, with the backing of the merchants, would take it seriously—Franklin had long since lost his enthusiasm for the plan. For his later attitude toward this revenue scheme, see his letter to Galloway of June 13, 1767, in *Writings,* V, 25–28.

4. Franklin Mss. (American Philosophical Society), LVIII, i, 36. The letter is dated December 21, 1766, and is incomplete.

In one branch of their duties the agents, including Franklin, may perhaps be charged with neglecting their opportunities in the months before the passage of the Stamp Act. There was singularly little effort made through newspaper or pamphlet to state the American case to the British public. Agents had before this played some part as propagandists, but the great epoch of American propaganda in England was yet to come, ushered in by the Stamp Act itself, and to no small degree directed by Franklin. The Stamp Act was foreordained; something, however, might be done to oppose other features of the new American policy. Two newspaper essays which appeared soon after his return to England, attacking the new trade regulations, bear evidences of his authorship.[5] Franklin also claimed credit for securing the deletion from the Mutiny Act of a provision empowering officers to quarter troops in private houses in America. It is certain that he was working hand in glove with Alderman Trecothick and the committee of North American merchants against this clause; and it is probable that he was the author of the published card of protest of the North American agents, and of two letters of expostulation, signed "An American," which appeared in *St. James's Chronicle* in April.[6] The second of these letters covered a wider range:

For my Part, Sir, I am not surprised at any Law that may be made at present with regard to our Colonies: A groundless Jealousy prevails towards them, and new Systems and Opinions have of late been adopted, of which the Americans have hitherto had no Conception.

5. "Observations," in the *London Chronicle,* January 15, 1765; and "North American," reprinted in the *Newport Mercury,* June 3, 1765, probably from the *Westminster Gazette.*

6. On Franklin and the Mutiny Act (5 Geo. III, *c.* 33), see *Writings,* IV, 388; V, 18. Bernard Faÿ, in his *Franklin, the Apostle of Modern Times,* p. 315, makes this a provision of the Stamp Act. In the Franklin Mss. (American Philosophical Society), L, ii, 55, is a draft in Franklin's own hand of a note to Welbore Ellis, Secretary at War: "Mr Glover & Mr Trecothic from the Committee of North American Merch[ts] present their respectful Compliments to Mr [Ellis—name struck out] Secretary at War, and request half an Hours Audience of him on the Mutiny Bill. . . ." The agents' card is in the *Newport Mercury,* July 8, 1765, reprinted from the *Gazetteer,* May 2, 1765; the letters by "An American" are in the *St. James's Chronicle,* April 18 and 23, 1765.

"Partial laws of trade" were denounced; and Englishmen were reminded that since the Americans "have by their Charters a complete Legislature within themselves, they should . . . be allowed the Privilege of taxing themselves." As for the Quartering Act, it "is in fact making slaves of them."

There is a point to which a People may be imposed on, and to that Point they will submit without much Murmur; and that Point once passed, dreadful will be the Consequences: The History of all Countries, and particularly our own, furnishes many Examples of this.

But Franklin did not yet realize that with the Stamp Act the point at which submission ends was actually passed for many of his fellow-countrymen. In July, he was to write his famous apologia to Charles Thomson:

Depend upon it, my good neighbour, I took every step in my power to prevent the passing of the Stamp Act. . . . We might as well have hindered the sun's setting. That we could not do. But since 'tis down, my Friend, and it may be long before it rises again, let us make as good a night of it as we can. We may still light candles.[7]

II

Everyone quotes this letter and draws the deduction that Franklin saw but dimly into the future. He saw no further into the American response to the Stamp Act, certainly, than all men in England, and, until Virginia spoke, most men in America. But there is an interesting sequel which has been overlooked. In September, Charles Thomson wrote a reply to Franklin to set him right upon the sentiments of the Americans; and in November Franklin procured the publication in the *London Chronicle,* through the agency of his friend William Strahan, of excerpts from this correspondence,[8] with the signatures suppressed, as part of an active campaign to reopen that issue which, in July, he had thought was pretty definitely closed.

7. *Writings,* IV, 390.
8. *London Chronicle,* November 16, 1765. See Franklin to Thomson, February 27, 1766, *Writings,* IV, 411.

Early in August Franklin was writing to John Hughes: "As to the Stamp Act, tho' we purpose doing our Endeavour to get it repeal'd, . . . yet the Success is uncertain."[9] The incentive to renew the battle was furnished partly by the more favorable complexion of the Rockingham ministry, chiefly by news from America. Long before Franklin had received his answer from Thomson, and apparently before he had been fully informed of his ominous unpopularity in Pennsylvania—this was the news from America which, it has sometimes been alleged, stirred him to new activity—other sensational dispatches from the colonies had at first disturbed him, and then plunged him into a vigorous campaign of publicity which was the prologue to the great battle for repeal. To John Hughes he had written calmly enough of the first political repercussions of the Stamp Act in Pennsylvania, but in evident alarm at the radical resolves of the Virginia Burgesses, which were provoking dangerous resentment at home. The "madness of the populace" in America and their "blind leaders" must be curbed; but equally the rising storm of disapproval in England must be stayed by a skillful pleading of America's case, lest worse befall. During the fall British public opinion grew steadily more hostile with the news of the American riots. For the next six months Franklin devoted himself with amazing industry and skill to propaganda.

The discovery of Franklin's specific contributions to the debate which began in August and September is a task of no little difficulty, and the conclusions here stated must at many points be regarded as tentative. As to his activity, especially in the later months of the controversy, there is plenty of testimony. Strahan was partly in the secret; in January he wrote to David Hall that "all this while too, he [Franklin] hath been throwing out Hints in the Public Papers, and giving Answers to such letters as have appeared in them, that required or deserved an Answer.—In this Manner is he now employed, with very little Interruption, Night & Day."[10] To Lord Kames, Franklin himself wrote: "You guessed aright in supposing

9. *Writings,* IV, 392.
10. *Pennsylvania Magazine of History,* X, 92.

that I would not be a *mute in that play.*"[11] Dr. John Fothergill and
other friends of the Pennsylvania agent rallied to his defense;[12] and
in 1767 the new *Pennsylvania Chronicle* devoted much space in
several of the early numbers to his rehabilitation. A long essay by
"A Lover of Justice" was inserted to prove that Franklin's activities
in aid of repeal, as a lobbyist and writer, had been persistent and
effective.[13] In succeeding numbers William Goddard reprinted nine
essays contributed by Franklin to London newspapers in 1765 and
1766. For lack of space Goddard omitted other pieces, but in his
explanation supplied a clue to identify two or three of the earliest
and most significant of these. For the rest it is possible to reach
certain conclusions by a critical use of internal evidence. With
regard to some items it can only be said that they reflect his ideas
or bear traces of having been revised by his hand. Even so, the
conclusion is well justified that Franklin became thus early the
engineer of the American propaganda machine in London. In this
capacity he reprinted the more notable pamphlets from America;
encouraged much writing in England; and himself wrote some of
the most persuasive essays. These activities, begun in 1765, he
continued throughout his residence as agent in England, especially
in the years through 1770; the greater part of this writing has not
hitherto been recognized as Franklin's. The widespread reprinting
of his pieces in the American papers raises the further interesting
question, as yet largely ignored, of his direct influence upon the
ideas as well as upon the polemic of the American Revolution.

One significant fact that emerges from a close inspection of his
propagandist writings between September, 1765, and the repeal of
the Stamp Act, and even more decisively from his unprinted private
musings on the controversy, is that as he elaborated the American
case he rapidly advanced in his own thinking to more radical views

11. *Writings,* V, 16.
12. Penn Papers (Mss. Historical Society of Pennsylvania), Official Correspondence, X, 35; Pemberton Papers (Mss. Historical Society of Pennsylvania), XXXIV, 142.
13. *Pennsylvania Chronicle,* February 9, 1767. See also the issues for
February 16, 23, March 9, 23, 1767. These pieces are incompletely reprinted
in *Writings,* IV, 393–399; V, 14–15.

of the character of American rights. When Bradford later published
a deadly parallel between Galloway's "Americanus" essay and
Franklin's *Examination*,[14] he revealed only a part of the distance in
ideas which had come to separate those two allies in Pennsylvania
politics. Yet Franklin in one respect kept closer touch with Galloway than with any other American: in his hope of perfecting, on a
liberal model, what he called a "consolidating union" with Great
Britain.

The Virginia Resolves, in the colonies an "alarm bell to the dis-
affected," raised other echoes in England. Among the Franklin
essays for which Goddard could find no room in his *Chronicle,*
some, he said, "are sign'd A Virginian, being in answer to some
Reflections cast on that Colony and Maryland."[15] An examination
of the London newspapers of this period has brought to light three
pieces, printed in September, 1765, which answer this description.[16]
Two were actually signed "A Virginian," and besides this significant
signature reveal such other internal evidences of Franklin's authorship that it is reasonable to assign them definitely to him. With the
third essay, signed "Equity," they fall into a familiar Franklin category of propitiatory argument. They contain a partial concession to
the views of the opposition; they develop an adroit parallel between
English and American motives and actions, and English and American rights; and they finally advance, by a Socratic route, to higher
ground of principle. In a *"P.S.* Quaere" appended to his second
letter, "A Virginian" touched, however tentatively, upon those
difficult questions of compact and of natural right on which singularly little is to be found, save by implication, in Franklin's
acknowledged publications:

Are the children of English parents that are born in foreign parts of
course subjects to our King? I ask only for information, though I am

14. *Pennsylvania Journal,* September 25, 1766.
15. *Pennsylvania Chronicle,* March 23, 1767.
16. "A Virginian," in *Lloyd's Evening Post,* September 2, 11, 1765 (the
letters were dated, respectively, August 23 and September 5); "Equity," in
the *Boston Evening-Post,* December 2, 1765, reprinted from the *Gazetteer,*
September 3, 1765.

inclined to think that they are not. And if they are not so naturally, what is it can make them so but their own consent? and if the first settlers then, that went over to America, had charters from the King, by which they and their posterity were to form assemblies, make laws, &c. is it not a kind of compact by which their posterity agree to become his subjects upon those conditions? Now if these charters can be made void by an Act of Parliament, will that very Act destroy the Compact by which they became subjects? I may be wrong in this particular, and, if I am, shall be glad to be set right in it.

Here is radical doctrine, surely, for 1765; especially radical for the cautious and pragmatic Franklin. Cautious and pragmatic he usually was in his admitted utterances, and even in his anonymous publications. But it is of great importance in the exploration of his mind to recognize that thus early he had traversed in speculation, however imperfectly and apologetically, pretty much the whole ground that would be covered in the next decade by the theoretical expounders of American rights.

Theory, however, was subordinated in most of Franklin's writing against the Stamp Act to arguments from expediency and material interest. Over the signatures "F.B.," "N.N.," "Homespun," "Pacificus Secundus," and probably also "Americus," "Justice," and "O,"[17] he resented the calumnies on the Americans circulated by "Tom Hint," "Vindex Patriae," and other "writers against the colonies." "Pacificus" drew his fire, not only as an advocate of the doctrine of virtual representation, which Franklin turned neatly into a paradox, but even more as an advocate of enforcement of the tax by military power—a threat which Franklin regarded as a very serious practical danger. He devoted much of his polemic in December and January to thwart it. To the charges of American ingratitude he repeatedly advanced the sacrifices of blood and treasure which the colonists had made in the last war—a war which

17. "Americus," in the *Newport Mercury,* February 3, 1766, reprinted from the *Public Ledger,* November 22, 1765; "Justice," in the *Newport Mercury,* February 17, 1766, probably from the *Gazetteer;* "O," in the *Boston Evening-Post,* March 17, 1766, reprinted from the *Gazetteer,* December 16, 1765.

he described as primarily in the interest of British trade—and reminded Englishmen that the riches of the colonies centered finally, through trade, in Britain. With characteristic frugality as a writer he got out and refurbished the arguments on taxation embodied in his letters of 1754 to Shirley; these indeed were printed, in February, 1766, in the *London Chronicle* and in several periodicals, no doubt at his instance. Another useful arsenal he found in his own Canada pamphlet of 1760, *The Interest of Great Britain Considered;* from it especially he drew his arguments from commercial expediency, based upon his former observations of the rapid increase of colonial population and trade. Indeed the recurrence, not merely of ideas and of arguments, but also of phraseology drawn from the Shirley letters and the Canada Pamphlet furnishes one of the best clues to Franklin's authorship of certain of the pamphlets as well as numerous newspaper essays in the Stamp Act debate.

The motives which impelled Franklin to draw the veil of anonymity over much of his writing in this period are not far to seek, though his enemies gave them the worst construction. His possession of a Crown appointment in the Post Office did not make him anti-American, as was insinuated; but it certainly confirmed him in his instinctive prudence. It is also true that he was shrewdly aware that his arguments for American rights would gain in effect in England if they seemed to come from a less interested source than a colonial agent. On occasion he posed in his essays as an Englishman, with neither kinsfolk nor property overseas. It was an age of anonymity in controversy, and such devices were neither uncommon nor, by contemporary standards, especially dishonest. But Franklin had to pay for his prudence in vituperation from the friends of the Penns and, probably, from the friends of the Massachusetts agent, De Berdt. One notable libeler of the Doctor—also an anonymous writer—in a letter from London, printed in the *Pennsylvania Journal,* charged that Franklin had basely kept silence in face of the threat to American liberties:

Several pens were employed to plead the cause of America, by every argument that might affect our sense of humanity, justice, or interest.

But why does not the Pennsylvania agent write? He has leisure and a masterly pen; The question was never answered.[18]

The question can now be answered, however, in a sense more favorable to Franklin's zeal and industry. His masterly pen was not idle. Besides numerous newspaper essays, it is probable that he wrote also certain pamphlets. That he set out to write one Stamp Act pamphlet early in 1766 can be shown beyond question. Among the Franklin manuscripts are eight folios, in his hand, of an intended tract, including two folios of a first draft and six folios of a revised version. That these were originally designed for pamphlet publication, rather than as newspaper essays, can be easily demonstrated. The draft is incomplete; so far as it goes it covers, with certain gaps, the history of the causes and development of the American disputes from the time of the failure of the Albany Plan of Union, so largely the work of Franklin, through the enactment of the new trade regulations, the Currency Act, and the Stamp Act; there are also reflections upon the misrepresentation of American conditions by British colonial officials. Even in the form in which it has survived it has distinctive quality. It promised to be an argument at least on the level of Franklin's well-known *Causes of the American Discontents* (1768). It has not been found possible to identify it with any of the numerous anonymous pamphlets of the time. Rather it seems probable that it was undertaken shortly before repeal, and then laid aside, unfinished, as a superfluous exercise. One passage Franklin salvaged in 1767 when he printed it in a letter to the *London Chronicle* as a quotation from an unnamed author: "one who had lived long in America, knew the people and their affairs extremely well—and was equally well acquainted with the temper and practises of government officers."[19]

18. "An Essay, Towards discovering the Authors and Promoters of the memorable Stamp Act, In a Letter from a Gentleman in London, to his friend in Philadelphia," *Pennsylvania Journal,* Supplement, September 18, 1766.

19. Franklin Mss. (American Philosophical Society), L, ii, 27, 30a, 31, 31a, 31b, 31c, 31d, 31e. A draft of the letter in the *London Chronicle,* April 9, 1767, is found in *ibid.,* p. 9.

The existence of this fragment of a pamphlet increases the probability that elsewhere among the unsigned political tracts which issued numerously from the English as from the American presses in that year may be discovered some one or more to which his name may reasonably be attached. Actually the present writer has found two such pamphlets, printed in London in December, 1765, and January, 1766, which are closely integrated in argument, and each of them is so intricately interwoven in materials and expression with Franklin's known writings over a long period—indeed from 1754 to 1775—that they seem clearly to belong to the Franklin canon. While the proof of these suspicions would strongly reinforce the case for Franklin's important role in the propaganda, and would help to define somewhat more clearly his ideas of the empire and of American rights, since one of the pamphlets asserts a claim to colonial home rule, it is here omitted because of the necessity of an elaborate textual analysis.

III

Behind the propaganda barrage the active political movement for the repeal of the Stamp Act and for the reform of the trade regulations got under way. Early in November, 1765, Franklin had a long audience with the young Lord Dartmouth, with whom he was greatly pleased; he was also invited to dine with Rockingham. He urged upon Dartmouth—probably also upon Rockingham—that "the general Execution of the Stamp Act would be impracticable without occasioning more Mischief than it was worth, by totally alienating the Affections of the Americans from this Country, & thereby lessening its Commerce." At the time he apparently thought that it was useless to press for immediate repeal; instead, he argued that Britain should suspend the act

for a Term of Years, till the Colonies should be more clear of Debt, & better able to bear it, & then drop it on some other decent Pretence, without ever bringing the Question of Right to a Decision. And I strongly recommended either a thorough Union with America, or that Government here would proceed in the old Method of Requisition, by which I was confident more would be obtained in the Way of voluntary Grant, than could probably be got by compulsory Taxes laid by Parliament. . . . That to send Armies & Fleets to enforce the Act, would not, in my Opinion, answer any good End.[20]

Finally he proposed to Dartmouth that upon the suspension of the act a royal commission of "three or four wise & good Men, Personages of some Rank & Dignity," be sent over to America to hear the complaints of the colonists, promise them redress, and endeavor "to convince & reclaim them by Reason, where they found them in the Wrong." The whole conversation with Dartmouth, as reported by Franklin, was a characteristic exhibition of his firm but cautious strategy of reconciliation, designed to avert that danger which he was already predicting from harsher measures—"of a future total Separation."

Suspension of the Stamp Act was the objective in early November; but a month later the agents were ready to press for immediate repeal. They had won powerful reinforcements from the mercantile group. On December 4, 1765, there assembled at the King's Arms Tavern a great meeting of the merchants trading to North America. From this meeting came the formation of that enterprising committee, headed by Barlow Trecothick, which more than any other agency was responsible for the repeal. The story of its activities has recently been told:[21] the drumming up of petitions for repeal from

20. "Extract of a Letter from B. F. to W[illiam] F[ranklin]," London, November 9, 1765, Charles Norton Smith Mss. (Historical Society of Pennsylvania), II, 44. This is a copy in the handwriting of William Franklin. The original letter, not at the moment available, is in the Mason collection of Franklin material recently acquired by Yale University. [At the time Professor Crane was writing his article the Mason collection was being catalogued. The original letter has not been found—it was probably sent by William Franklin to one of his father's Pennsylvania friends as ammunition with which to defend him. See *The Papers of Benjamin Franklin* (New Haven, 1968), XII, 361 (ed.).]

21. L. S. Sutherland, "Edmund Burke and the First Rockingham Ministry," *English Historical Review*, XLVII, 46–70. At several points this new and illuminating exposition of the twofold movement for repeal and trade reform can be supplemented by a reading of the many extracts dealing with the movement from letters from London which were published in the

the trading and manufacturing towns and the arrangement of hearings, such as Franklin's, before the Commons. A temporary alliance of the North American and West Indian committees paved the way for an unprecedented mercantile domination of that session of Parliament: before the coalition of these naturally discordant interests was dissolved, it resulted, not merely in repeal of the Stamp Act, but also in a partial reform of the American trade regulations.

Franklin's connections with the committee of London merchants trading to North America are, however, a matter of dispute. He was charged with standing outside the movement and only raising his voice, in his examination, after the success of the repeal agitation had already been determined by a private poll of the Commons; but this testimony comes from a discredited source.[22] To be sure, Franklin's relations with the Massachusetts agent, De Berdt, a member of the committee, were very cool, and this may have limited his cooperation. There is evidence, however, that he was twice present at meetings of the committee. His association with Trecothick and an earlier merchants' committee in the previous spring will be recalled.

The climax of Franklin's propaganda against the Stamp Act, if not of the development of his privately held political views, was reached on the occasion of his famous examination before the House of Commons in February, 1766. The affair was elaborately stage-managed. The groundwork had been well laid by the committee of North American merchants; and it is known that Franklin himself concerted with friendly members of the Commons those leading questions which gave him his opportunity to score heavily against the feasibility of the measure. His answers were quite as ready to the hostile questions of Grenville and other opponents of repeal, which suggests that he had carefully prepared the whole case. He drew largely for his arguments from his own previously

colonial newspapers in the early months of 1766. In particular it appears that trade reform was the original purpose of the merchants, but that they were persuaded, probably by the arguments of the colonial agents, to concentrate first upon repeal.

22. *Pennsylvania Journal,* Supplement, September 18, 1766.

printed essays. Moreover, he probably came into the House well armed with notes. Indeed there exist among his manuscripts two sets of memoranda which bear strong indications that they were prepared for this occasion. Certainly they were drawn up during the height of the agitation for repeal; and several striking parallels between them and the printed *Examination* point to a closer connection.[23]

The notes in question also include a number of ideas and arguments which Franklin did not develop in his examination, if the printed text can be supposed to be reasonably complete. The most interesting of these additions are the suggestions of "Three Ways of avoiding these Inconveniences"[24]—the inconveniences, that is, of parliamentary taxation. This passage brings into interesting conjunction the three expedients which, since 1754, Franklin had formulated to solve the imperial problem in America. The synthesis is far from complete—indeed the suggestions were offered as alternative ideas. The first alternative, discussed at some length, was his current proposal, concurred in by Otis but repugnant to most Americans, of colonial representation at Westminster. The arguments that were stressed for this solution seem to have been contrived rather for British than for American ears. The second suggestion was the plan of the Albany Congress, drafted by Franklin, for a common council to represent the colonial assemblies. The third, barely listed here, was the proposal which Franklin had made to Grenville early in 1765 as a substitute for the Stamp Act, "the Paper Money Scheme." Of these three choices only the first was actually developed by Franklin in his examination, and then only in a negative sense, to deny the right of Parliament to tax the colonies until properly qualified by the admission of colonial members.

23. Franklin Mss. (American Philosophical Society), L, ii, 46, 51. These parallels include two of the most famous passages in the *Examination:* the description of the altered temper of the Americans toward Great Britain after 1763; and the long discussion of colonial participation in the last French war and the character of the war as one for the supremacy of a British interest, the Indian trade. See *Writings,* IV, 418–419, 436–439.

24. Franklin Mss. (American Philosophical Society), L, ii, 51.

In the examination, as is well known, Franklin in general skill-fully avoided the knotty questions of the basis of the colonial claims; and he asserted the claim for exemption from taxation within the narrow limits of internal taxation. On this head one passage has often been cited as an example of his suppleness in argument. He had admitted that the distinction between external and internal taxation did not exist in the language of the charter; might not the colonists, he was asked, "by the same interpretation, object to the Parliament's right of external taxation?" "A[nswer]. They never have hitherto. Many arguments have been lately used here to shew them, that there is no difference, and that, if you have no right to tax them internally, you have none to tax them ex-ternally, or make any other law to bind them. At present they do not reason so; but in time they may possibly be convinced by these arguments."[25] Commentators have emphasized in this passage the prophecy—or threat—implied in the phrases "at present" and "in time." Is it not quite as significant that Franklin was speaking here in the third person, not in the first? Again he declared, in the same tone of reporting the sentiments of the Americans rather than argu-ing his own views: "The authority of parliament was allowed to be valid in all laws, except such as should lay internal taxes. It was never disputed in laying duties to regulate commerce."[26] Here, too, one detects, as so often in Franklin's writings, the suggestion of an *arrière pensée*. The influence of the organized merchants, who had prepared the scene for the examination, was continuously exerted in 1766 to suppress the discussion of large constitutional issues. Franklin, with his usual caution, was not unsympathetic with these tactics, and in his examination brought them to brilliant perfection. Indeed, throughout the whole of his newspaper and pamphlet polemic, in the years after the repeal of the Stamp Act as well as at this time, when he advanced the more limited claims of the Ameri-cans, he generally wrote in the character of a reporter of the principles held overseas. His own views he kept prudently in re-serve, even in his correspondence, until, around 1768, he began to

25. *Writings,* IV, 446.
26. *Ibid.,* p. 419.

communicate them, in strict confidence, to a few of his American friends. In consequence, those students who have read only his published political essays, and have then encountered these later revealing letters, have concluded that it was not until some years after the Stamp Act excitement, when new measures had raised new issues, that Franklin began to revise his views of Parliamentary authority and of American rights in the direction of home rule.

IV

Luckily there exist certain clues to the well-kept secret of his private opinions in the winter of 1765–1766. It was Franklin's habit to enter comments in the margins of his copies of the controversial tracts. Many such revealing marginalia are to be found in the pamphlets still preserved from Franklin's library. Some of these were reproduced, not too completely or accurately, by Jared Sparks and John Bigelow; but the latest Franklin editor, Smyth, regarded them as too "crude and fragmentary" to deserve much attention. Actually they are of first-rate importance, and it is curious that they have not been carefully studied to trace the workings of Franklin's mind on imperial problems before the Revolution. There are difficulties, to be sure, in determining in certain instances just when the notes were set down. Several of the pamphlets in question were printed in 1769 and 1770, and were apparently annotated by Franklin in those years, when he had already given the clue to his ideas of colonial autonomy in letters to his son and to Samuel Cooper. There are, however, three annotated tracts of 1765 and 1766 in which the marginalia bear indications of strict contemporaneity; in the case of the more important of these the evidence is especially strong. The three are: a collection of colonial charters; William Knox, *The Claim of the Colonies to an Exemption from Internal Taxes imposed by Authority of Parliament, Examined* (1765); and *Protest against the Bill to Repeal the American Stamp Act, of Last Session* (1766).[27]

27. On Franklin's library and the present location of Franklin's copies of the controversial pamphlets of this period, some of them annotated, see

When the Americans, in 1765, began to question the validity of
Parliamentary taxation, their first appeal, generally, was to their
charters. The charters therefore acquired a new interest for the
English public. Their texts were now published in the periodicals,
and separately as pamphlets.[28] Franklin possessed himself of one
such collection which he indexed in the margins for ready reference;
at numerous points he underscored the text and entered brief notes.
Naturally he did not overlook those charter clauses which defined
a power of taxation in the colonial governments.[29] Several times,
too, he emphasized the grant to the colonies of legislative powers.
One may perhaps infer that thus early he was gathering ammunition upon the larger issue, as yet remote from most men's minds,
of colonial legislative autonomy. Elsewhere in his marginalia the
evidence passes from inference to certainty.

The proofs appear in his comments, probably contemporaneous
with the Stamp Act controversy, in the Knox pamphlet; and rather
more decisively in the marginalia of the first Lords' *Protest* (1766),
which were quite certainly written down close to the time of its
surreptitious publication. Here the notes have the unmistakable
character of memoranda for a contemplated reply—such a reply as
might have been made with effect in the spring of 1766, but which
Franklin would hardly have planned to write at a later time.[30]

George Simpson Eddy, "Dr. Benjamin Franklin's Library," *Proceedings of
the American Antiquarian Society*, n.s., XXXIV, 206–226. Franklin's copy of
the charters is in the Historical Society of Pennsylvania; the other two items
are in the New York Public Library.

28. F. J. Hinkhouse, *The Preliminaries of the American Revolution as
seen in the English Press, 1763–1775* (1926), pp. 93–94; and advertisements,
as in the *Daily Advertiser*, January 11, 1766.

29. Franklin was uncomfortably aware of the reservation in the Pennsylvania charter of which the Grenvillites made so much: "King covenants not
to tax but by Assembly or Act of Par^t" was his entry opposite this clause.
When he noted the point in Knox, *The Claim of the Colonies* (p. 5), he
wrote: "A Right that never existed cannot be a Right *Reserved*. . . . Qu^y If
the Parliament had before no such Right, it would not be given to them by
Words in the Charter?" See also his argument in his examination, *Writings*,
IV, 445.

30. At the head of the title-page is a mutilated entry: ". . . mean by a
thorough Inquisition of the Point to procure a Settlement of Rights." Again,

No such reply to the protesting peers was printed, probably because public interest in the American question evaporated so quickly after repeal. But the ideas discoverable in these marginalia were clearly those which Franklin held in the spring of 1766.

These ideas, it soon became apparent, struck at the roots of the doctrine of Parliamentary sovereignty in the colonies. "The Sovereignty of the Crown I understand," Franklin wrote in the margin of the first *Protest*. "The Sov^y of the British Legislature out of Britain, I do not understand."[31] In January, 1766, in a newspaper letter signed "N.N.," he had already argued that the extent of Parliamentary power in the dominions was a moot point, yet to be settled authoritatively. But meanwhile Parliament had adopted the resolutions of right which were incorporated in the Declaratory Act. In his examination Franklin roundly asserted that the Americans would think these resolutions "unconstitutional and unjust."[32] "It is to be wish'd it had not asserted it," he wrote of the Declaratory Act in his copy of the first *Protest*, "or asserted it with some Limitation as when *qualified* etc"; and in his copy of the second *Protest* he entered an emphatic counterprotest against the Declaratory Act.[33]

Usually Franklin preferred an indirect to a frontal attack upon Parliamentary sovereignty. "Anxious about preserving the Sovereignty of this Country?" he wrote on the first *Protest*. "Rather be

opposite the record of the vote in the House of Lords on repeal, is the memorandum: "Comp[limen]t the Lords . . . Proof of my Opinion of their Goodness in the Freedom with which I purpose to examine their Protests." And following a passage in which the peers had contested the right of the Americans to be exempt from a due share of the imperial burdens, he wrote: "Repeat on this Head all that has been done & paid by America.—King's Message, Parl^t Grants, &c." Where the Lords alleged that the last war was entered upon "for the interest and security of those Colonies," Franklin wrote: "The fact deny'd. State the Cause & Effect of the War. The expensive Manner of Carrying it on &c." Others of these marginalia are in the same style of hints for an intended rejoinder.

31. *Protest against the Bill to Repeal the American Stamp Act* (1766), p. 11.

32. *Gazetteer,* January 11, 1766, reprinted in the *Pennsylvania Chronicle,* March 9, 1767; *Writings,* IV, 421.

33. Jared Sparks, ed., *The Works of Benjamin Franklin,* 10 vols. (Boston, 1840), IV, 209–210; *Protest,* p. 13.

so about preserving the Liberty. We shall be so about the Liberty of America, that your Posterity may have a free Country to come to, where you will be rec^d with open Arms." In this passage Franklin set down, more succinctly than elsewhere, a train of argument, based upon the rights of the subject rather than upon an analysis of Parliamentary powers, which was a favorite theme in his political writing. The note might, indeed, be taken as a summary of one of the suspected Franklin pamphlets published late in January, 1766.

In 1766 as clearly as in 1770, Franklin drew a sharp distinction between realm and dominions. "The Colonies," he remarked in his *Examination,* "are not supposed to be within the realm; they have assemblies of their own, which are their parliaments, and they are, in that respect, in the same situation with Ireland."[34] In the marginalia he repeated the distinction again and again. When the protesting peers denounced as "a most dangerous doctrine" the asserted colonial opinion "that the obedience of the subject is not due to the Laws and Legislature of the Realm, farther than he in his private judgment shall think it conformable to the ideas he has formed of a free constitution,"[35] Franklin commented: "The Danger easily removed. The Subject in America only. America not in the Realm of England or G.B. No man in America thinks himself exempt from the Jurisdiction of the Crown & and their own Assemblies—or has any such private Judgm^t." The power of taxation, the Lords declared, "cannot be properly, equitably or impartially exercised, if it does not extend itself to all the members of the state. . . ."[36] Franklin agreed, but now unmistakably defined the empire as a loose personal union in the Crown: "right; but we are different States. Subject to the King." When Knox, in his attack on the charter exemptions, contended that the constitution of Great Britain "acknowledges no authority superior to the legislature, consisting of king, lords, and commons,"[37] Franklin queried: "Does this Writer imagine that wherever an Englishman settles, he is Subject to the

34. *Writings,* IV, 441.
35. *Protest,* p. 12.
36. *Ibid.,* p. 6.
37. William Knox, *The Claim of the Colonies* (1765), p. 8.

Power of Parliamᵗ?" Knox's description of the colonists as subjects of Great Britain[38] he rejected in a note which goes all the way in its denial of Parliamentary sovereignty over the colonies: "The People of G. Britain are Subjects of the King. G.B. is not a Sovereign. The Parliament has Power only *within the Realm.*" Again, when the Lords in the first *Protest* referred to the dependency of the colonies "on the imperial Crown and Parliament of Great Britain,"[39] Franklin underlined "Parliament" and supplied this note: "Thrust yourselves in with the Crown in the Government of the Colonies. Do your Lordships mean to call the Parliament *imperial*[?]"

Franklin, it is clear, had come by 1766 to reject in principle the idea of the imperial character of Parliament as then constituted, and was certainly aware that the implication of this denial extended far beyond the immediate debate over taxation. To be sure, he recognized that in these private views he was ahead of his time, ahead, indeed, of most American sentiment.[40] When the Lords charged that the case which the Americans were making against taxation without representation actually "extends to all other laws,"[41] he entered no denial on his own behalf, but remarked, in language strikingly similar to that which he had used in his examination upon the more restricted topic of internal and external taxation: "It is so reason'd here, not there, but in time they may be convinc'd."

Now any such theory of colonial legislative autonomy within the empire was vulnerable at two points, as the later debates were to demonstrate: in point of law, and in the light of practice and

38. *Ibid.*

39. *Protest,* p. 4. Franklin, to be sure, struck out the second sentence, but apparently because it rested upon a strained reading of the text. Franklin also wrote "Neg." in the margin opposite this passage.

40. There was, to be sure, a good deal of home-rule sentiment and expression in America from the beginning of the controversy, as Professor C. F. Mullett has clearly shown in his "Colonial Claims to Home Rule (1764–1775)," *University of Missouri Studies,* II, No. 4 (1927).

41. *Protest,* p. 10. This claim, the text continued, "must (if admitted) set them absolutely free from any obedience to the power of the British Legislature." Franklin commented: "but not to the Power of the Crown."

precedent. To the latter difficulty Franklin gave rather more attention than to the former. His own arguments were often drawn from
history; but as a reasonable man he had to recognize that, since the
Restoration at all events, Parliament had often legislated for
America. This difficulty he confronted in his own thinking during
the Stamp Act discussions, and thus early formulated his reply—
not, on the whole, a very convincing one. At the head of his notes
for a reply to the first Lords' *Protest* he wrote: "We have submitted
to your Laws, no Proof of our acknowledging your Power to make
them. Rather an Acknowledgment of their Reasonableness or of
our own Weakness." Knox, in his pamphlet, asserted: "I find
almost as many instances of the parliament's exercising supreme
legislative jurisdiction over the colonies, as there have been sessions
of parliament since the first settlement of America by British subjects."[42] Franklin's reply was categorical: "All Usurpations of
Power not belonging to them; many unjust."

Franklin's theory of usurpation was modified by a parallel doctrine of consent. This was most clearly stated, perhaps, in a letter
to Thomas Cushing written in 1771:

My opinion has long been that Parliament has originally no Right to
bind us by any kind of Law whatever without our Consent. We have
indeed in a manner consented to some of them, at least tacitly. But
for the future methinks we should be cautious how we add to those
Instances, and never adopt or acknowledge an Act of Parliament but
by a formal Law of our own. . . .[43]

42. *The Claim of the Colonies,* p. 9. Knox specified, among other such
acts, those "restraining their commerce; prohibiting the carriage or exporta-
tion of their manufactures from one colony to another; taxing the produc-
tions of one colony when brought into another." Franklin underscored these
lines, and wrote: "Wicked." When the Lords referred to "the wise policy" of
the Navigation Act and subsequent trade laws (*Protest*, p. 11), Franklin
observed: "The Policy *wise* with regard to foreigners. Selfish with Reg[d] to
Colonies." Opposite the prediction of evils which would follow "that
absolute freedom of trade, which they appear to desire," he wrote "Qu[y].
Other Advantages of Colonies besides Commerce. Selfishness of Commercial
Views."
43. *Writings,* V, 324–325.

When English writers brought forward the precedents of the Post Office, the Hat Act, or the Navigation Acts, Franklin was ready to acknowledge a tacit consent which gave those statutes separately a validity in America, but which manifested no general consent and hence conferred no general legislative powers. In some fashion or other laws binding upon the Americans must receive their assent: in their own assemblies, in a common council representing the assemblies, in a properly representative Parliament, or, as in the past, in the crude fashion of colonial submission to reasonable legislation. With respect to taxation, at least, Franklin made this very clear. "The Trust of Taxing America," he wrote in 1766, "was never reposed by the People of America in the Legislature of Gr. Britain."[44]

The logical corollary of such a denial of Parliamentary sovereignty as Franklin was shadowing forth as early as these Stamp Act days was a claim to the complete legislative independence of the colonial assemblies. But Franklin, a pragmatist, for some time refused to be entirely logical. In 1766 and 1767, he was content to formulate the lesser claim to *internal* legislative autonomy. To Lord Kames, in April, 1767, he communicated his doubts of the sovereignty of Parliament, but added, sensibly: "On the other hand, it seems necessary for the common good of the empire, that a power be lodged somewhere, to regulate its general commerce: this can be placed nowhere so properly as in the Parliament of Great Britain."[45] Here was a practical concession such as John Adams, among others, was willing to make as late as 1774. Franklin at first rationalized it, not too ingenuously, in the distinction between internal and external taxes. By 1768, he was ready to throw this distinction overboard; to his son he wrote: "I shall not give myself the trouble to defend it." The real grievance, he had come to think, was not that Britain taxed her exports to the colonies—all countries had a power to tax their exports to foreign countries—but that she

forbids us to buy the like manufactures from any other country. This she does, however, in virtue of her allowed right to regulate the com-

44. In the margin of the *Protest,* p. 7.
45. *Writings,* V, 20–21.

merce of the whole empire, allowed I mean by the Farmer, though I think whoever would dispute that right might stand upon firmer ground, and make more of the argument. . . .[46]

Not the logic of his constitutional theory, but his economic liberalism and his strong sense that America was a rapidly expanding and maturing community urged him forward to a radical view of the empire as a commonwealth of free peoples joined in allegiance to the king.

Franklin, however, was not always content to define and justify this conception of the true colonial constitution as a loose personal union. He was, after all, very much an imperialist himself, often stirred to eloquence by dreams of the future power and grandeur of a Greater Britain. In certain moods he could counsel a return to the good old way as it had been happily practiced before the late innovations in the government of colonies. At other times he advanced beyond home rule to advocate the creation of a more perfect union of realm and dominions. He was in such a mood when, in 1766, he wrote in his copy of the first *Protest:* "The Agitation of the Question of Right makes it now necessary to settle a Constitution for the Colonies."[47]

Unfortunately only the vague outlines of Franklin's "constitution" are discernible. It is well known that more than once he proposed the admission of colonial representatives to the Parliament at Westminster, but it has not been so clearly understood that this was a detail in his scheme for a "consolidating union." He seems to have been influenced in this direction during the Stamp Act crisis by his correspondence with the Scottish jurist and *philosophe,* Henry Home, Lord Kames, and no doubt by Galloway. In a belated reply to a letter from Kames of December, 1765, now lost, he wrote in 1767: "I am fully persuaded with you, that a *Consolidating Union,* by a fair and equal representation of all parts of this empire in Parliament, is the only firm basis on which its political grandeur and prosperity can be founded."[48] By such means a "supreme legis-

46. *Ibid.,* pp. 115–116.
47. *Protest,* p. 15.
48. *Writings,* V, 17–18, 21. Cf. "Letter concerning the Gratitude of America," January 6, 1766, *ibid.,* IV, 400–404.

lature" would *for the first time* be created. "There is yet no such Thing," Franklin wrote in his copy of the first *Protest*. "It is indeed wanted and to be wish'd for."[49] In a letter of May 9, 1766, to Cadwallader Evans, he was somewhat more explicit: "It would certainly contribute to the strength of the whole, if Ireland and all the dominions were united and consolidated under one common council for general purposes, each retaining its particular council or parliament for its domestic concerns."[50] The creation of such a "consolidating union" must be the result of some such formal act of union as had earlier united England and Scotland: an act which by "ascertaining the relative Rights and Duties of each" would put an end to disruptive disputes.[51]

These liberal imperial ideas of 1766 Franklin continued to propound, at least in his more hopeful and idealistic moods, till almost the eve of his departure from England. Yet even in 1766, in more realistic moments, he had begun to despair of a solution upon any such broad basis of imperial federation. To Evans he had recalled the tale of Friar Bacon and Friar Bungay, with its fatalistic theme: time is, time was, time is past. "The time has been, when the colonies might have been pleased with it," he wrote to Kames in 1767: "they are now *indifferent* about it; and if it is much longer delayed, they too will *refuse* it."[52] To Galloway, whose faith was more persistent in those schemes of federation which each had developed, not without mutual counsel and encouragement, since Stamp Act days, Franklin wrote early in 1774:

I wish most sincerely with you that a Constitution was formed and settled for America, that we might know what we are and what we have, what our Rights and what our Duties, in the Judgment of this Country as well as in our own. Till such a Constitution is settled,

49. *Protest*, p. 8. See also *Writings*, V, 260, for another expression of this view in 1770.

50. *Writings*, IV, 456.

51. See Franklin to Samuel Cooper, June 8, 1770, *ibid.*, V, 261. The quotation is from Franklin to Joseph Galloway, January 11, 1770 (Ms. William L. Clements Library).

52. *Writings*, IV, 456; V, 17. See also "Francis Lynn," *ibid.*, V, 168. The germ of these passages is to be found in Franklin Mss. (American Philosophical Society), L, ii, 46b.

different Sentiments will ever occasion Misunderstandings. But if 'tis to be settled, it must settle itself, nobody here caring for the Trouble of thinking on't.[53]

Thus Franklin was thrown back upon his other position, also well outlined in his thinking as early as 1766, of colonial autonomy. His classic statement of this contention occurs in a letter to his son, written in 1768, in which he rejected alike the "half-wayhouse" of the Pennsylvania Farmer and also what he described as the Boston doctrine of the "subordination" of the assemblies to a Parliament whose power to make laws for them they at the same time denied:

Something might be made of either of the extremes; that Parliament has a power to make *all laws* for us, or that it has a power to make *no laws* for us; and I think the arguments for the latter more numerous and weighty, than those for the former. Supposing that doctrine established, the colonies would then be so many separate states, only subject to the same king, as England and Scotland were before the union.[54]

This utterance has been thought to mark Franklin's conversion to the radical doctrine of colonial autonomy, and to place him, even in 1768, well in advance of most of the theorists of the American Revolution. In almost every point it had been anticipated by Franklin himself during the Stamp Act crisis. His advanced ideas, to be sure, he only partially revealed at the time, and in later propaganda he often prudently withdrew to a more moderate debating position. But it would seem that he revealed the true history of his political ideas when, shortly before he left England, he wrote: "from a thorough Enquiry (on Occasion of the Stamp Act) into the Nature of the Connection between Britain and the Colonies, I became convinced, that the Bond of their Union is not the Parliament, but the King."[55]

53. Letter of February 18, 1774 (Ms. William L. Clements Library).
54. *Writings*, V, 115.
55. *Ibid.*, VI, 260.

✪

Setting Metes and Bounds

Until these last revisions [on American rights to fish off the coast of Newfoundland or in the Gulf of St. Lawrence] peace seemed stalled over some cod and haddock. Franklin chose now to put in his oar by producing a paper from his pocket upon which he had itemized the American claims for reparations. "Remember," he reminded the British, "the first principle of the treaty is equality and reciprocity. You demand payment of us of debt and restitution or compensation to the refugees. If a draper had sold a piece of cloth to a man upon credit and then sent a servant to take it from him by force, and afterward brought his action for the debt, would any court of law or equity give him his demand without obliging him to restore the cloth?" he argued with his homely logic. Citing the carrying off of goods from Boston, Philadelphia, and the Southern states, and the burning of towns, he suggested the propriety of now submitting claims for such damages.[1] Adams chimed in with an account of goods carried off from Boston to Halifax by Gage's soldiers; Franklin remembered the rifling of his

---

From pp. 378–385, 458–459 in *The Peacemakers: The Great Powers and American Independence* by Richard B. Morris. Copyright © 1965 by Richard B. Morris. Reprinted by permission of Harper & Row, Publishers.

1. Benjamin Franklin's counterproposal, "An Article proposed and read to the Commissioners before signing the preliminary articles, with a state of facts." A. H. Smyth, ed., *The Writings of Benjamin Franklin*, 10 vols. (New York, 1905–1907), VIII, 632n.; copy in Adams Family Papers (Massachusetts Historical Society), Microfilm No. 359.

own library in Philadelphia; Jay thought of a number of items, and Laurens reminded the negotiators of the plundering of Negroes and plate from the Carolinas. The removal of Negro slaves from Charleston and Savannah had been one of the scandals of the British evacuation, and had already called forth remonstrances to the British from Jay and Adams. "The name of an Englishman is in very bad repute in these Southern Provinces," Vaughan had told Oswald. "God forbid that there should be any foundation" for such charges! Oswald in turn had protested to Strachey.[2]

With the temperature reaching the boiling point, a recess was called. Oswald, Fitzherbert, and Strachey withdrew. Should they refer the issues of the fisheries and the Loyalists back to London? Even had the Americans been agreeable to allowing the issues to remain *in statu quo* during the eight days or so that it would take to get word back from England, there would have been political risks in deferring the settlement until after Parliament convened. However, the Americans expressly reserved the right to introduce "any new articles which they might think expedient." Fearing that Franklin's insistence that reparations be placed on the agenda would open a Pandora's box and "unhinge the whole negotiation," and confronted with the fact that the titular British negotiator, Richard Oswald, was unwilling to put up a fight to whittle down further the concessions on the fisheries, Fitzherbert and Strachey bowed to the inevitable.

On their return to the room Fitzherbert declared that, "upon consulting together and weighing everything as maturely as possible," he and Strachey had advised Oswald "to strike" with the Americans according to the terms the American commissioners had stated as their ultimata on the fishery and the Loyalists. Had

2. Benjamin Vaughan to Richard Oswald, November 14; Oswald to Strachey, November 15; to Thomas Townshend, November 15, 1782; John Barry to Thomas Townshend, November 27, 1782. Foreign Office Papers (Public Record Office, London), 95/511, 27/2, 97/157. According to William Petty's later recollection, Oswald had told him that Benjamin Franklin threatened to sell the German prisoners unless the Negroes were restored or paid for. Rufus King, *Life and Correspondence*, IV, 94.

we not assented to the fishery article, Strachey stated, there would have been no treaty at all.[3] This concession on the part of the British was no wholesale surrender, however. What the peace commissioners now settled upon was something even more restrictive than Adams' compromise version of November 28. The changes in the article they agreed to not only watered "right" to "liberty" as regards the coastal fishery, but also involved abandoning the liberty of curing and drying on Cape Sable, as well as the explicit permission to be granted American fishermen to rent land for curing and drying their fish. Instead, the "liberty" of drying and curing was restricted to the period of time that these coastal regions remained "unsettled." Thereafter, it would "not be lawful" for the fishermen to use the land for that purpose "without a previous agreement" with "the inhabitants, proprietors, or possessors of the ground."[4]

The Americans made additional compromises. They now accepted an obligation binding Congress merely to recommend "earnestly" to the legislatures of the states that they provide for the restitution of the property of both "real British subjects" and persons "resident in districts in the possession of His Majesty's arms, and who have not borne arms against the said United States"; and permitting persons "of any other description" to move freely

3. Benjamin Franklin to Robert R. Livingston, December 5, 1782, *Writings,* VIII, 632–634; Alleyne Fitzherbert to Thomas Robinson, November (17) 29, 1782, Manchester Papers, 1220, No. 1 (William L. Clements Library, University of Michigan); to William Petty, December 4, 1782, Shelburne Papers (William L. Clements Library, University of Michigan), p. 71; to Strachey, December 19, 1782, Lamson-Strachey Mss. (Library of Congress).

4. Three "projects" of the fisheries article are in Adams Family Papers (Massachusetts Historical Society), Microfilm No. 359. The first is a version of John Adams' November fourth proposal; the second, in John Adams' hand, is, except for the omission of the words "agreed that," the final version contained in the November thirtieth treaty; the third, save for an inversion in the last sentence, is the same as John Adams' draft of November twenty-eighth. Richard Oswald confessed that by mistake he had thrown "the fishing minutes" into the fire along with a batch of unimportant papers. Oswald to Strachey, December 18, 1782, Shelburne Papers (William L. Clements Library, University of Michigan), p. 70.

within the United States for twelve months unmolested in their
efforts to obtain restitution of such of their properties as may have
been confiscated. It was further agreed "that there shall be no
future confiscations made, nor any prosecutions commenced against
any person or persons, for or by reason of the part which he or
they may have taken in the present war." This moral rather than
legal obligation left the door open a crack, but the separate states,
following a vindictive course, soon proceeded to slam it shut.[5]
No provision for indemnification of patriots was secured, but, of
course, the Americans never seriously expected it. In an expansive
mood, the Americans agreed to the payment of all debts due to
British merchants rather than restricting them to those incurred
before 1775, as in Jay's provisional draft.[6]

Despite these concessions, the Americans felt they had put in a
good day's work. At dinner that Friday evening Adams was asked
if he wanted fish. "No," he laughed, "I have had a pretty good
meal of them today." "I am glad to hear it," Ridley rejoined, "as
I know that a small quantity would not satisfy you." "Thanks be
to God," Adams wrote Elbridge Gerry of Marblehead, "that our
Tom Cod are safe in spite of the malice of enemies, the finesse of
allies, and the mistakes of Congress," although he was curiously
imprecise about letting the folks back home know just what the
Americans had won. He could afford to be in an expansive mood.
"Doctor Franklin has behaved well and nobly, particularly this
day," he declared, an enormous concession for an Adams to make,
but he had been agreeably impressed by Franklin's stout stand on
the Mississippi and the fisheries, as well as by his willingness to

5. Later Caleb Whitefoord insisted that the Americans "did admit" the
British claim for indemnification of the Loyalists but did not insist upon
indemnification for their own people. *Whitefoord Papers*, p. 202. For loose
papers summarizing the arguments of the Americans on the refugees, see
Adams Family Papers (Massachusetts Historical Society), Microfilm
No. 488.

6. Richard Oswald to Thomas Townshend, November 30, 1782, Foreign
Office Papers (Public Record Office, London), 95/511, 97/157; Shelburne
Papers (William L. Clements Library, University of Michigan), 70:416.

complete the preliminaries without further consultation with the French court.[7]

Toward his colleague from New York Adams was even more generous. He had previously eulogized Jay as a diplomat who achieved results by technical mastery as distinguished from those seeking results from "dresses, horses, balls, or cards." If the French knew as much of Jay's negotiations as they do of mine, he recorded in his journal, they "would very justly give the title with which they have inconsiderately decorated me, that of *Le Washington de la Négotiation,* a very flattering Compliment indeed, to which I have not a right, but sincerely think it belongs to Mr. Jay." Adams rejoiced at the "entire coincidence of principles and Opinions" which had obtained between Jay and himself, and never failed to pay tribute to the New Yorker for the central role he played in the transactions.[8]

Signing was set for the next day, Saturday, November 30. To Caleb Whitefoord, a fellow Scot of Oswald, the omens seemed propitious, as it happened to be St. Andrew's Day. The parties foregathered at Oswald's lodgings at the Grand Hotel Muscovite, on the same street, rue des Petits Augustins, where the Jays were staying. The principals compared treaty drafts. The Americans pointed out that Strachey had left out the twelve-month limitation of time permitted the refugees to reside in America in order to try to recover their estates. Franklin and Jay looked surprised, and insisted that the limitation be put back, which was done.[9] Laurens managed to get a clause inserted forbidding the carrying off of Negroes or other property of American inhabitants by the evacuating forces. Oswald agreed.

7. Ridley, *Diary,* November 29, 1782; L. H. Butterfield, ed., *Diary and Autobiography of John Adams,* 4 vols. (Cambridge, Mass., 1961), III, 64; John Adams to Elbridge Gerry, December 14, 1782, Adams Family Papers (Massachusetts Historical Society).

8. John Adams to Arthur Lee, October 10, 1782; Butterfield, ed., *Diary,* III, 82, 85; Benjamin Rush, *Autobiography* (Princeton, 1948), p. 215 (1792).

9. Richard Oswald to Thomas Townshend, November 30, 1782, Colonial Office Papers (Public Record Office, London), 5/8–3.

Just before the signing, according to stories widely circulated at the time, Franklin stepped out of the room and returned wearing the very coat that he had worn in January, 1774, on the occasion of his public humiliation by Solicitor General Wedderburn before a committee of the Privy Council. Franklin on that occasion had been excoriated for his part in exposing Massachusetts' Tory Governor, Thomas Hutchinson. For his role in revealing the Governor's confidential letters Franklin had been dismissed from his post of Deputy Postmaster General for America. No one believed that he would ever forget that scorching rebuke. Now, on the occasion of his triumph, and as an affront both to the King "and the whole British nation," he allegedly donned the suit of figured blue Manchester velvet that he had worn on that less happy occasion. Although Franklin had a flair for the dramatic in the matter of costumery, he was too big a man to let personal spite mar a solemn moment, and this legend is entirely without substance. The fact is that the doctor never left the room, never changed his coat, and wore at the signing ceremony a suit of black cloth in keeping with the period of mourning which had been decreed by the court of Versailles for the demise of a German prince. When the story was later called to his attention he indignantly disclaimed it, as did Caleb Whitefoord, an eyewitness, and Lord Mountstuart, who reached Paris shortly after the signing. The latter made a point of reporting that "everything passed in the simplest manner with great civility and decorum on all sides."[10]

The parties affixed their signatures to duplicate originals of both the preliminary treaty and the separate article. According to protocol, Richard Oswald, representing the more venerable state, signed first on behalf of the erstwhile monarch of a now free and independent people, and then the Americans in strict alphabetical order. Whitefoord and William Temple Franklin, as secretaries to their respective commissions, duly attested the signatures. Seals

10. *Whitefoord Papers,* pp. 200, 201n.; Mountstuart to Liston, December 20, 1782, Mountstuart Letter Book, Additional Mss. 36, 804 (British Museum).

were affixed, and a signed original turned over to each side for transmission to their principals. Curiously enough, the original which went to the Americans has never been found, and we must be content with the single original text in London's Public Record Office.[11]

The signing over, the participants rode out to Passy together to celebrate the event. There they were joined by some French guests, one of whom took occasion to rub salt into the wounds. Turning to the British, he harped on the theme of "the growing greatness of America," and predicted that "the Thirteen United States would form the greatest empire in the world."

"Yes, sir," Caleb Whitefoord replied, "and they will *all* speak English; every one of 'em."[12]

The great moment had passed, and France was not permitted to share therein. The Americans, in accordance with their settled purpose, had concluded the preliminaries without the advice of the French court. However, the evening before the signing Franklin dashed off a note to Vergennes apprising him of the event about to take place, and promising to forward a copy of the articles of peace. This he did almost at once, but without the separate secret article.*[13] Rather clumsily Adams disclosed that the agree-

11. Draft of alterations proposed in Papers of John Jay (Special Collections, Columbia University Libraries); copies of preliminaries in *ibid; Papers of Benjamin Franklin* (Yale University Library); Adams Family Papers (Massachusetts Historical Society), Microfilm No. 103; Colonial Office Papers (Public Record Office, London), 5/8–3; Papers of the Continental Congress (National Archives), pp. 106, 135, 1 (minus separate article); Shelburne Papers (William L. Clements Library, University of Michigan), pp. 34, 70:405; Francis Wharton, ed., *The Revolutionary Diplomatic Correspondence of the United States,* 6 vols. (Washington, 1889), VI, 96–100; Hunter Miller, ed., *Treaties and Other International Acts of the United States of America, 1776–1863,* 8 vols. (Washington, 1931–1948), II, 96–107.

12. *Whitefoord Papers,* p. 187.

* Concerning the boundary between the United States and Florida; Britain recovered Florida in the general peace settlement [ed.].

13. See Correspondance Politique, États-Unis (Ministère des Affaires Étrangères, Paris), 22:502–507; Benjamin Franklin to John Adams, December 3, 1782, Adams Family Papers (Massachusetts Historical Society);

ment covered more than was in Vergennes' copy. On November 5 the Duc de La Vauguyon paid him a call. Adams' own journal tells what happened: "I showed him our preliminary treaty," he records, "and had some difficulty to prevent his seeing the separate article; but I did prevent him from seeing anything of it but the words 'Separate Article.' "[14] The British were careful not to disclose the secret article to Rayneval in London, but they did hasten to assure him that the fishing rights granted the Americans did not pose a future conflict in the area that was being set aside for the fishermen of France.[15]

Having deliberately violated the instructions of Congress in pursuing their course apart from the French, the Americans defended their action in a letter to Secretary Livingston and in words penned, appropriately, by John Jay. "As we had reason to imagine that the articles respecting the boundaries, the refugees, and fisheries did not correspond with the policy of this Court, we did not communicate the preliminaries to the Minister until after they were signed," and not "even then," they admitted, did they inform him of the *separate* article.[16]

Privately Vergennes was shocked at the liberal concessions England had made to her rebellious subjects, thereby stripping him of a heavy club he might have wielded against the adversary to secure Gibraltar, concessions in India, and other demands of the

---

E. Edwards (Bancroft) to Strachey, December 4, 1782, Foreign Office Papers (Public Record Office, London), 97/157. At Charles Gravier's request Benjamin Franklin marked "with a strong red line" the boundaries of the United States settled by the preliminaries. Benjamin Franklin to Gravier, December 6, 1782, Correspondance Politique, Angleterre (Ministère des Affaires Étrangères, Paris), 539:168.

14. Butterfield, ed., *Diary*, III, 90.

15. Joseph de Rayneval to Charles Gravier, December 4, 1782, Correspondance Politique, Angleterre, 539:155–156.

16. Commissioners to Robert R. Livingston, December 14, 1782, Charles Francis Adams, ed., *Works of John Adams*, 10 vols. (Boston, 1850–1856), VII, 18–20. Although the original draft is in the handwriting of John Adams, the paragraph touching their action toward the French court is in John Jay's hand. For Henry Laurens' private dissent from this paragraph, see Ridley, *Diary*, July 1783.

Bourbon partners. After looking over the articles he remarked to Rayneval, "The English buy peace rather than make it," adding, "Their concessions exceed all that I could have thought possible." His Undersecretary in reply characterized the treaty with the Americans as a "dream." "I am persuaded," he wrote, "that the English Ministers in making it have the defection of the Americans in view." "The unhappy news" of the signing, he soon pointed out, seriously weakened his position as a negotiator with Lord Shelburne.[17] Vergennes was most upset about the fisheries provisions, as he felt that they violated France's exclusive rights which, by his interpretation, were affirmed by the Treaty of Commerce with America of 1778. Unfortunately, what had been done could not easily be undone. "Our opinion could not influence the negotiations," the Comte later complained to La Luzerne, "since we knew nothing of their details, and because they were completed in the most sudden, unforeseen, and, I might say, extraordinary manner."[18]

When Franklin and Laurens paid their respects to Vergennes some days after the signing, the French Minister remarked that "the abrupt signing of the articles" by the Americans "had little in it which could be agreeable to the King." Although the conversation was amicable, if restrained, Vergennes urged Franklin not to send the provisional treaty on to Congress. Such "an intelligence with England," he argued, "might make the people in America think a peace was consummated, and embarrass Congress, of whose fidelity I had no suspicion."[19] Franklin and his colleagues

17. Charles Gravier to Joseph de Rayneval, December 4, 1782; de Rayneval to Gravier, December 12, 25, 1782. Correspondance Politique, Angleterre, 539:158–159, 220–222, 314–317.

18. Charles Gravier to Chevalier Anne César de La Luzerne, July 21, 1783, Correspondance Politique, États-Unis, 25:67–68; cf. also January 22, April 12, 1783, *ibid.*, 23:72; 24:33.

19. Charles Gravier to Chevalier Anne César de La Luzerne, December 19, 1782, Wharton, ed., VI, 151. Gravier's displeasure was no secret from other diplomats. Mercy d'Argenteau to Prince Wenzel Kaunitz-Rietberg, December 6, 1782, Staatskanzlei, Diplomatische Korrespondenz, Frankreich (Haus-, Hof-, und Staatsarchiv, Vienna), 0412–0428.

could not take this plea seriously. Their own responsibilities as commissioners made it incumbent upon them to report to Congress as promptly as possible the course they had taken. On the evening of December 15 Vergennes was disturbed to learn from Franklin that the Americans had received a British passport for protection of an American vessel called the *Washington,* Captain Barney commanding, by which they intended to send dispatches to America, including the transmittal of the preliminary articles. With the presumption that only the doctor among the four commissioners could have ventured to take, Franklin suggested that this vessel offered a safe mode of conveyance for any part of the financial aids that America had lately requested of France, and concluded, "I fear that Congress will be reduced to despair when they find that nothing is yet obtained."

Vergennes felt that the tone of Franklin's letter was "so singular" that it was his duty to reply. "I am at a loss, sir," he remarked, "to explain your conduct and that of your colleagues on this occasion." He pointed out that the Americans had concluded their preliminaries without the communication with the court of France that Congress had prescribed. Worse still, he declared, "You are about to hold out a certain hope of peace to America without even informing yourself on the state of the negotiation on our part."[20]

Franklin proved more than equal to the challenge posed by Vergennes' rebuke. "It was certainly incumbent on us to give Congress as early an account as possible of our proceedings," he replied. What will they think if they hear the news "by other means without a line from us?" He assured Vergennes that nothing had been agreed to in the preliminaries "contrary to the interests of France," and that no peace was to take place between England and America "till you have concluded yours." He conceded that the American commissioners may have been indiscreet in not consulting the Comte before signing the preliminaries, but softened

20. Benjamin Franklin to Charles Gravier, December 15, 1782; Gravier to Franklin, December 15, 1782. Wharton, ed., VI, 137–138, 140.

the blow by confessing, "We have been guilty of neglecting a point of *bienséance*." This, he assured the Comte, was not from want of respect to the King, "whom we all love and honor." Now that the "great work" has been "so nearly brought to perfection," Franklin expressed the hope that it would "not be ruined by a single indiscretion of ours. And certainly the whole edifice sinks to the ground immediately if you refuse on that account to give us any further assistance. . . . *The English, I just now learn, flatter themselves they have already divided us,*" he deftly added. "I hope this little misunderstanding will therefore be kept secret, and that they will find themselves totally mistaken."[21]

If the English, who learned of this misunderstanding almost at once through their spy Edward Bancroft,[22] had counted on the French terminating their assistance to America, they were to be speedily disillusioned. Despite his private bitterness Vergennes did not think it prudent to insist that Franklin withhold the preliminaries or to refuse the doctor's request for more money.[23] The same ship that set out for Philadelphia with the American peace preliminaries also carried the first installment of the last French loan of six million livres.[24] Not until France and Spain had settled their preliminary terms with England did Vergennes feel it safe to turn off the spigot. Meantime an open breach was avoided. At Versailles a formal declaration was drafted in French to be made by the American commissioners reaffirming their adherence to

21. Benjamin Franklin to Charles Gravier, December 17, 1782, Wharton, ed., VI, 143, 144.

22. Alleyne Fitzherbert to Thomas Robinson, December 18, 1782, Foreign Office Papers (Public Record Office, London), 27/3, wherein Benjamin Franklin's position toward the alliance is contrasted with John Jay's more critical attitude.

23. This latter point he also made to Joseph de Rayneval, December 30, 1782, Correspondance Politique, Angleterre, 539:374–375, 380–381. See also Charles Gravier to Chevalier Anne César de La Luzerne, December 19, 24, 1782, Correspondance Politique, États-Unis, 22:562–563, 586–587; Henri Doniol, *Histoire de la Participation de la France à l'Établissement des États-Unis d'Amérique,* 5 vols. (Paris, 1886–1892), V, 192–194, 198–199.

24. Ridley, *Diary,* December 30, 1782.

the French alliance. A preliminary version was drawn up at the start of the year; a final version bore the date January 20, 1783, "done at Passy," and was apparently intended to accompany the Declaration of the Cessation of Hostilities which the Americans issued on the occasion of the signing of the Franco-Spanish preliminaries with England. The circumstances surrounding these drafts are still shrouded in mystery. Whether or not Franklin tried to persuade his colleagues to affix their signatures to the document cannot now be ascertained, as the extant papers of the American commissioners have nothing directly to say on the subject. A fair inference, however, may be drawn from a letter Jay wrote Lafayette from Rouen on January 19. Expressing surprise that anyone should entertain doubts of "American good faith," he asserted, "America has so often repeated her professions and assurances of regard" for the treaty with France "that I hope she will not impair her dignity by making any more of them." Evidently Jay's colleagues felt the same way, for the unsigned drafts still repose in the archives of the Quai d'Orsay.[25]

Without detracting from Shelburne's astute manipulations which resulted in his driving a wedge between the French and American allies, albeit at a heavy price,[26] one should not minimize the dexterous performance of the Americans who secured peace while maintaining the semblance of the alliance at the same time. As long as the Americans were in a position to make calls upon their French ally,[27] the British could not hope in the final round of talks

25. See Declaration of American Commissioners, January 2 (draft); also January 20, 1783 (unsigned) (both in French). Correspondance Politique, États-Unis, 23:14–15, 70–71. See also John Jay to Stephen Sayre, December 15, 1782, Papers of John Jay (Special Collections, Columbia University Libraries); to Lafayette, January 19, 1783, H. P. Johnston, ed., *Correspondence and Public Papers of John Jay,* 4 vols. (New York, 1890–1893), III, 25.

26. See Harlow, *Founding of Second British Empire,* I; Clarence W. Alvord, *Lord Shelburne and the Founding of British-American Goodwill* (London, 1925), p. 18; R. W. Van Alstyne, *The Rising American Empire* (New York, 1960), p. 68.

27. See contract between King of France and the United States, February 25, 1783, Treaty Ser. No. 83 1/2 (National Archives); Papers of the Continental Congress (National Archives), 145:323–327.

to water down the vast concessions they had made America by way of preliminaries.

. . . . . .

Within days after the signing of the definitive treaties the brothers Montgolfier, French inventors, demonstrated a successful balloon ascension in Paris. By the late fall of 1783 flights as long as twenty-five minutes had been made across the Seine, and to an altitude of almost ten thousand feet. People chose to forget the long war that had just ended and to ignore the new war clouds then darkening the eastern sky. In Paris the talk was of nothing but balloons. "Don't you begin to think of taking your passage in one next spring?" Sally Jay wrote to John, who had gone on a trip to England. Caught up in the fad, seamstresses planned balloon petticoats to permit air travel, and serious thinkers argued that balloons upset the new balance of power and would give France military supremacy.[28]

Air travel and air domination may have seemed like flights of fancy in the year 1783, but the revolutionary age which the American war for independence heralded proved a reality that few European statesmen grasped. Neither of the Bourbon partners had much to fear from America, a French foreign office memorandum pointed out to the Spaniards by way of consolation. The new nation could be expected to share the lethargy of other republics, compounded by sectional rivalries.[29] In downgrading the

28. Among the numerous references to the balloon ascensions in the correspondence of the peace commissioners may be cited: Benjamin Franklin on Balloons, August 30, John Bigelow, ed., *The Complete Works of Benjamin Franklin*, 10 vols. (New York, 1887–1888), X, 155; John Jay to Gouverneur Morris, July 20, 1783; to Robert Morris, September 12, 1783; to William Livingston, September 12, 1783; Sarah to John Jay, November 27, 1783, *Papers of John Jay* (Special Collections, Columbia University Libraries); Barthelemy to Hennin, October 14, 1783, Hennin Papers (Institut de France).

29. [Charles Gravier, Joseph de Rayneval, or Comte de Montmorin] Reflections on the peace (Archivo Histórica Nacional, Estado Series, Madrid), 4203:1; Goltz to Frederick II, December 13, 1782; Frederick II to Thulemeier, May 26, 1783. Marvin L. Brown, *American Independence Through Prussian Eyes* (Durham, N.C., 1959), pp. 127, 128, 201.

durable character of the American republic Vergennes by no means stood alone among the statesmen of Europe. Baron von der Goltz, the Prussian Ambassador at Paris, saw in America "only a people poor, exhausted, and afflicted with the vices of corrupt nations." His monarch, the great Frederick, predicted that "little by little, colony by colony, province by province," the Americans would "rejoin England and their former footing."[30]

Men of little vision and less faith could not discern the shape of things to come. It was this prescience with which the American commissioners were endowed which rendered their diplomacy at once so effectual and by the same token so distasteful to their European counterparts, save for visionaries like Oswald and Hartley. Franklin, Jay, and Company were instruments of a new revolutionary society. They were principals in a great confrontation of the Old Order and the New. The Old Order, in which even adversaries were bound together by ties of blood and caste, was unaccustomed to treating as equals men of lesser social rank. With its balance-of-power politics, its pseudo-Machiavellian ethics, and its objectives of limited gains, the Old Order could not comprehend revolutionary ends, which, in the rhetoric of the day so faithfully reported from America by Barbé-Marbois, could accept "no middle ground" between "slavery and liberty."[31]

True, the peace of Paris and Versailles of 1783 was no *diktat* forced upon a conquered people, but rather a negotiated peace with an adversary who had managed, aside from North America, to avoid humiliating defeat. Such a peace involved concessions on both sides. What was so remarkable about the achievements of the American commissioners was that where they compromised it was on inessentials and where they conceded it was to yield the trivial. From beginning to end they remained unswerving on the

30. Philosophes like the Abbé Morellet, on the other hand, recognized the revolutionary impact of America and its peculiar advantages stemming from the absence of a feudal structure (Morellet to William Petty, April 22, 1782, *Lettres à Shelburne*, pp. 190–192).

31. Barbé-Marbois to Charles Gravier, April 12, 1782, Correspondance Politique, États-Unis, 21:45.

score of obtaining both absolute independence and a continental domain for thirteen littoral states. On the main objectives of national survival they proved uncompromising.[32] Because the American commissioners resolutely contended for the right of a sovereign people to choose their own form of government and because they secured grudging recognition of that right from the Old Order, a free people is eternally in their debt.

Years later in Paris Bonaparte was to tell Robert R. Livingston, "You have come to a very corrupt world."[33] Jay and Adams had discovered that for themselves long before. The peacemaking began as an encounter between innocence and guile, but the Americans rapidly acquired a measure of sophistication sufficient for the task at hand. Neophytes in the arts of secret diplomacy at the start, they were the peers of their Old World counterparts at the finish. "Undisciplined marines as we were," Adams commented, "we were better tacticians than was imagined."[34]

32. T. Pownall, *A Memorial Addressed to the Sovereigns of America* (London, 1783).

33. Robert R. Livingston papers cited by Dangerfield, *Livingston,* p. 311; but cf. Madame de Staël, *Oeuvres,* 17 vols. (Paris, 1821), XV, 47–48.

34. John Adams to Elbridge Gerry, December 14, 1782, Adams Family Papers (Massachusetts Historical Society).

✪

The Political Theory of Benjamin Franklin

Can any new thing be written of Benjamin Franklin? Is there a corner of his magnificent mind or an aspect of his towering influence that is not the most familiar public property? He has had a dozen or more notable biographers and a legion of faithful investigators of one or another of his activities and interests.[1] In his own writings, public as well as private, he examined himself with discrimination and revealed himself with candor.[2]

Yet much remains to be hypothesized and verified in what Carl Van Doren liked to call the "Franklin science." We need a new and revised edition of his complete writings,[3] an expanded

---

From Clinton Rossiter, "The Political Theory of Benjamin Franklin," *The Pennsylvania Magazine of History and Biography* (July 1952), pp. 259–293. Reprinted by permission of The Historical Society of Pennsylvania.

1. No attempt will be made here to give even a fragmentary bibliography of works by and about Franklin. See the card catalogue of any convenient library, as well as Carl Van Doren, *Benjamin Franklin* (New York, 1938), pp. 785–788; Carl Becker, *Benjamin Franklin* (Ithaca, N.Y., 1946), pp. 41–42; R. E. Spiller, *et al.*, eds., *Literary History of the United States* (New York, 1948), III, 507–515; P. L. Ford, *Franklin Bibliography* (Brooklyn, N.Y., 1889); F. L. Mott and C. E. Jorgenson, eds., *Benjamin Franklin, Representative Selections* (New York, 1936), pp. cli–clxxiii.

2. Carl Van Doren, ed., *Benjamin Franklin's Autobiographical Writings* (New York, 1948).

3. The best editions now available are Jared Sparks, ed., *The Works of Benjamin Franklin*, 10 vols. (Boston, 1840); and A. H. Smyth, ed., *The Writings of Benjamin Franklin*, 10 vols. (New York, 1905–1907). [See Bibliographical Note at the end of this volume (ed.).]

bibliography, a scientific biography, additional calendars of his papers (which are spread throughout the Western World), and a Franklin dictionary. We need a fuller biography than Van Doren's, something "half again as long," as Van Doren himself promised not long before his death;[4] we need a fuller one than that, something with the sweep and detail of the Freeman *Washington*. And certainly we can expect and welcome a constant flow of articles and monographs that will question and perhaps revise some of the accepted interpretations of Franklin's special accomplishments and talents.

This article proposes to do exactly that. Convinced that the literature on Franklin's political theory falls well below the high level of analysis reached by the literature on his religion, scientific achievements, diplomacy, personal life, and political career, I should like to re-examine this important part of his thought, paying particular attention to those democratic ideas he expressed and acted upon during his and America's colonial period. I have no intention of pronouncing even a single final judgment on Franklin's political theory, but I do think it essential to "question and perhaps revise" certain assumptions about this aspect of his many-sided philosophy.

The pattern of Franklin's political theory is as perplexing as it is intriguing, as elusive as it is important. He was an able and productive political pamphleteer. He reflected with peculiar accuracy the changing political moods of eighteenth-century America, and was looked upon as the representative colonial by the keenest observers of his time. He helped to introduce to the American mind four or five fundamental assumptions about government and society. Yet he was never in the ordinary sense a theorist or philosopher in the field of political science.

The proof of this startling observation lies in Franklin's own writings: the sum total of his strictly philosophical musings about government and politics would fill, quite literally, about two printed pages. He wrote authoritatively about scores of events and

4. Carl Van Doren, *et al.*, *Meet Dr. Franklin* (Philadelphia, 1943), p. 223.

problems that had persuaded men far less speculative than he to philosophize at length about the nature and purpose of government, but his arguments were descriptive, statistical, propagandistic, and totally lacking in any appeal to fundamentals.[5] He was the one American patriot to write influentially about the events of 1763–1776 without calling upon natural law, the rights of man, and the social contract.

If ever Franklin expressed a clear and conscious thought on such matters as the origin of government or the nature of authority, the research for this article, which has led through a half-dozen libraries and several hundred letters, pamphlets, and rough scribblings, has been unable to find it. He seems to have been constitutionally incapable of the kind of writing done by Williams, Wise, Mayhew, Otis, and almost every other political actor in colonial or Revolutionary America. If just one small trickle of theory had leaked through somewhere out of the vast structure of his political writings, we might rejoice to have found the sure source of his ideas. The amazing fact that he never once permitted this to happen leaves us wondering if perhaps this refusal to philosophize was not the result of a calculated, rigidly observed rule of political argument.

His early and unhappy venture into speculation about the cosmos could well have conditioned his subsequent thinking about politics. "The great uncertainty I found in metaphysical reasonings disgusted me, and I quitted that kind of reading and study for others more satisfactory."[6] The nature of his task should also be remembered: the bulk of his political arguments consisted of letters to the English press, not speeches to the American as-

5. The most characteristic examples are the eleven letters entitled "The Colonist's Advocate" (1770), printed in V. W. Crane, ed., *Benjamin Franklin's Letters to the Press, 1758–1775* (Chapel Hill, N.C., 1950), pp. 167–209.
6. To Benjamin Vaughan, November 9, 1779, *Writings*, VII, 412. Even Franklin's rough drafts and memoranda—for example, those preserved in the American Philosophical Society—are wholly practical and unspeculative in character. Franklin Papers (American Philosophical Society), L, i, 7–9, 13; ii, 4, 9–12, 24, 31, 46, 48, 50, 51.

semblies; he could hardly have rung the changes on natural rights and revolution in the *London Chronicle* or *Public Advertiser*. And certainly one piece like his *Rules by which a Great Empire may be reduced to a Small One*[7] was worth a hundred passionate appeals to God and nature in the attempt to sway British opinion. In any case, there is no acceptable explanation why Benjamin Franklin, of all people, should have been one of the least philosophical statesmen in American history.

Were the person under analysis anyone but Franklin, this article would end here, or rather would never have been begun. Yet we are dealing with the great democrat of colonial America, and somehow we must wring from his practical arguments the political faith that he doggedly refused to make articulate. One method of accomplishing this obstinate feat is to describe Franklin's beliefs as other men saw them. This is a technique not ordinarily to be trusted, but in a case like this it is the only alternative to no technique at all. And we have reasonable evidence, drawn particularly from Franklin's consistent actions in support of the popular cause, that he did indeed espouse the principles ascribed to him by friend and foe. These principles may be reduced to two major headings: the teachings of John Locke and radical Whiggery.

It is impossible to estimate accurately the extent of Franklin's dedication to the philosophy of natural law and natural rights. As a scientist, skeptic, and unprejudiced student of universal history, he could not have missed the inconsistencies and historical distortions in Locke's *Second Treatise*. On the other hand, his pragmatic mind, which was always more concerned with the effects of a political philosophy than with its logic or symmetry, would have been the first to recognize the usefulness to the popular cause of a system based so squarely on the notion of government by the consent of the governed. Among the bits of evidence that Franklin accepted the dominant theory of his time and class are these: he studied and admired "the great Mr. Locke's" philosophical writ-

7. *Writings*, VI, 127–137. This essay was first printed in *The Gentleman's Magazine*, September 1773.

ings,[8] and was hardly less devoted to Algernon Sidney;[9] as a member of the Committee of Five he read over and endorsed Jefferson's "rough draft" of the Declaration of Independence;[10] and he was widely credited, especially in England, with the authorship of *Common Sense,* which Paine had published anonymously in Philadelphia. It was even rumored that the Queen had caught the Prince of Wales red-handed with "Dr. Franklin's pamphlet Common Sense."[11]

Scattered through Franklin's pamphlets, letters, and notes are other witnesses to his tacit acceptance of Locke's renowned theory, phrases and sentences that glimmer here and there in the great gray mass of his practical arguments. To quote these out of context would be unfair to Franklin, and indeed quite misleading. It must therefore suffice to state the general impression they leave: that Franklin endorsed as useful doctrines the state of nature (in which all men are free and equal),[12] and social contract,[13] natural law, natural rights (including "life, liberty, and property," as well as freedom of inquiry, expression, petition, religion and migration),[14] and the happiness and safety of the people as the purpose of government. As the most conspicuous Revolutionary of 1776 Franklin could hardly have doubted the rights of resistance and revolution, but we may search his writings in vain for any clear statement of this doctrine.[15]

The only elements in the natural rights–natural law theory

8. *Writings,* I, 179, 243; II, 387 n.

9. Franklin's Ramsay, pp. 28, 52. (See below, Note 31.)

10. Julian Boyd, *The Declaration of Independence* (Princeton, 1945), pp. 16 ff., and references there cited.

11. *Pennsylvania Evening Post,* January 11, 1777.

12. Franklin's Ramsay, pp. 8, 10, 14; Franklin's Wheelock, p. 7.

13. Franklin's Ramsay, pp. 9, 10, 15, 51–54.

14. *Ibid.,* pp. 51–52; "I think People should be left at Liberty to go where they can be happiest." Franklin to Jonathan Shipley, March 10, 1774 (Yale Library).

15. For glimpses of the Lockean theory in his published writings, see *Writings,* II, 25–28, 293; VI, 260, 298; IX, 293; X, 59–60, 72; *Works,* II, 323, 556; Crane, *Letters to the Press,* pp. 55–56, 169. For glimpses in the marginalia, see Franklin's *Good Humour,* pp. 18–20; Franklin's Ramsay, pp. 8–10, 15, 24, 28, 51–52.

that Franklin seems to have enlarged upon were property and equality. Although in general he shared the popular view of the sanctity of property—"Does not *every Man's Feelings* Declare that his Property is not to be taken from him without his Consent?"[16]—he seems to have entertained a somewhat more radical, socially minded view of the importance of any one man's possessions in relation to the commonweal. The Franklin touch is manifest in this passage:

All Property, indeed, except the Savage's temporary Cabin, his Bow, his Matchcoat, and other little Acquisitions, absolutely necessary for his Subsistence, seems to me to be the Creature of public Convention. Hence the Public has the Right of Regulating Descents, and all other Conveyances of Property, and even of limiting the Quantity and the Uses of it. All the Property that is necessary to a Man, for the Conservation of the Individual and the Propagation of the Species, is his natural Right, which none can justly deprive him of: But all Property superfluous to such purposes is the Property of the Publick, who, by their Laws, have created it, and who may therefore by other Laws dispose of it, whenever the Welfare of the Publick shall demand such Disposition. He that does not like civil Society on these Terms, let him retire and live among Savages. He can have no right to the benefits of Society, who will not pay his Club towards the Support of it.[17]

Franklin's belief in equality was the obverse of his well-known impatience with "places, pensions, and peerages,"[18] with the stupidity and injustice of legalized inequalities of any description.[19] His thoughts on this subject were expressed as usual in extremely untheoretical language, but occasionally a sentence appears in the progress of his argument that belies a belief in equality as the key principle of organization of free society. Franklin came to this belief gradually, for in his earlier years he flirted with the

16. Franklin's Ramsay, p. 27.
17. To Robert Morris, December 25, 1783, *Writings,* IX, 138.
18. *Ibid.,* VII, 172.
19. See *ibid.,* IX, 161–168, for his low opinion of the Cincinnati and their abortive attempt to "form an Order of *hereditary Knights,* in direct opposition to the solemnly declared Sense of their Country." See also *ibid.,* VI, 371.

doctrine of the stake-in-society. In the end his naturally democratic sympathies triumphed resoundingly. Near the close of his life, in arguing against property as a qualification for the suffrage, he had this to say to the proponents of aristocracy:

The Combinations of Civil Society are not like those of a Set of Merchants, who club their Property in different Proportions for Building and Freighting a Ship, and may therefore have some Right to vote in the Disposition of the Voyage in a greater or less Degree according to their respective Contributions; but the important ends of Civil Society, and the personal Securities of Life and Liberty, these remain the same in every Member of the society; and the poorest continues to have an equal Claim to them with the most opulent, whatever Difference Time, Chance, or Industry may occasion in their Circumstances.[20]

In general, then, it is safe to say that Franklin believed in the natural rights–natural law philosophy as much as he could believe in any body of doctrine, and that he subscribed with extra fervor to the basic Lockean belief in "a Society in which the Ruling Power is circumscribed by previous Laws or Agreements."[21] Like all the men of his time he put his faith in limited government, government in which the rulers were the servants of the people.[22]

In considering Franklin a radical Whig the men of his time were recognizing his kinship with scores of other representatives of the popular party in the colonial assemblies. With Pitt and King William as their heroes, the Glorious Revolution as their golden age, and the uncorrupted British Constitution as the noblest of all governmental systems,[23] the colonial Whigs were preparing the ground in which American democracy was to flourish. The battle cry of the good Whig, in the colonies as in England, was

20. *Ibid.,* X, 59–60; see also VI, 291.
21. Franklin's Ramsay, p. 15.
22. See especially his whimsical speech to the Convention of 1787, in Max Farrand, *The Records of the Federal Convention* (New Haven, Conn., 1911), II, 120, as well as Franklin's Ramsay, pp. 33–34.
23. *Writings,* V, 133; Franklin Papers (American Philosophical Society), L, i, 4b, 8, 11.

"Liberty!"—by which he meant constitutionalism, representation, government by "the people" (those who had some property), "the rights of Englishmen,"[24] and a system of "balanced government" in which the legislature was actually dominant. Through most of his life, indeed through all of it as a colonial, Franklin was in the van of the liberty-loving Whigs, which explains his hope to settle his colony's constitution "firmly on the Foundations of Equity and English Liberty."[25] Not all of the Colonial Whigs—Franklin's friend Joseph Galloway, for example—were able to make the transition to independence, fewer still from there to democracy. Franklin seems to have had no trouble. He was a notable specimen of that uncommon species, the man who grows more democratic with age, fame, respectability, and the gout.

Among Franklin's literary remains was a printed paper, endorsed in his hand with the statement "Some Good Whig Principles." In point of fact these principles push well beyond sound Whiggery into radical country, which explains why he found them especially "good." These could just as easily have been his own words as he arrived in the mother country in 1764.

It is declared,

First, That the government of this realm, and the making of laws for the same, ought to be lodged in the hands of King, Lords of Parliament, and Representatives of *the whole body* of the freemen of this realm.

Secondly, That *every man* of the commonalty (excepting infants, insane persons, and criminals) is, of common right, and by the laws of God, *a freeman*, and entitled to the free enjoyment of *liberty*.

Thirdly, That liberty, or freedom, consists in having *an actual share* in the appointment of those who frame the laws, and who are to be the guardians of every man's life, property, and peace; for the *all* of one man is as dear to him as the *all* of another; and the poor man has

24. For examples of Franklin's concern for English rights, see *Writings*, III, 233; V, 80–81; Crane, *Letters to the Press*, pp. 10–11, 44, 56, 112, 174. And see generally Conyers Read, "The English Elements in Benjamin Franklin," *The Pennsylvania Magazine of History and Biography*, LXIV (1940), 314–330.

25. To Galloway, June 10, 1758 (Yale Library).

an *equal* right, but *more* need, to have representatives in the legislature than the rich one.

Fourthly, That they who have *no* voice nor vote in the electing of representatives, *do not enjoy* liberty; but are absolutely *enslaved* to those who have votes. . . .

And, sixthly and lastly, . . . that it is *the right* of the commonalty of this realm to elect a *new* House of Commons once in *every year*, according to the ancient and sacred laws of the land. . . .[26]

Two more preliminary observations, and we shall be ready to outline Franklin's special contributions to the American democratic tradition. The first touches upon his habits of thought. The methods Franklin employed in weighing political issues were hardly less significant than the decisions he reached. We will have a good deal less trouble with his political mind if we will remember that he was a pragmatist, insisting that all ideas be judged by their effects; a scientist, distrusting dogma and prizing free inquiry; a skeptic, doubting all certainty and never "wholly committed" to any cause or truth;[27] and a generalist, ranging through all disciplines and integrating them masterfully into one grand comprehension of human knowledge.

The second point concerns the location of his recorded ideas. For the most part they are the same as for the other great figures of his time, who wrote copiously, influentially, and with absolutely no system. Pamphlets on current issues, letters to the press,[28] private correspondence, and formal papers are the categories of authorship in which his contributions are to be sought.[29] Hardly less important are the so-called "marginalia," notes made by

26. *Writings*, X, 130–131; see also VI, 128, 214–215. Franklin's favorite club in London was known as the "Honest Whigs." Van Doren, *Franklin*, pp. 421–422.

27. Becker, *Franklin*, p. 35.

28. It is to this problem that Verner W. Crane has devoted years of patient labor. The end result, *Benjamin Franklin's Letters to the Press, 1758–1775*, is a triumph in the Franklin science.

29. Under the last heading I would include the thoroughly prepared "Examination of Dr. Benjamin Franklin, Etc., in the British House of Commons," *Writings*, IV, 412–448.

Franklin in the margins of his copies of other men's pamphlets. Some of these notes are testimony to a universal human urge, the urge to scribble "This Wiseacre," "No!," "Childish," "All mere Quibbling," and "A Falsity!" alongside the brash paragraphs of enemy pamphleteers. Most of them, however, were written in a serious, searching vein, for they were one of his favorite methods of preparing retorts to the press. Although his most important editor, Albert H. Smyth, considered these scribblings "crude and fragmentary," "never intended for publication," and therefore not worth printing,[30] other scholars have valued them highly. These precious indications, in Franklin's own hand, of his innermost thoughts on the great issues of the 1760's are preserved in the Library of Congress, the New York Public Library, the Yale Library, the Athenaeum of Philadelphia, and the Historical Society of Pennsylvania. They are a unique source of his political ideas.[31]

Franklin's specific contributions to the aggregate of libertarian principles inherited by the Revolutionary generation were a patchwork of utility, reason, and warm human sympathy. Some of his offerings were directly and consciously bestowed on his fellow citizens. Some were working principles of method and attitude that he was content to practice and to let other men imitate or spin out into theories of democracy. All were essential ingredients

---

30. *Ibid.,* IV, V.

31. Fragments of the marginalia are in *Works,* IV, 206–232, 281–301; *Writings,* X, 234–240; *The Pennsylvania Magazine of History and Biography,* XXV (1901), 307–322, 516–526, and XXVI (1902), 81–90, 255–264; American Antiquarian Society, *Proceedings,* XXXIV (New Series), 217–218. The pamphlets in which the most revealing marginalia are to be found are (1) *The Claim of the Colonies to an Exemption from Internal Taxes* (London, 1765); (2) *Good Humour: or, a Way with the Colonies* (London, 1766); (3) Allen Ramsay, *Thoughts on the Origin and Nature of Government* (London, 1769); (4) Matthew Wheelock, *Reflections Moral and Political on Great Britain and her Colonies* (London, 1770). Item 1 is in the New York Public Library, item 2 (in photostat) in the Yale Library, items 3 and 4 in the Library of Congress. They are cited here as Franklin's *Claim of the Colonies,* Franklin's *Good Humour,* Franklin's Ramsay, and Franklin's Wheelock.

of the new way of life and thought that he represented so magnifi-
cently before the rulers and people of Europe. Political pragmatism,
conciliation and compromise, freedom of speech and press, economic individualism, and federalism were the essentials of American democracy to which Franklin devoted special attention.

POLITICAL PRAGMATISM

Pragmatism as a rule of conscious political action has never had a
more eminent exponent than Benjamin Franklin.[32] There were
great pragmatists before this greatest of pragmatists. The political
history of colonial America was written by men who had "the
attitude of looking away from first things, principles, 'categories,'
supposed necessities; and of looking towards last things, fruits,
consequences, facts."[33] But in Franklin's life and political arguments this method became an acknowledged, if yet nameless,
American fundamental. William James, in his memorable lectures
on pragmatism in 1906 and 1907, described this philosophy as
"a new name for some old ways of thinking." Franklin might have
been perplexed by the label, but he would certainly have recognized
his own ways of thinking. No man could have been less concerned
with origins and first principles, or more concerned with consequences and facts. The character of his natural science left its
mark on his political science. He was perhaps the most thorough-
going utilitarian America has produced.

Franklin's political pragmatism was simply one influential expression of his general attitude toward life and its problems. He
was not a political philosopher; he was not a philosopher at all.
He was a man prepared to investigate and discuss every principle
and institution known to the human race, but only in the most
practical and unspeculative terms. He limited his own thought
process to the one devastating question: *Does it work?,* or more

32. See particularly the excellent chapter "Benjamin Franklin: Student of
Life," contributed by R. E. Spiller to *Meet Dr. Franklin,* pp. 83–103.
33. William James, *Pragmatism: A New Name for Some Old Ways of
Thinking* (New York, 1907), pp. 54–55.

exactly, *Does it work well?* Most men who call themselves pragmatists, especially in politics, examine the evidence of consequences
and facts from a predetermined observation post constructed out of
strongly held articles of faith. They are pragmatists within limits,
within a context that itself may not be put to the test and may well
be an irrational inheritance or a rationalized faith. Not so Franklin,
who seemed willing to subject even his most basic beliefs, if they
could be called that, to the test of experience. He was a democrat,
radical Whig, and friend of liberty because democracy, Whiggery,
and liberty had demonstrated themselves to his uncommitted
mind to be the best practical solutions to the problems facing
men in society. He had proved and found solid the very context
of his pragmatism.

Perhaps the most convincing example of Franklin's consistent
devotion to political pragmatism was his well-known attitude on
the usefulness of organized religion. Himself a pagan skeptic
with no need for ministerial intervention, he nevertheless had pronounced and favorable views of the value of religion to a free and
stable society. He had decided, after much observation in Boston
and Philadelphia, that one of the essentials of self-government was
a high level of public morality. He had decided further that such
a condition of public morality was largely the product of organized
religion. The churches and sects of New England and the middle
colonies had helped create a collective state of mind conducive
to habits of self-reliance and self-government. It had nourished
the way of life that his other observations had already taught him
to be the most blessed for the average man. Organized religion
had "worked," and worked well, in the colonies. It must therefore be supported, even by the skeptic. Franklin went to church,
when he went to church, because it was "decent and proper," not
because he believed. In his proposals that led to the founding of
the Academy of Philadelphia, he advocated the teaching of history
because it would "also afford frequent Opportunities of showing
the Necessity of a *Publick Religion,* from its Usefulness to the
Publick; the Advantage of a Religious Character among private
Persons; the Mischiefs of Superstition, etc., and the Excellency of

the CHRISTIAN RELIGION above all others antient or modern."[34] He had abandoned logical deism because "this doctrine, though it might be true, was not very useful." He turned back to give support to Christianity because this doctrine, though it might be untrue, was highly indispensable to his kind of society.

Education, too, was important because useful. Franklin's faith in education had a dozen outlets. The American Philosophical Society, the Library Company, the University of Pennsylvania, and the Franklin Funds of Boston and Philadelphia are present-day reminders of his high regard for formal and informal education of all classes, ages, and conditions of men. The famous *Proposals Relating to the Education of Youth in Pensilvania* (1749)[35] are utilitarian to the core. The modern reader cannot suppress the pleasant suspicion that Franklin's ideal academy would be geared to turn out the maximum number of young Franklins.

The proprietary government of Pennsylvania, the target of his early popularism, was likewise put to the test, but found wanting. Franklin could easily have based his mistrust of this system on principle alone, but preferred to condemn it for its harmful effects. In a characteristic passage from the aptly titled *Cool Thoughts on the Present Situation* (1764), he launched this pragmatic attack on the proprietary system:

> Considering all Circumstances, I am at length inclin'd to think, that the Cause of these miserable Contentions is not to be sought for merely in the Depravity and Selfishness of human Minds. . . . I suspect therefore, that the Cause is radical, interwoven in the Constitution, and so become of the very Nature, of Proprietary Governments; and will therefore produce its Effects, as long as such Governments continue. And, as some Physicians say, every Animal Body brings into the World among its original Stamina the Seeds of that Disease that shall finally produce its Dissolution; so the Political Body of a

34. *Writings,* II, 393. For other examples of his regard for the usefulness of religion, see J. M. Stifler, *The Religion of Benjamin Franklin* (New York, 1925), pp. 8, 15, 17, 40, 118; *Writings,* IX, 521.

35. *Writings,* II, 386–396; also III, 16–17; X, 9–32. See generally Thomas Woody, *Educational Views of Benjamin Franklin* (New York, 1931).

Proprietary Government, contains those convulsive Principles that will at length destroy it.

I may not be Philosopher enough to develop those Principles, nor would this Letter afford me Room, if I had Abilities, for such a Discussion. The *Fact* seems sufficient for our Purpose, and the *Fact* is notorious, that such Contentions have been in all Proprietary Governments, and have brought, or are now bringing, them all to a Conclusion.[36]

A final example of Franklin's political pragmatism was his oft-repeated warning of the unworkability of laws that outrage a people's fundamental opinions. This was the sort of argument—calling attention to consequences rather than constitutional rights—with which he attempted to dissuade the advocates of harsh measures for the colonies. He even printed small cards describing "The Result of England's Persistence in Her Policy Towards the Colonies."

History affords us many instances of the ruin of states, by the prosecution of measures ill suited to the temper and genius of their people. The ordaining of laws in favour of *one* part of the nation, to the prejudice and oppression of *another,* is certainly the most erroneous and mistaken policy. An *equal* dispensation of protection, rights, privileges, and advantages, is what every part is entitled to, and ought to enjoy; it being a matter of no moment to the state, whether a subject grows rich and flourishing on the Thames or the Ohio, in Edinburgh or Dublin. These measures never fail to create great and violent jealousies and animosities between the people favoured and the people oppressed; whence a total separation of affections, interests, political obligations, and all manner of connexions, necessarily ensue, by which the whole state is weakened, and perhaps ruined for ever![37]

Franklin's supremely practical observation, "the *Fact* seems sufficient for our Purpose, and the *Fact* is notorious," has become a major working principle of this race of pragmatists, and to him and his popular writings must go at least some of the credit.

36. *Writings,* IV, 228–229.
37. *Ibid.,* VI, 290–291; Franklin's *Good Humour,* p. 18.

CONCILIATION AND COMPROMISE

Franklin placed extraordinary value in the spirit and techniques of conciliation and compromise. By nature and experience he was disposed to seek peace and harmony in whatever controversy he might have wandered into by design or accident. His nature was skeptical and undogmatic; he could even doubt his own opinions. The benign speech that James Wilson delivered for him on the last day of the Convention of 1787 was characteristic of a lifetime of active political argument.

I confess that I do not entirely approve of this Constitution at present, but Sir, I am not sure I shall never approve it: For having lived long, I have experienced many instances of being obliged, by better information or fuller consideration, to change opinions even on important subjects, which I once thought right, but found to be otherwise. It is therefore that the older I grow the more apt I am to doubt my own judgment, and to pay more respect to the judgment of others. Most men indeed as well as most sects in religion, think themselves in possession of all truth, and that wherever others differ from them it is so far error. Steele, a Protestant, in a dedication tells the Pope, that the only difference between our two churches in their opinions of the certainty of their doctrine, is, the Romish Church is infallible, and the Church of England is never in the wrong. But tho' many private persons think almost as highly of their own infallibility as of that of their Sect, few express it so naturally as a certain French lady, who in a little dispute with her sister, said, I don't know how it happens, Sister, but I meet with nobody but myself that's *always* in the right. *Il n'y a que moi qui a toujours raison.*

In these sentiments, Sir, I agree to this Constitution, with all its faults, if they are such; because I think a general Government necessary for us, . . . I consent, Sir, to this Constitution, because I expect no better, and because I am not sure that it is not the best. The opinions I have had of its errors I sacrifice to the public good. I have never whisper'd a syllable of them abroad. Within these walls they were born, and here they shall die. . . .

On the whole, Sir, I cannot help expressing a wish, that every member of the Convention who may still have objections to it, would with me on this occasion doubt a little of his own infallibility, and to make *manifest* our *unanimity,* put his name to this Instrument.[38]

Experience confirmed this natural faith in conciliation. He was a shrewd observer of proceedings in the Junto, the Assembly, and a thousand public meetings. He noted the differing consequences of the differing ways in which men might hold and express the same opinions. Having decided that the spirit of compromise was an essential of political success and the basis of stable, peaceful, effective self-government, he acted in character by laying down rules that would improve himself and others in this important respect.

I made it a rule to forbear all direct contradiction to the sentiments of others and all positive assertion of my own. I even forbade myself . . . the use of every word or expression in the language that imported a fixed opinion, such as "certainly," "undoubtedly," etc.; and I adopted instead of them, "I conceive," "I apprehend," or "I imagine" a thing to be so or so, or "It so appears to me at present." When another asserted something that I thought an error, I denied myself the pleasure of contradicting him abruptly and of showing immediately some absurdity in his proposition; and in answering I began by observing that in certain cases or circumstances his opinion would be right, but that in the present case there "appeared" or "seemed to me" some difference, etc. I soon found the advantage of this change in my manners: The conversations I engaged in went on more pleasantly; the modest way in which I proposed my opinions procured them a readier reception and less contradiction; I had less mortification when I was found to be in the wrong, and I more easily prevailed with others to give up their mistakes and join with me when I happened to be in the right.[39]

The Junto conducted its discussions deliberately in this spirit.

38. *Writings,* IX, 607–609; Farrand, *Records of the Federal Convention,* II, 641–643. I have used the copy in the Library of Cornell University transcribed by Franklin for Charles Carroll.

39. Max Farrand, ed., *The Autobiography of Benjamin Franklin* (Berkeley, Cal., 1949), pp. 112–113; also pp. 21–22.

Our debates were to be under the direction of a president, and to be conducted in the sincere spirit of enquiry after truth, without fondness for dispute or desire of victory; and to prevent warmth, all expressions of positiveness in opinion or of direct contradiction were after some time made contraband and prohibited under small pecuniary penalties.[40]

Franklin never made the mistake of identifying conciliation and compromise with democracy, of regarding this spirit as an end in itself. In the Assembly and before the House of Commons his "desire of victory" was keen and apparent, but he was certain that victory would be easier to gain if "fondness for dispute" were erased from his nature or at least not betrayed in debate. He could take a firm stand, even commit himself to an advanced position, as he did with few qualms in subscribing to the Declaration of Independence, but he was satisfied that first he had explored all possible alternatives and had done his best to avoid the final break.

The significance of conciliation and compromise for successful democracy has never been examined satisfactorily in philosophical terms. It is to be deeply regretted that Franklin could never bring himself to theorize in letter or pamphlet about this fundamental principle of his personal code and public faith. It "worked well," and that was enough for him. Yet any political theorist who attempts to fix with finality the place of conciliation and compromise in the American democratic tradition will be well advised to study Franklin's political conduct. His life argues powerfully that democracy depends on men with a nice feeling for the proper balance between faith and skepticism, principle and compromise, tenacity and conciliation. Franklin was boasting, not complaining, when he wrote from London to his American posterity: "Hence it has often happened to me, that while I have been thought here too much of an American, I have in America been deem'd too much of an Englishman."[41]

He could hardly have given himself a finer compliment.

40. *Ibid.*, p. 73. See *Writings,* II, 393–394, for his thoughts in this vein in connection with the Academy.
41. *Writings,* VI, 260, 262. See also the piece in Crane, *Letters to the Press,* pp. 107–108.

FREEDOM OF SPEECH AND PRESS

Franklin was a shrewd and influential defender of the twin freedoms of speech and press. As the leading printer and journalist of the middle colonies, as a scientist dedicated to free inquiry and international exchange of information,[42] and as a politician convinced that discussion and compromise were the essence of self-government, he had the most intense personal reasons for championing freedom of expression.

Through seventy years he never wavered in his belief in the social usefulness of freedom of speech, nor ever shrank from active conflict with those who would suppress it. In 1722, when Benjamin was only sixteen years old, his brother James was "taken up, censured, and imprisoned for a month" for printing in his *New-England Courant* a political piece that "gave offence to the Assembly."

During my brother's confinement, which I resented a good deal notwithstanding our private differences, I had the management of the paper, and I made bold to give our rulers some rubs in it, which my brother took very kindly, while others began to consider me in an unfavourable light as a young genius that had a turn for libelling and satire. My brother's discharge was accompanied with an order from the House (a very odd one) that "James Franklin should no longer print the paper called the *New England Courant*." There was a consultation held in our printing house amongst his friends in this conjuncture. Some proposed to elude the order by changing the name of the paper; but my brother seeing inconveniences in that, it was finally concluded on as a better way to let it be printed for the future under the name of "Benjamin Franklin."[43]

42. See Gladys Meyer, *Free Trade in Ideas: Aspects of American Liberalism Illustrated in Franklin's Philadelphia Career* (New York, 1941).

43. *Autobiography*, p. 25. Actually it was a later issue, that of January 14, 1723 (in which James Franklin's disrespect for the clergy was a bit too carelessly flaunted), that persuaded the General Court to forbid further publication under his name.

The piece in which the apprentice "made bold to give our rulers some rubs" was the eighth of his communications to the *Courant* from "Silence Dogood." In this letter he quoted at length the most famous of *Cato's Letters,* which he presented as an "Abstract from the London Journal." Even over a pseudonym it was a bold swipe at authority, and the wonder is that Benjamin did not follow James to jail.

Without Freedom of Thought, there can be no such Thing as Wisdom; and no such Thing as publick Liberty, without Freedom of Speech; which is the Right of every Man, as far as by it, he does not hurt or controul the Right of another: And this is the only Check it ought to suffer, and the only Bounds it ought to Know.

This sacred Privilege is so essential to free Governments, that the Security of Property, and the Freedom of Speech always go together; and in those wretched Countries where a Man cannot call his Tongue his own, he can scarce call any Thing else his own. Whoever would overthrow the Liberty of a Nation, must begin by subduing the Freeness of Speech; a *Thing* terrible to Publick Traytors. . . .

The Administration of Government is nothing else but the Attendance of the *Trustees of the People* upon the Interest and Affairs of the People: And as it is the Part and Business of the People, for whose Sake alone all publick Matters are, or ought to be transacted, to see whether they be well or ill transacted; so it is the Interest, and ought to be the Ambition, of all honest Magistrates, to have their Deeds openly examined, and publickly scan'd. . . .

Misrepresentation of publick Measures is easily overthrown, by representing publick Measures truly; when they are honest, they ought to be publickly known, that they may be publickly commended; but if they are knavish or pernicious, they ought to be publickly detested.[44]

Franklin carried these youthful beliefs through seventy years of political storms. To freedom of speech he was "wholly committed."

The publisher of the *Pennsylvania Gazette* had considerable direct influence upon the development of a free and responsible

44. *Writings,* II, 25–28; *New-England Courant,* July 9, 1722. This piece from the writings of Thomas Gordon and John Trenchard was reprinted again and again in the colonial press throughout the pre-Revolutionary period.

colonial press. Like the best papers in London the *Gazette* adopted a policy of neutrality in public controversies. Franklin refused to make his paper the organ of the anti-Proprietary party, but threw its columns open to opinions from all sides. At the same time, he kept constant watch on the political winds that blew and weathered several storms by discreetly reefing his sails. As long as freedom of the press was uncertain in Pennsylvania he was careful merely to antagonize, not enrage, the Proprietary party. Meanwhile, he did his best to cement this freedom by printing a responsible journal, by calling attention to the value of differing opinions, and by publishing an account of the trial of John Peter Zenger.

By 1750 the press in England and the colonies had achieved a remarkable measure of freedom. Franklin, who wrote to the *Public Advertiser* that "Free Government depends on Opinion, not on the brutal Force of a Standing Army,"[45] made full use in England of what he had helped create in America: an unlicensed, uncensored press in which the public could find all important issues thoroughly, even controversially, debated.

Franklin's most influential statement on freedom of press was "An Apology for Printers," which appeared in the *Gazette* June 10, 1731.[46] This "apology" is worth quoting at length, for it is a remarkably accurate representation of the principles of a free press that governed popular thinking in eighteenth-century America.

Being frequently censur'd and condemn'd by different Persons for printing Things which they say ought not to be printed, I have sometimes thought it might be necessary to make a standing Apology for my self, and publish it once a Year, to be read upon all Occasions of that Nature. . . .

I request all who are angry with me on the Account of printing things they don't like, calmly to consider these following Particulars.

1. That the Opinions of Men are almost as various as their Faces; an Observation general enough to become a common Proverb, *So many Men so many Minds.*

45. Crane, *Letters to the Press,* p. 193.
46. *Writings,* II, 172–179. This piece was reprinted in other journals, e.g., *South-Carolina Gazette,* October 14, 1732.

2. That the Business of Printing has chiefly to do with Mens Opinions; most things that are printed tending to promote some, or oppose others.

3. That hence arises the peculiar Unhappiness of that Business, which other Callings are no way liable to; they who follow Printing being scarce able to do any thing in their way of getting a Living, which shall not probably give Offence to some, and perhaps to many;
. . .

5. Printers are educated in the Belief, that when Men differ in Opinion, both Sides ought equally to have the Advantage of being heard by the Publick; and that when Truth and Error have fair Play, the former is always an overmatch for the latter: Hence they chearfully serve all contending Writers that pay them well, without regarding on which side they are of the Question in Dispute. . . .

10. That notwithstanding what might be urg'd in behalf of a Man's being allow'd to do in the Way of his Business whatever he is paid for, yet Printers do continually discourage the Printing of great Numbers of bad things, and stifle them in the Birth. I my self have constantly refused to print anything that might countenance Vice, or promote Immorality; tho' by complying in such Cases with the corrupt Taste of the Majority I might have got much Money. . . .

To this shrewd and useful set of working principles should be added a reflection penned by Franklin in a private letter more than a half-century later.

It is a pleasing reflection, arising from the contemplation of our successful struggle, . . . that liberty, which some years since appeared in danger of extinction, is now regaining the ground she had lost, that arbitrary governments are likely to become more mild and reasonable, and to expire by degrees, giving place to more equitable forms; one of the effects this of the art of printing, which diffuses so general a light, augmenting with the growing day, and of so penetrating a nature, that all the window-shutters despotism and priestcraft can oppose to keep it out, prove insufficient.[47]

The old man at Passy was not so lucid as he had been in London or Philadelphia, but his faith in the power of truth and the influence of the printed word was as strong as ever. The most eminent

47. *Writings,* IX, 102.

exponent of freedom of speech and press in colonial America, Franklin went to his republican grave secure in the knowledge that he had done as much as any other man to advertise these great liberties to the American political consciousness.

ECONOMIC INDIVIDUALISM

Many Americans would argue that Franklin's reputation as a herald of democracy should rest in the first instance upon his solid contributions to the doctrine of economic individualism. Certainly no one, whether friend or foe of the American system, would deny that our political democracy is underpinned and conditioned by a well-defined set of economic principles and institutions. The American economic and political systems, like the American economic and political traditions, have always been inseparable, mutually nourishing elements of "the American way of life." American democracy has been, in the best and truest sense of the terms, *middle-class, bourgeois, free-enterprise* democracy. The twentieth-century trend toward governmental regulation and the welfare state has, if anything, sharpened our comprehension of this historical truth.

In the light of this truth Franklin's significance is unmistakable. As a self-made business success he represented to the world the rise to prominence of the American bourgeoisie; as an author and moralist he preached to "the middling people" the personal virtues that a nation of businessmen was to practice and cherish; as the best-known economist in colonial America he was a respected foe of mercantilism and advocate of the liberating principles of *laissez faire*.[48]

The first and second of these points may be considered together, for Franklin's moralizing was an unsolicited testimonial to his own "way to wealth." Father Abraham's formula for worldly success— *"Industry* and *Frugality"*—was a catalogue of virtues that Franklin

48. See generally L. J. Carey, *Franklin's Economic Views* (Garden City, N.Y., 1928); W. A. Wetzel, *Benjamin Franklin as an Economist* (Baltimore, 1895).

had not come by naturally. He had cultivated these qualities consciously in order to win financial independence, and he saw no reason why they could not be cultivated by other men in business. The way in which he preached these virtues is still worth noticing. The unique features of the American democratic culture owe a good deal to these words from *The Way to Wealth:*

It would be thought a hard Government that should tax its People one-tenth Part of their *Time,* to be employed in its Service. But *Idleness* taxes many of us much more, if we reckon all that is spent in absolute *Sloth,* or doing of nothing, with that which is spent in idle Employment or Amusements, that amount to nothing. *Sloth,* by bringing on Diseases, absolutely shortens Life. *Sloth, like Rust, consumes faster than Labour wears; while the used Key is always bright,* as *Poor Richard* says. *But dost thou love Life, then do not squander Time, for that's the stuff Life is made of,* as *Poor Richard* says. How much more than is necessary do we spend in sleep, forgetting that *The sleeping Fox catches no Poultry,* and that *There will be sleeping enough in the Grave,* as *Poor Richard* says.

If Time be of all Things the most precious, wasting Time must be, as *Poor Richard* says, *the greatest Prodigality;* since, as he elsewhere tells us, *Lost Time is never found again; and what we call Time enough, always proves little enough:* Let us then up and be doing, and doing to the Purpose; so by Diligence shall we do more with less Perplexity. *Sloth makes all Things difficult, but Industry all easy,* as *Poor Richard* says; and *He that riseth late must trot all Day, and shall scarce overtake his Business at Night;* while *Laziness travels so slowly, that Poverty soon overtakes him,* as we read in *Poor Richard,* who adds, *Drive thy Business, let not that drive thee;* and *Early to Bed, and early to rise, makes a Man healthy, wealthy, and wise.*

So what signifies *wishing* and *hoping* for better Times. We may make these Times better, if we bestir ourselves. *Industry need not wish,* as *Poor Richard* says, *and he that lives upon Hope will die fasting. There are no Gains without Pains; then Help Hands, for I have no Lands,* or if I have, they are smartly taxed. And, as *Poor Richard* likewise observes, *He that hath a Trade hath an Estate; and he that hath a Calling, hath an Office of Profit and Honour;* but then the *Trade* must be worked at, and the Calling well followed, or neither the *Estate* nor the *Office* will enable us to pay our Taxes. If we are industrious, we shall never starve; for as *Poor Richard* says, *At the working*

Man's House Hunger looks in, but dares not enter. Nor will the Bailiff or the Constable enter, for *Industry pays Debts, while Despair encreaseth them,* says *Poor Richard.* What though you have found no Treasure, nor has any rich Relation left you a Legacy, *Diligence is the Mother of Goodluck* as *Poor Richard* says *and God gives all Things to Industry.* Then *plough deep, while Sluggards sleep, and you shall have Corn to sell and to keep,* says *Poor Dick.* . . . 'Tis true there is much to be done, and perhaps you are weak-handed, but stick to it steadily; and you will see great Effects, for *Constant Dropping wears away Stones,* and by *Diligence and Patience the Mouse ate in two the Cable;* and *Little Strokes fell great Oaks,* as *Poor Richard* says in his Almanack, the Year I cannot just now remember.

Methinks I hear some of you say, *Must a Man afford himself no Leisure?* I will tell thee, my friend, what Poor Richard says, *Employ thy Time well, if thou meanest to gain Leisure; and, since thou art not sure of a Minute, throw not away an Hour.* Leisure, is Time for doing something useful; this Leisure the diligent Man will obtain, but the lazy Man never; so that, as *Poor Richard* says *A Life of Leisure and a Life of Laziness are two Things.* Do you imagine that Sloth will afford you more Comfort than Labour? No, for as *Poor Richard* says, *Trouble springs from Idleness, and grievous Toil from needless Ease. Many without Labour, would live by their Wits only, but they break for want of Stock.* Whereas Industry gives Comfort, and Plenty, and Respect: *Fly Pleasures, and they'll follow you. The diligent Spinner has a large Shift; and now I have a Sheep and a Cow, everyBody bids me good Morrow;* all which is well said by *Poor Richard.* . . .

So much for Industry, my Friends, and Attention to one's own Business; but to these we must add *Frugality,* if we would make our *Industry* more certainly successful. A Man may, if he knows not how to save as he gets, *keep his Nose all his Life to the Grindstone,* and die not worth a *Groat* at last. *A fat Kitchen makes a lean Will,* as *Poor Richard* says; and

> Many Estates are spent in the Getting,
> Since Women for Tea forsook Spinning and Knittıng,
> And Men for Punch forsook Hewing and Splitting.

If you would be wealthy, says he, in another Almanack, *think of Saving as well as of Getting: The Indies have not made Spain rich, because her Outgoes are greater than her Incomes.*

Away then with your expensive Follies, and you will not then have so much Cause to complain of hard Times, heavy Taxes, and charge-able Families; for, as *Poor Dick* says,

> Women and Wine, Game and Deceit,
> Make the Wealth small and the Wants great.

And farther, *What maintains one Vice, would bring up two Children.* You may think perhaps, that a *little* Tea, or a *little* Punch now and then, Diet a *little* more costly, Clothes a *little* finer, and a *little* Enter-tainment now and then, can be no *great* Matter; but remember what *Poor Richard* says, *Many a Little makes a Mickle;* and farther, Beware of little *Expences; A small Leak will sink a great Ship;* and again, *Who Dainties love, shall Beggars prove;* and moreover, *Fools make Feasts, and wise Men eat them.*[49]

Whether industry and frugality were qualities of Puritan origin —whether Franklin was, as many scholars have insisted,[50] a mid-dleman between Cotton Mather[51] and John D. Rockefeller—is a question of scant meaning for his status as prophet of American capitalism. The young Franklin could easily have read about the pleasant consequences of industry and frugality in several non-Calvinistic writers, or could have learned them from the Quaker merchants of Philadelphia.[52] Indeed, it is highly probable that this lesson, too, was learned pragmatically, out of his own experience. In any case, his unsophisticated, straightforward writings on the ingredients of business success—the prefaces to *Poor Richard, The Way to Wealth,* and after his death the priceless *Autobiogra-phy*—were translated and retranslated into a dozen languages, printed and reprinted in hundreds of editions, read and reread by millions of people, especially by millions of young and impression-able Americans. The influence of these few hundred pages has been matched by that of no other American book.

49. *Writings,* III, 409–413.
50. See especially the famous (and distorted) treatment of Franklin in Max Weber, *The Protestant Ethic and the Spirit of Capitalism* (London, 1930), pp. 48–51; A. W. Griswold, "Three Puritans on Prosperity," *New England Quarterly,* VII (1934), 475, 483–488.
51. Franklin's tribute to Mather is in *Writings,* IX, 208–209.
52. F. B. Tolles, "Benjamin Franklin's Business Mentors: The Philadel-phia Quaker Merchants," *William and Mary Quarterly,* 3rd Series, IV (1947), 60–69.

Industry and frugality can hardly be called political principles. Yet as the central elements in the American creed of economic individualism their influence upon our politics has been pronounced and lasting. The character of a nation cannot be other than the aggregate of the characters of its citizens, and the American democracy surely owes a healthy portion of its past and present character to the fact that many of its citizens have done their best to imitate the Franklin of the *Autobiography*. The frugal, industrious, self-reliant, community-minded businessman and farmer —the typical American—lives even today in the image of "Benjamin Franklin, printer." Carlyle was not too far from the truth when he looked at Franklin's portrait and exclaimed, "There is the father of all the Yankees."

The Puritan virtues, if we may call them that, do not add up to an especially pleasant and well-rounded personality. Franklin, however, never intended that they should stand alone, and such persons as D. H. Lawrence[53] have done the great bourgeois no honor in confusing his full-bodied character with that of the mythical Poor Richard. All that Franklin was trying to tell his fellow Americans in the prefaces to the almanacs was that first things must be attended to first: when a man had worked and saved his way to success and independence, he could then begin to live a fuller or even quite different life. This is what Franklin had in mind when he had Father Abraham declare, "Be *industrious* and *free;* be *frugal* and *free.*"[54] The expansion of America is evidence enough that as elements of a larger tradition, as facets of a whole personality, industry and frugality have given fiber alike to nation and individuals. The American mind stands fast in the belief that these virtues are indispensable props of freedom and independence, for as Father Abraham observed, "A Ploughman on his Legs is higher than a Gentleman on his Knees."

We must be extremely cautious in presenting Franklin as an early advocate of *laissez faire.* Like Jefferson and Lincoln he has been rudely appropriated and glibly quoted as the patron saint of

---

53. *Studies in Classic American Literature* (New York, 1923), pp. 13–31.
54. *Writings,* III, 417.

some of our most conservative movements and organizations. And like Jefferson and Lincoln he was a good deal more benevolent, progressive, and community-minded than those who now call him to judgment against all social legislation.

Franklin's most imposing service to the triumph of *laissez faire* was his attack on the restrictive doctrines of mercantilism. He was a colonial tradesman who resented the assignment of America to an inferior economic position. He was a friend of liberty who disliked the efforts of any exploiting group—whether proprietors, princes, priests, or English manufacturers—to prevent the mass of men from realizing their full capabilities and impulses toward freedom. Small wonder that he had no use for mercantilist policies. His central position in the controversy over Parliament's power to legislate for the colonies and his cordial relations with the French Physiocrats[55] strengthened his earlier, provincial convictions that free trade among all nations and colonies was the way to peace and economic prosperity,[56] and that mercantilism, like all unnecessary tampering with "the order of God and Nature," was unwise, unjust, unprofitable, and ultimately unworkable.[57] It is amusing, and highly instructive, to notice the very different thought processes by which Franklin and the Physiocrats arrived at identical conclusions about the unwisdom of government regulation of the economy and the beauties of free trade. The Physiocrats regarded free trade as part of their "natural order"—"that order which seemed obviously the best, not to any individual whomsoever, but to rational, cultured, liberal-minded men like the Physiocrats. It was not the product of the observation of external facts; it was the revelation of a principle within."[58] Nothing could have been far-

55. On "Franklin and the Physiocrats," see Carey, *Franklin's Economic Views,* Chap. 7. For evidence of Franklin's acceptance of most of their teachings, see *Writings,* V, 155–156, 200–202.

56. *Writings,* II, 313–314, 232–237; *Works,* II, 366.

57. See especially his letter to Richard Jackson, May 9, 1753, in Carl Van Doren, ed., *Letters and Papers of Benjamin Franklin and Richard Jackson* (Philadelphia, 1947), p. 34.

58. C. Gide and C. Rist, *A History of Economic Doctrines* (Boston, n.d.), p. 9.

ther removed from Franklin's pragmatic method of fixing his gaze upon effects and consequences.[59]

Perhaps the clearest evidence of Franklin's devotion to a free economy is to be found in a copy of George Whatley's *The Principles of Trade* in the Library of Congress. This antimercantilist tract was published in 1765 and was republished in 1774 with many new notes. The Library of Congress copy,[60] a second edition, bears this inscription on the flyleaf—"The gift of Doctr. B. Franklin to Th. Jefferson"—and this note on page two—"Notes marked B. F. are Doctr. Franklin's." Some of the most important notes in the book are marked "B. F." in Jefferson's hand, and there is little doubt that these were indeed Franklin's contributions to Whatley's new edition. Whatley spoke in his preface of "some very respectable Friends" who had indulged him "with their Ideas and Opinions."[61] The most significant of "B. F.'s" ideas was the note on pages thirty-three and thirty-four, a hard-packed essay containing at least four phrases found elsewhere in Franklin's writings. The spelling is Whatley's, but the words are Franklin's:

Perhaps, in general, it wou'd be beter if Government medled no farther wide Trade, than to protect it, and let it take its Cours. Most of the Statutes, or Acts, Edicts, Arets and Placaarts of Parliaments, Princes, and States, for regulating, directing, or restraining of Trade; have, we think, been either political Blunders, or Jobbs obtain'd by artful Men, for private Advantage, under Pretence of public Good. When Colbert asembled some wise old Merchants of France; and desir'd their Advice and Opinion, how he cou'd best serve and promote Comerce; their Answer, after Consultation, was, in three words only, *Laissez nous faire*. Let us alone. It is said, by a very solid Writer of

59. Examples of his wholly practical arguments against mercantilism may be found in Crane, *Letters to the Press,* pp. 94–99, 116–119, 180–181.

60. *Library of Congress Quarterly Journal of Current Acquisitions,* VIII (1950), 78.

61. Franklin has been given a little too much credit for the decline of mercantilism, for it is still assumed by many writers that he had significant face-to-face influence on Smith. The case for this thesis rests on extremely unreliable evidence. See particularly T. D. Eliot, "The Relations between Adam Smith and Benjamin Franklin," *Political Science Quarterly,* XXXIX (1924), 67–96.

the same Nation, that he is wel advanc'd in the Science of Politics, who knows the ful Force of that Maxim *Pas trop gouverner:* Not to govern too strictly, which, perhaps, wou'd be of more Use when aply'd to Trade, than in any other public Concern. It were therefore to be wish'd that Comerce were as fre between al the Nations of the World, as it is between the several Countrys of England.

In his own writings, too, Franklin was outspoken in his praise of the new principles of *laissez faire* that were shortly to be more scientifically demonstrated by Adam Smith and others.[62] He did as much as any American to dig the grave of mercantilism. In an age when liberalism was strongly and naturally opposed to governmental regulation of the economy, a passage such as this was a hard blow for freedom:

It seems contrary to the Nature of Commerce, for Government to interfere in the Prices of Commodities. Trade is a voluntary Thing between Buyer and Seller, in every Article of which each exercises his own Judgment, and is to please himself. . . . Where there are a number of different Traders, the separate desire of each to get more Custom will operate in bringing their goods down to a reasonable Price. It therefore seems to me, that Trade will best find and make its own Rates; and that Government cannot well interfere, unless it would take the whole Trade into its own hands . . . and manage it by its own Servants, at its own Risque.

Franklin's limitations as a *laissez-faire* economist should be clearly understood. In addition to the obvious and characteristic fact that he refused to draw together his scattered arguments against mercantilism into a balanced economic philosophy, there are several points that should be considered by modern economic individualists who insist upon invoking his illustrious shade: his strong, quite Jeffersonian agrarian bias ("Agriculture is the great Source of Wealth and Plenty"[63]); his community-minded views

62. *Writings,* IV, 469–470.
63. To Jonathan Shipley, September 13, 1775 (Yale Library). See also *Writings,* V, 202; IX, 245–246; X, 61, 121–122; Carey, *Franklin's Economic Views,* Chap. 8; C. R. Woodward, "Benjamin Franklin: Adventures in Agriculture," in *Meet Dr. Franklin,* pp. 179–200; E. D. Ross, "Benjamin Franklin

on the nature of private property;[64] his perception of the social evils of emergent industrialism ("Manufactures are founded in poverty"[65]); his vigorous opposition to government by plutocracy;[66] his consistent hostility to the erection of tariff barriers;[67] and his refusal to pursue the pound after 1748. Franklin was an economic individualist, not because he had any mystic faith in the utility of the profit motive or in the benefits of an industrial society, but because "individualism was synonymous with that personal independence which enabled a man to live virtuously."[68] Franklin could hardly have foreseen the great concentrations of wealth and economic power that were to signal the successes of American free enterprise, but we may rest assured that he would have found them poisonous to the simple, friendly, free, communal way of life he hoped his countrymen would cultivate and cherish. In any case, he did much to shape the economy that in turn has helped shape the American governmental system.

FEDERALISM

In most political theories or popular traditions federalism has been at best a convenient technique of constitutional organization; more often than not it has been passed over completely. In the United States of America it has been an article of faith. The Republic was founded upon the concept of limited government, and the existence of the states, semisovereign entities with lives and powers of their own, has always been considered the one trustworthy limit upon all urges toward centralized absolutism. The federal principle is something more fundamental and emotion-provoking than just one more check in a system of checks and balances.

---

as an Eighteenth-Century Agricultural Leader," *Journal of Political Economy*, XXXVII (1929), 52–72.

64. See Note 63.
65. *Writings*, IV, 49; see also VI, 13; VIII, 611.
66. *Ibid.*, X, 59.
67. *Ibid.*, VIII, 261; IX, 19, 63, 241, 614–615.
68. V. W. Crane, *Benjamin Franklin, Englishman and American* (Baltimore, 1936), p. 54.

Franklin made rich contributions to the theory and practice of American federalism. Almost alone among Americans of the mid-eighteenth-century he saw, as usual from a wholly practical point of view, the solid advantages that each colony would derive from a solemn union for certain well-defined purposes. He was far ahead of the men about him in abandoning provincialism for an inter-colonial attitude—too far, it would seem, for his efforts to speed up the slow development of American federalism ended in a magnificent but preordained failure.

Franklin tells the story of his great adventure in intercolonial diplomacy so frugally and honestly that it would be absurd to hear it from anyone but him:

In 1754 war with France being again apprehended, a congress of commissioners from the different Colonies was by an order of the Lords of Trade to be assembled at Albany, there to confer with the chiefs of the six nations concerning the means of defending both their country and ours. Governor Hamilton having received this order, acquainted the House with it, . . . naming the Speaker (Mr. Norris) and myself to join Mr. Thomas Penn and Mr. Secretary Peters as commissioners to act for Pennsylvania. . . . we met the other commissioners at Albany about the middle of June. In our way thither, I projected and drew up a plan for the union of all the Colonies under one government, so far as might be necessary for defence and other important general purposes. . . . I ventured to lay it before the Congress. It then appeared that several of the commissioners had formed plans of the same kind. A previous question was first taken whether a union should be established, which passed in the affirmative unanimously. A committee was then appointed, one member from each colony, to consider the several plans and report. Mine happened to be preferred, and with a few amendments was accordingly reported. By this plan the general government was to be administered by a president-general appointed and supported by the Crown and a grand council to be chosen by the representatives of the people of the several Colonies met in their respective Assemblies. The debates upon it in Congress went on daily hand in hand with the Indian business. Many objections and difficulties were started, but at length they were all overcome, and the plan was unanimously agreed to, and copies ordered to be transmitted to the Board of Trade and to the Assemblies of the several provinces. Its fate was singular. The Assemblies did not adopt it, as they all thought there was too much *prerogative* in it; and in England it was judged to have too much of the *democratic*. The Board of Trade therefore did not approve of it; nor recommend it for the approbation of His Majesty; . . .[69]

The powers of the president-general and grand council were sharply limited by the purpose of the proposed union—defense of the frontier. They were directed to four specific problems: Indian treaties "in which the general interest of the colonies may be concerned"; war and peace with the Indians; purchases and settlement of western lands; and regulation of Indian trade. To these ends the union was further authorized to "raise and pay soldiers," "build forts," and "equip vessels," as well as to "make laws, and lay and levy such general duties, imposts, or taxes, as to them shall appear most equal and just." Representation on the council was to be proportioned to each colony's contributions to the common treasury, and the council was protected against dissolution or prorogation by the president-general.[70] Finally, the interests of the mother country were secured by subjecting all laws to the scrutiny and possible veto of the king-in-council.

The Albany Plan was not so much the creation of one man's lively genius as the product of several fine minds working toward a long-contemplated goal, with all arrangements conditioned sharply by the fear of offending a shortsighted Crown and stubborn colonies. Yet it was Franklin's plan that was preferred to all others and was adopted by the commissioners with very few changes. If he did not have a well-developed understanding of the federal principle, he did recognize the advantages and delicacies of confederation-for-defense. The Albany Plan is a landmark on the

69. *Autobiography*, pp. 159–160. See also his three letters of 1754 to Governor Shirley, *Writings*, III, 231–241. These were reprinted in the *Pennsylvania Chronicle*, January 16, 1769.

70. For the documents of the Albany Plan, see *Writings*, III, 197–227, 231–241. See generally Mrs. L. K. Mathews, "Benjamin Franklin's Plans for a Colonial Union, 1750–1775," *American Political Science Review*, VIII (1914), 393–412.

rough road that was to lead through the first Continental Congresses and the Articles of Confederation to the Constitution of 1787. It was a notable expression of Franklin's dominant faith in cooperative effort in a common cause. He never ceased believing that in this matter at least he was right and other men wrong.

I am still of opinion it would have been happy for both sides the water if it had been adopted. The Colonies so united would have been sufficiently strong to have defended themselves; there would then have been no need of troops from England; of course the subsequent pretence for taxing America and the bloody contest it occasioned would have been avoided. But such mistakes are not new; history is full of the errors of states and princes.[71]

In June, 1775, as delegate to the Second Continental Congress, Franklin proposed a plan, "Articles of Confederation and Perpetual Union" for the "United Colonies of North America,"[72] which was based on his Albany Plan and several other instances of federation in colonial experience. The Congress was not ready for any such radical step, but again Franklin had pointed the way for other men to follow. In the crucial matter of representation Franklin, a "large-state" man with no shred of provincial prejudice, was strongly opposed to the Articles of Confederation eventually adopted. Representation in his proposed Congress was to be proportioned to population.[73] He was not entirely satisfied with the solution adopted by the Convention of 1787, but he was strong in his final faith in federal union.

Although somewhat outside the scope of this article, Franklin's opinions on the questions of imperial federation and the power of Parliament to legislate for the colonies deserve brief mention. He was a perfect representative of the process of trial and error, of backing and filling, through which the leading colonials were moving toward the "dominion theory" finally implied in the Declaration of Independence. Having passed and repassed through the intermediate stages—acknowledgment of Parliament's power to

71. *Autobiography*, p. 161.
72. *Writings*, VI, 420–425.
73. Franklin Papers (American Philosophical Society), L, i, 35.

legislate for the colonies,[74] advocacy of colonial representation in Parliament (an old favorite of Franklin's),[75] assertion of the fine-spun distinction between internal and external taxation,[76] simultaneous and confusing assertion of the distinction between taxation for revenue and taxation for regulation of commerce[77]—Franklin took final refuge in the useful conclusion that the colonies, as equals of the mother country, were united to her only "by having one common sovereign, the King."[78] Under this interpretation of the colonial system, the achievement of independence, at least on paper, involved nothing more than renouncing allegiance to a tyrannical king.[79]

AUTHENTIC DEMOCRACY

One final observation must be made and supported before we can close the circle of Franklin's political philosophy: in thought, action, and argument he was a warmhearted democrat, in the best and fullest sense of the word. Origin, temperament, environment, and experience all helped to produce the leading democrat of the age. The last of these, experience, was especially instrumental. The delightful fact that Franklin, as he saw more and more of the way the world did its business, grew more and more sour on the sup-

74. *Writings,* III, 207. The "rights of Englishmen" would limit this power in the colonies as in England. *Ibid.,* III, 232–241.

75. *Ibid.,* III, 238–241; Crane, *Letters to the Press,* pp. 59, 59 n., 72, 129 n.; Franklin's *Good Humour,* p. 22.

76. *Writings,* IV, 424; Crane, *Letters to the Press,* pp. 53–54.

77. *Writings,* IV, 421, 428; Crane, *Letters to the Press,* pp. 201–203; Franklin's *Good Humour,* p. 20; Franklin's *Claim of the Colonies,* p. 8; Franklin's *Wheelock,* pp. 26, 29, 44, 48–50; Franklin's *Ramsay,* p. 62.

78. *Writings,* V, 260; see also IV, 445–446; V, 114–115, 280; VI, 260–261; Crane, *Letters to the Press,* pp. 46–49, 110–112, 134–138. See generally C. F. Mullett, *Colonial Claims to Home Rule* (Columbia, Mo., 1927); Carl Becker, *The Declaration of Independence* (New York, 1922), Chap. 3; C. H. McIlwain, *The American Revolution: A Constitutional Interpretation* (New York, 1924). For Franklin's conversion, see V. W. Crane, "Benjamin Franklin and the Stamp Act," Colonial Society of Massachusetts, *Publications,* XXXII, 56–77, and *Benjamin Franklin: Englishman and American,* pp. 72–139.

79. For an unguarded version of Franklin's mature opinion of the power of Parliament, see his *Claim of the Colonies,* pp. 5–13.

posed merits of monarchy and aristocracy leads us to believe that his democracy, too, was of pragmatic origin. Whatever the explanation, there is convincing proof of his ever-growing respect for the capacity of ordinary men to govern themselves. His faith in the judgment of the people was not completely uncritical, but it was a faith on which he was willing to act.[80]

One example was the manner in which Franklin refused to abandon the tenets of radical Whiggery, but rather refined and republicanized them into a profoundly democratic system of constitutional principles. Franklin was one of the few old revolutionaries at the Convention of 1787 who did not embrace the new faith in the separation of powers. He signed the document willingly, believing that it was the best obtainable under the circumstances, and hoping that it would not frustrate the natural course of democratic progress. Yet he would have preferred a constitution with these radically different arrangements: a plural executive, unsalaried and probably elected by the legislature; a unicameral legislature, with representation proportioned to population; annual elections for all holders of public office, including officers of the militia; universal manhood suffrage, with no bow to property;[81] a straightforward, unqualified bill of rights; and an easy method of formal amendment.[82]

Since he practiced what he preached and "doubted a little of his own infallibility," he did not find it necessary to withdraw from the convention. Yet his constitutional notions make clear that he was very much in sympathy with the radical opposition to the Consti-

80. *Writings*, V, 134; VIII, 451–452; IX, 330, 638; X, 7; Farrand, *Records of the Federal Convention*, II, 204–205, 249.

81. Franklin characterized the "forty-shilling freehold" act as "an infamous Breach of Trust & Violation of the Rights of the Freeholders." Franklin's Ramsay, pp. 42–45.

82. Evidence of these principles is to be found in *Writings*, III, 197–227, 307–320; VI, 420–425; IX, 169–170, 590–604, 674; X, 54–60, 501–502. See also Farrand, *Records of the Federal Convention*, I, 47, 48, 54, 61, 77–78, 81–85, 98–99, 103, 106, 197–200, 216, 427, 450–452, 488–489; II, 65, 120, 204, 208; M. R. Eiselen, *Franklin's Political Theories* (Garden City, N.Y., 1928), Chaps. 8–12. The Pennsylvania Constitution of 1776 was more to Franklin's liking. See J. P. Selsam, *The Pennsylvania Constitution of 1776* (Philadelphia, 1936).

tution. The one point at which he departed from their doctrine may well have been decisive: having abandoned the provincial attitude before most of the anti-Federalists were born, Franklin had little sympathy for their antinational point of view. The old imperialist had great faith in the advantages of a "general government." He hoped out loud that each member of the proposed Congress would "consider himself rather as a Representative of the whole, than as an Agent for the Interests of a particular State."[83] And he even supported a motion that "the national legislature ought to be empowered to negative all laws, passed by the several States, contravening, in the opinion of the national legislature, the articles of union . . . or any Treaties subsisting under the authority of the union."[84] Franklin's final political faith was as "national" as it was "democratical." He was one of the few men in America unafraid to use both of these adjectives in public.

Another example of Franklin's progress toward an ever-purer democratic faith was his change in attitude on the question of Negro slavery. Although the Junto had taken an early stand against slavery, the organizer of the Junto was not above dealing in "likely young Negroes" as a sideline. In time he came to see the monstrous injustice of the thing, and gave full backing to several organizations devoted to freeing and educating the Negro slave. His last public act was performed as President of the Pennsylvania Society for Promoting the Abolition of Slavery, when he signed a memorial to the House of Representatives calling for measures to discourage the slave trade. His last public writing was a letter to the *Federal Gazette* satirizing the arguments of a Georgia Congressman in defense of this traffic.[85] By the time of his death he had expressed all the fundamental economic and ethical arguments against slavery, as-

83. *Writings,* IX, 596.
84. Farrand, *Records of the Federal Convention,* I, 47. The last phrase was his own contribution.
85. *Writings,* X, 86–91; also 66–68, 127–129. See generally V. W. Crane, "Benjamin Franklin on Slavery and American Liberties," *The Pennsylvania Magazine of History and Biography,* LXII (1938), 1–11; R. I. Shelling, "Benjamin Franklin and the Dr. Bray Associates," *ibid.,* LXIII (1939), 282–293; A. S. Pitt, "Franklin and the Quaker Movement against Slavery," Friends Historical Association *Bulletin,* XXXII (1943), 13–31; Carey, *Franklin's Economic Views,* Chap. 4.

serting in particular that it was unjust, unnatural, and inhuman, and a corrupting menace to free institutions and love of liberty.

Finally, Franklin was firmly in the popular ranks in his sanguine opinion of the nature of political parties. He did not consider them "factions," but natural products of free government, ventilators of public issues, and effective instruments of the popular will. In *The Internal State of America,* an undated but late sociological musing, Franklin had these characteristic words to say on a problem that gave some of the framers sleepless nights:

It is true that in some of our States there are Parties and Discords; but let us look back, and ask if we were ever without them? Such will exist wherever there is Liberty; and perhaps they help to preserve it. By the Collision of different Sentiments, Sparks of Truth are struck out, and political Light is obtained. The different Factions, which at present divide us, aim all at the Publick Good; the Differences are only about the various Modes of promoting it. Things, Actions, Measures and Objects of all kinds, present themselves to the Minds of Men in such a Variety of Lights, that it is not possible we should all think alike at the same time on every Subject, when hardly the same Man retains at all times the same Ideas of it. Parties are therefore the common Lot of Humanity; and ours are by no means more mischievous or less beneficial than those of other Countries, Nations and Ages, enjoying in the same Degree the great Blessing of Political Liberty.[86]

These are the thoughts of a wise, kindly, democratic old man who looked upon cooperation-through-organization as the motive power of free society.

Conclusions are dangerous, especially when they deal with great men, even more so when the great man in question has already been rounded off by Becker and Van Doren.[87] This conclusion

86. Franklin Papers (Library of Congress), X, 2263–2264; *Writings,* X, 120–121. For earlier judgments, see *Writings,* II, 110, 232, 233, 295; III, 319–320.

87. See Becker, *Franklin,* pp. 31–37; Van Doren, *Franklin,* pp. 260–262, 781–782, *Meet Dr. Franklin,* pp. 1–10, 221–234, and his review of Becker in *William and Mary Quarterly,* 3rd Series, IV (1947), 231–234. An old evaluation of Franklin that has stood up well is Theodore Parker, *Historic Americans* (Boston, 1908), pp. 1–40.

will therefore be narrow and apposite. Skirting any evaluation of Franklin's complete character and accomplishments, omitting any further mention of his influence on the American tradition, it will confine itself rigidly to one date and place—February 13, 1766, in the British House of Commons—and one question: What political faith did Franklin express and represent as he stood before the members and answered their questions about British North America?[88]

First, he represented a pattern of popular political thought, ancient in origin, but new in sweep. The more perceptive gentlemen, among them Franklin's well-wishers, could look behind his spare phrases and see the mind of a whole continent in political ferment. Here before them was visible evidence that the people of the colonies were thinking in terms, not only of the constitutional rights of Englishmen, but of the natural rights of all men. Whiggery, under several names and guises, had swept America, and the ultimate Whig was now at the bar. It must have been an unsettling experience for some of the members to hear the blessed words "unjust," "unconstitutional," "liberties," "privileges," and "common consent" drop from the lips of this middling person.

Second, Franklin represented new habits of thinking about political and social problems. However legalistic and theoretical were most of the arguments out of Boston and Philadelphia, his brand of persuasion was more typical of the average colonial mind. Franklin's method was an informed, hardheaded appeal to facts. "The *Fact* seems sufficient for our Purpose, and the *Fact* is notorious." His case for the repeal of the Stamp Act could be compressed in the warning, "It doesn't work; it never will." America's favorite argument was seeing its first heavy duty.

He likewise represented the incipient fact of American federalism. Himself a uniquely *American* official—"I am Deputy Postmaster-General of North-America"—he breathed the Continental spirit that was soon to power the final drive toward independence. He could tell the House that "every assembly on the continent,

88. This great "examination" is in *Writings*, IV, 412–448. It was widely reprinted in the colonial press.

and every member in every assembly" had denied Parliament's authority to pass the Stamp Act. From this day forward, throughout the next nine years, Franklin was unofficial ambassador for all the colonies. The American Union was hastening to be born, and the sign of union was Dr. Franklin.

Next, Franklin represented the growing American conviction that the colonies were marked for a future state of "glory and honor" that would dwarf that of the mother country. As early as 1752 Poor Richard had echoed the widespread belief that America was a God-ordained haven for the oppressed of every land:

> Where the sick Stranger joys to find a Home,
> Where casual Ill, maim'd Labour, freely come;
> Those worn with Age, Infirmity or Care,
> Find Rest, Relief, and Health returning fair.
> There too the Walls of rising Schools ascend,
> For Publick Spirit still is Learning's Friend,
> Where Science, Virtue, sown with liberal Hand,
> In future Patriots shall inspire the Land.

God's plans for America were even more challenging than that:

I have long been of opinion, that *the foundations of the future grandeur and stability of the British empire lie in America;* and though, like other foundations, they are low and little now, they are, nevertheless, broad and strong enough to support the greatest political structure that human wisdom ever yet erected.[89]

A different sort of empire, cast loose from the mother country, was to rise on this foundation and to satisfy the prophecies of destiny that Franklin had pronounced.

Finally, and most important, Franklin stood before Commons and the world as the representative colonial. This person who knew so much more about America than anyone else, who talked of rights and resistance so confidently, this was no Belcher or Hutchinson, no placeman or royal governor, but a new breed of man to be heard in such high places. Although Franklin was ac-

89. Franklin to Lord Kames, January 3, 1760, *Works,* VII, 188.

tually the most extraordinary man of the century, on that memorable day he was the true colonial—self-contained, plain-spoken, neither arrogant nor humble, the visible expression of the new way of life and liberty that was to occupy the continent. And as men looked in wonder at him and America, so he and America looked in disbelief at England. The eyes of the colonists seemed open for the first time to the corruption and self-interest that cankered and degraded all British politics. The New World was at last face to face with the Old, and about to reject it for something more wholesome. The Old World would realize too late that Franklin spoke for a multitude even then turning away to a faith of its own when he said of the British nation, "It knows and feels itself so universally corrupt and rotten from Head to Foot, that it has little Confidence in any publick Men or publick Measures."[90]

Now that these things have been written, now that Franklin has surrendered his identity to colonial democracy, perhaps it would be proper to rescue him and end this article with our attention fixed on him alone. He was, after all, Dr. Benjamin Franklin, the most amazing man America has produced, as untypical in the whole as he was typical in his parts. And in fixing our attention we must recall the one conviction that brought harmony to this human multitude: the love of liberty—in every land, in every time, and for every man.

God grant, that not only the Love of Liberty, but a thorough Knowledge of the Rights of Man, may pervade all the Nations of the Earth, so that a Philosopher may set his Foot anywhere on its Surface, and say, "This is my Country."[91]

This was Franklin's political faith.

90. To Galloway, February 17, 1758, March 13, 1768, and April 20, 1771 (Yale Library).
91. To David Hartley, December 4, 1789, *Writings,* X, 72.

GERALD STOURZH

✪

Reason and Power in Benjamin Franklin's Political Thought

Perhaps no period of modern history has been more a victim of generalization than the Age of Enlightenment. The worship of reason and progress and belief in the essential goodness and perfectibility of human nature are most commonly associated with the eighteenth-century climate of opinion. Many of the stereotypes which have been applied to it have automatically been transferred to Benjamin Franklin. Already to contemporaries of his old age, Franklin seemed the very personification of the Age of Reason. Condorcet, who had known Franklin personally, summed up his description of Franklin's political career as follows: "In a word, his politics were those of a man who believed in the power of reason and the reality of virtue."[1] In Germany, an admirer was even more enthusiastic: "Reason and virtue, made possible through reason alone, consequently again reason and nothing but reason, is the magic with which Benjamin Franklin conquered heaven and earth."[2] This is also the judgment of posterity. F. L. Mott and

From Gerald Stourzh, "Reason and Power in Benjamin Franklin's Political Thought," *The American Political Science Review,* Vol. XLVII (1953), pp. 1092–1115.

1. A. Condorcet O'Connor and M. F. Arago, eds., *Oeuvres du Marquis de Condorcet,* 2nd ed., 12 vols. (Paris, 1847–1849), III, 420.

2. Georg Forster, "Erinnerungen aus dem Jahre 1790," in "Kleine Schriften," *Georg Forsters saemmtliche Schriften,* ed. by his daughter, 9 vols. (Leipzig, 1843), VI, 207.

Chester E. Jorgenson, who have so far presented the most acute analysis of Franklin's thought and its relationship to the intellectual history of his time, do not hesitate to call him "the completest colonial representative" of the Age of Enlightenment.[3] Unanimous agreement seems to exist that Franklin was "in tune with his time."[4]

This essay will attempt to show that these generalizations, instead of illuminating the essence of Franklin's moral and political philosophy, tend rather to obscure some of the mainsprings of his thought and action. Our investigation rests upon the assumption that man's understanding of politics is inseparable from his conception of human nature. Consequently, this reappraisal of Franklin's political thought will subject his views on human nature to close scrutiny; it is hoped that this procedure may lead to a rejection of some of the clichés to which he has fallen victim.

THE "GREAT CHAIN OF BEING"

Many of the notions which are commonly applied to the eighteenth century, such as the belief in progress and in the perfectibility of human nature, are significant chiefly with respect to the currents of thought and action related to the American and French revolutions, and do little to deepen our understanding of earlier developments. So it is to the first half of the eighteenth century that we must now turn. We are prone to overlook the extraordinary difference in age which separated Franklin from the other Founding Fathers of the Republic. Franklin was born in 1706, twenty-six years before Washington, twenty-nine years before John Adams, thirty-

3. F. L. Mott and Chester E. Jorgenson, eds., *Benjamin Franklin, Representative Selections with Introduction, Bibliography, and Notes* (New York, 1936), p. xiii.

4. Carl Becker, review of the Franklin Institute's *Meet Dr. Franklin*, in *American Historical Review*, L (October 1944), 142. Cf. Henry Steele Commager's statement that it was the faith in reason which gave unity to Franklin's life, in "Franklin, the American," review of Carl Van Doren's *Benjamin Franklin*, in *The New York Times Book Review*, October 9, 1938, p. 1. Charles A. Beard explicitly referred to Franklin as an outstanding example of American writers on progress in his introduction to J. B. Bury, *The Idea of Progress* (New York, 1932), p. xxxvii.

seven years before Jefferson, thirty-nine years before John Jay, forty-five years before James Madison, and fifty-one years before Alexander Hamilton.

Franklin's fame as a social and natural philosopher rests mainly on the achievements of his middle and late years. One needs to remember, however, that he was a moral philosopher long before he became a natural philosopher and before he advised his fellow men how to acquire wealth.[5] At the age of twenty-two, he formed a "club for mutual improvement,"[6] the Junto, where great emphasis was laid on moral or political problems. Whether self-interest was the root of human action, whether man could attain perfection, whether "encroachments on the just liberties of the people"[7] had taken place—all these things were matters of discussion at Franklin's club. Already at the age of nineteen, during his first stay in London, he had printed his first independent opus, *A Dissertation on Liberty and Necessity, Pleasure and Pain*.[8] This piece showed

5. Even after having achieved world-wide fame as a natural philosopher, he observed that we deserve reprehension if "we neglect the Knowledge and Practice of essential Duties" in order to attain eminence in the knowledge of nature. A. H. Smyth, ed., *The Writings of Benjamin Franklin*, 10 vols. (New York, 1905–1907), IV, 22.

6. *Autobiography, Writings*, I, 22.

7. James Parton, *Life and Times of Benjamin Franklin*, 2nd ed., 2 vols. (Boston, 1897), I, 160. See also *Writings*, II, 89. The authors who so far have most closely scrutinized Franklin's political thought do not see the relevance of many of the younger Franklin's remarks on human nature, arbitrary government, or the nature of political dispute to his concept of politics. See M. R. Eiselen, *Franklin's Political Theories* (Garden City, N.Y., 1928), p. 13; R. D. Miles, "The Political Philosophy of Benjamin Franklin" (unpublished dissertation, University of Michigan, 1949), p. 36; Mott and Jorgenson, p. lxxxii. The most recent work in this field, Clinton Rossiter's "The Political Theory of Benjamin Franklin," *Pennsylvania Magazine of History and Biography*, LXXVI (July 1952), 259–293, pays no attention to Franklin's conception of human nature and his attitude towards the problem of power and the ends of political life. Rossiter's contention (p. 268) is that Franklin "limited his own thought process to the one devastating question: *Does it work?, or more exactly, Does it work well?"* Franklin, however, like everybody else, had certain ends and goals in view, and the question "Does it work?" is meaningless without the context of certain basic desiderata.

8. This little work has been omitted in the Smyth edition of Franklin's writings, because "the work has no value, and it would be an injury and an

that no trace was left of his Presbyterian family background. The secularization of his thought had been completed.[9] Gone were the Puritan belief in revelation and the Christian conception of human nature which, paradoxically, included the notion of the depravity of man, as well as of his uniqueness among all created beings.[10] Franklin's *Dissertation* shows that he was thoroughly acquainted with the leading ideas of his time. The early decades of the eighteenth century were characterized by the climate of opinion which has been aptly called "cosmic Toryism."[11] Pope's *Essay on Man*

offence to the memory of Franklin to republish it." *Writings*, II, vi. It is, however, reprinted as an appendix to Parton, Vol. I, and has since been republished independently with a bibliographical note by Lawrence C. Wroth (New York, 1930).

9. See Herbert Schneider, "The Significance of Benjamin Franklin's Moral Philosophy," *Columbia University Studies in the History of Ideas*, II (1918), 298.

10. In his *Autobiography*, Franklin acknowledges his debt to Shaftesbury and Collins for becoming "a real doubter in many points of our religious doctrine." *Writings*, I, 244. The question of Franklin's attitude toward the great moral philosophers and of their influence upon him is considerably more difficult to determine than the same question with regard to John Adams or Thomas Jefferson. With the exception of authors named in the *Autobiography*, comments on books Franklin read are extremely rare. His library has not been preserved; there is, however, a list of books known to have been in Franklin's library at the time of his death (compiled by Dr. George Simpson Eddy in Princeton University; photostat in the library of the American Philosophical Society in Philadelphia). See also Mr. Eddy's article "Dr. Benjamin Franklin's Library," *Proceedings of the American Antiquarian Society*, New Series, XXXIV (October 1924), 206–226. Except for comments in some English pamphlets, there exist nothing like the voluminous marginal notes of John Adams and Jefferson. Also he was not able to keep up a correspondence like Adams' or Jefferson's, discussing great problems from the perspective of a long life in retirement after the great events of their lives had taken place. Immersed in public business almost until his death, Franklin does not seem to have had much time left over for reading. Benjamin Rush told John Adams that "Dr. Franklin thought a great deal, wrote occasionally, but read during the middle and later years of his life very little." October 31, 1807, in Benjamin Rush, *The Letters of Benjamin Rush*, L. H. Butterfield, ed., 2 vols. (Princeton, 1951), II, 953. For a compilation of the authors with whom Franklin was acquainted, see Lois Margaret MacLaurin, *Franklin's Vocabulary* (Garden City, N.Y., 1928), Chap. 1, and Mott and Jorgenson, p. lv.

11. Basil Willey, *The Eighteenth Century Background* (London, 1940), Chap. 3, *passim*.

and many pages of Addison's *Spectator*—both of which Franklin admired—most perfectly set forth the creed of a new age. Overshadowing everything else, there was joy about the discoveries of the human mind, which had solved the enigma of creation:

> Nature and Nature's Laws lay hid in Night:
> GOD said, *Let Newton be!* and all was Light.[12]

The perfection of that Great Machine, the Newtonian universe, filling humanity with admiration for the Divine Watchmaker, seemed to suggest that this world was indeed the best of all possible worlds. Everything was necessary, was good. Pope's "Whatever is, is right" is the key phrase of this period. The goodness of the Creator revealed itself in His giving existence to all possible creatures. The universe "presented the spectacle of a continuous scale or ladder of creatures, extending without a break from the worm to the seraph."[13] Somewhere in this "Great Chain of Being," to use a favorite phrase of the period,[14] there must be a place for man. Man, as it were, formed the "middle link" between lower and higher creatures. No wonder, then, that Franklin chose as a motto for his *Dissertation* the following lines of Dryden:

> Whatever is, is in its Causes just,
> Since all Things are by Fate; but purblind Man
> Sees but a part o' th' Chain, the nearest Link,
> His Eyes not carrying to the equal Beam
> That poises all above.[15]

12. Pope's epitaph intended for Newton's tomb.

13. Willey, pp. 47–48.

14. See A. O. Lovejoy, *The Great Chain of Being* (Cambridge, Mass., 1936). This brilliant analysis of that complex of ideas has been applied to Franklin only once, although it offers important clues for an understanding of Franklin's conception of human nature. Arthur Stuart Pitt in "The Sources, Significance, and Date of Franklin's 'An Arabian Tale,' " *Publications of the Modern Language Association,* LVII (March 1942), 155–168, applies Lovejoy's analysis to one piece of Franklin's and does not refer to relevant writings of Franklin's youth in which this idea may also be found. Pitt's article is valuable in pointing out the sources from which Franklin could have accepted the idea directly, namely Locke, Milton, Addison, and Pope.

15. Parton, I, 605.

The consequences of the conception of the universe as a Great Chain of Being for Franklin's understanding of human nature are highly significant. To be sure, man had liberated himself from the oppression of Original Sin, and in his newly established innocence he hailed the Creator and praised the Creation. But if the depravity of human nature had been banished, so had man's striving for redemption, man's aspiration for perfection. There was nothing left which ought to be redeemed. Indeed, in the new rational order of the universe, it would not seem proper to long for a higher place in the hierarchy of beings. Man's release from the anguish of Original Sin was accompanied by a lowering of the goals of human life. "The imperfection of man is indispensable to the fullness of the hierarchy of being." Man had, so to speak, already attained the grade of perfection which belonged to his station. From the point of view of mortality, then, what this amounted to was a "counsel of imperfection—an ethics of prudent mediocrity."[16]

Quiet contentment with, and enjoyment of, one's place in the Great Chain of Being must have been a comforting creed for the wealthy and educated classes of the Augustan age:

> Order is Heav'n's first law; and this confest,
> Some are, and must be, greater than the rest,
> More rich, more wise.[17]

This was not the optimism of progress, which we usually associate with the eighteenth century. It was an optimism of acceptance;[18] for the rich and complacent, the real and the good, seemed indeed to coincide.

Not so for Benjamin Franklin. Late in his life, in 1771, he referred to "the poverty and obscurity in which I was born and bred." His innate desire for justice and equality, his keen awareness of existing conditions of injustice and inequality, finally his own experience of things which he could not possibly call just or good—

16. Lovejoy, pp. 199, 200.
17. Alexander Pope, "An Essay on Man," Epistle 4, in *Selected Works,* Modern Library ed. (New York, 1948), p. 127.
18. Willey, p. 56.

for instance, he tells us that his brother's "harsh and tyrannical treatment of me might be a means of impressing me with that aversion to arbitrary power that has stuck to me through my whole life"[19]—all this contravened the facile optimism of the Augustan age.

Franklin, indeed, accepted the cosmological premises of his age (as witness the above-quoted motto of the *Dissertation*). But his conclusions make the edifice of "cosmic Toryism"—so imposing in Pope's magnificent language—appear a mockery and an absurdity. Franklin's argumentation was simple enough: God being all-powerful and good, man could have no free will, and the distinction between good and evil had to be abolished. He also argued that pain or uneasiness was the mainspring of all our actions, and that pleasure was produced by the removal of this uneasiness. It followed that *"No State of Life can be happier than the present, because Pleasure and Pain are inseparable."* The unintentional irony of this brand of optimism cannot be better expressed than in young Franklin's conclusion:

I am sensible that the Doctrine here advanc'd, if it were to be publish'd, would meet with but an indifferent Reception. Mankind naturally and generally love to be flatter'd: Whatever sooths our Pride, and tends to exalt our Species above the rest of the Creation, we are pleas'd with and easily believe, when ungrateful Truths shall be with the utmost Indignation rejected. "What! bring ourselves down to an Equality with the Beasts of the Field! With the *meanest* part of the Creation! 'Tis insufferable!" But, (to use a Piece of *common* Sense) our *Geese* are but *Geese* tho' we may think 'em *Swans;* and Truth will be Truth tho' it sometimes prove mortifying and distasteful.[20]

The dilemma which confronted him at the age of nineteen is characteristic of most eighteenth-century philosophy: "If nature is good, then there is no evil in the world; if there is evil in the world, then nature so far is not good."[21]

19. *Autobiography, Writings,* I, 226, 247 n.
20. Parton, I, 617.
21. Carl Becker, *The Heavenly City of the Eighteenth Century Philosophers* (New Haven, 1932), p. 69.

Franklin cut this Gordian knot by sacrificing "Reason" to "Experience." He turned away from metaphysics for the quite pragmatic reason that his denial of good and evil did not provide him with a basis for the attainment of social and individual happiness:

> Revelation had indeed no weight with me, as such; but I entertain'd an opinion that, though certain actions might not be bad *because* they were forbidden by it, or good *because* it commanded them, yet probably these actions might be forbidden *because* they were bad for us, or commanded *because* they were beneficial to us. . . .[22]

To achieve useful things rather than indulge in doubtful metaphysical speculations, to become a doer of good—these, then, became the principal aims of Franklin's thought and action.[23]

This fundamental change from the earlier to the later Enlightenment—from passive contemplation to improvement, from a static to a dynamic conception of human affairs—did contribute to the substitution of the idea of human perfectibility for the idea of human perfection—a very limited kind of perfection, as we have seen; but it was by no means sufficient to bring about the faith in the perfectibility of human nature. Something else was needed: proof that "social evils were due neither to innate and incorrigible disabilities of the human being nor the nature of things, but simply to ignorance and prejudices."[24] The associationist psychology, elaborating Locke's theory of the malleability of human nature, provided the basis for the expansion of the idea of progress and perfectibility from the purely intellectual domain into the realm of moral and social life in general. The Age of Reason, then, presents us with a more perplexing picture than we might have supposed.

Reason, after all, may mean three different things: reason as a faculty of man; reason as a quality of the universe; and reason as a temper in the conduct of human affairs.[25] We might venture the

22. *Autobiography, Writings,* I, 296. See also *Writings,* VII, 412.
23. See *Writings,* I, 341; II, 215; III, 145; IX, 208; X, 38.
24. Bury, p. 128.
25. This distinction is Roland Bainton's. See his "The Appeal to Reason and the American Revolution," in Conyers Read, ed., *The Constitution Reconsidered* (New York, 1938), p. 121.

generalization that the earlier Enlightenment stressed reason as the quality of the Newtonian universe, whereas the later Enlightenment, in spite of important exceptions, exalted the power of human reason to mold the moral and social life of mankind.[26] Franklin's "reason," as we shall see presently, is above all a temper in the conduct of human affairs.

This discussion is important for a correct understanding of Franklin's position in the center of the crosscurrents of the Age of Enlightenment. The fact that the roots of his thought are to be found in the early Enlightenment is not always realized, or, if realized, not always sufficiently explained. Julian P. Boyd, in his introduction to Carl Becker's biographical sketch of Franklin, states that Franklin and Jefferson believed "that men would be amenable to rational persuasion, that they would thereby be induced to promote their own and their fellows' best interests, and that, in the end, perfect felicity for man and society would be achieved."[27] These ideas are certainly suggestive of the later Enlightenment, and appear to be more applicable to Jefferson than to Franklin. Carl Becker himself asserts, somewhat ambiguously and with undue generalization, that Franklin "was a true child of the Enlightenment, not indeed of the school of Rousseau, but of Defoe and Pope and Swift, of Fontenelle and Montesquieu and Voltaire."[28] There is little evidence that this school prophesied the achievement of perfect felicity for man and society.

Bernard Mandeville, a personal acquaintance of Franklin, joined the chorus of those who proclaimed the compatibility of human imperfection and the general harmony. "Private Vices, Public Benefits" was the subtitle of his famous *Fable of the Bees,* which Franklin owned and probably read. Mandeville's paradoxical doctrines must have been a powerful challenge to Franklin's young

26. Cf. A. O. Lovejoy's statement: "The authors who were perhaps the most influential and the most representative in the early and mid-eighteenth century, made a great point of reducing man's claims to 'reason' to a minimum." " 'Pride' in Eighteenth Century Thought," in *Essays in the History of Ideas* (Baltimore, 1948), p. 68.

27. Carl Becker, *Benjamin Franklin* (Ithaca, 1946), p. ix.

28. *Ibid.,* p. 31.

mind. "The Moral Virtues," Mandeville asserted in terms reminiscent of Machiavelli, "are the Political Offspring which Flattery begot upon Pride." While arguing that men are actuated by self-interest and that this self-interest promotes the prosperity of society as a whole, Mandeville maintains a rigorous standard of virtue, declaring those acts alone to be virtuous "by which Man, contrary to the impulse of Nature, should endeavour the Benefit of others, or the Conquest of his own Passions out of a Rational Ambition of being good."[29]

By making ethical standards so excessively rigorous, Mandeville rendered them impossible of observance, and indirectly (though intentionally) pointed out their irrelevance for practical life. The very rigor of his ethical demands in contrast to his practical devices suggests that Mandeville lacked "idealism." This was not the case with Franklin. The consciously paradoxical Mandeville could offer no salvation for the young Franklin caught on the horns of his own dilemma. Shaftesbury, Mandeville's *bête noire*—whose works were already familiar to Franklin—had a more promising solution. In his *Inquiry Concerning Virtue or Merit* (1699), Shaftesbury had asserted that man by nature possesses a faculty to distinguish and to prefer what is right—the famous "moral sense."

Franklin's option for Shaftesbury was made clear from his reprinting two dialogues "Between Philocles and Horatio, . . . concerning Virtue and Pleasure" from the *London Journal* of 1729 in the *Pennsylvania Gazette* of 1730. In the second dialogue, reason was described as the chief faculty of man, and reasonable and morally good actions were defined as actions preservative of the human kind and naturally tending to produce real and unmixed happiness. These dialogues until recently have been held to be Franklin's own work; however, a reference in the *Autobiography* to a "Socratic dialogue" and "a discourse on self-denial," tradi-

29. Bernard Mandeville, *The Fable of the Bees*, F. B. Kaye, ed., 2 vols. (Oxford, 1924), I, 48–49, 51. Franklin owned Mandeville's work, according to a list in the Mason-Franklin Collection of the Yale University Library. He was introduced to Mandeville during his first stay in London. *Writings*, I, 278.

tionally interpreted as concerning the two dialogues between Philocles and Horatio, recently has been shown to concern two pieces published in the *Pennsylvania Gazette* of 1735. The first piece is a dialogue between Crito and Socrates, never before correctly attributed to Franklin, in which he asserted that the "SCIENCE OF VIRTUE" was "of more worth, and of more consequence" to one's happiness than all other knowledge put together; in the second piece, a discourse on self-denial, Franklin combated the (Mandevillean) idea that "the greater the *Self-Denial* the greater the Virtue." Thirty-three years later, Franklin was still following Shaftesbury when he exhorted: "Be in general virtuous, and you will be happy." However, we shall see later that Franklin, in the last analysis, was not as far removed from Mandeville's pessimism as these cheerful views would suggest. His was a sort of middle position between Mandeville's "realism" and Shaftesbury's "idealism."[30]

THE IDEA OF PROGRESS

The restraining influence of the idea of the Great Chain of Being retained its hold on Franklin after his return to a more conventional recognition of good and evil. In his "Articles of Belief" of 1728 he said that "Man is not the most perfect Being but one, rather as there are many Degrees of Beings his Inferiors, so there are many Degrees of Beings superior to him."[31] Franklin presented the following question and answers to the discussions in the Junto:

Can a man arrive at perfection in his life, as some believe; or is it impossible, as others believe?

30. The proof that the two dialogues between Philocles and Horatio were not written by Franklin and the identification of the two other pieces have been furnished by Alfred O. Aldridge, "Franklin's 'Shaftesburian' Dialogues Not Franklin's: A Revision of the Franklin Canon," *American Literature,* XXI (May 1949), 151–159. See also *Writings,* I, 343; II, 168–169. The discourse on self-denial is printed in John Bigelow, ed., *The Complete Works of Benjamin Franklin,* 10 vols. (New York, 1887–1888), I, 414–417. The last quote, written in 1768, is in *Writings,* V, 159.

31. *Writings,* II, 92; see also X, 124, and Note 14 above.

Answer. Perhaps they differ in the meaning of the word *perfection.* I suppose the perfection of any thing to be only the greatest the nature of the thing is capable of. . . .

If they mean a man cannot in this life be so perfect as an angel, it may be true; for an angel, by being incorporeal, is allowed some perfections we are at present incapable of, and less liable to some imperfections than we are liable to. If they mean a man is not capable of being perfect here as he is capable of being in heaven, that may be true likewise. But that a man is not capable of being so perfect here, is not sense. . . . In the above sense, there may be a perfect oyster, a perfect horse, a perfect ship; why not a perfect man? That is, as perfect as his present nature and circumstance admit.[32]

We note here the acknowledgment of man's necessarily "imperfect" state of perfection. However, it is striking to see that Franklin refused to employ this theory as a justification of the status quo. Within certain bounds, change, or progress for the better, was possible. Many years later, Franklin was to use exactly the same argument in the debate on the status of America within the British Empire. A pro-English writer had presented the familiar argument of "cosmic Toryism" (and of conservatism in general, of course): "To expect perfection in human institutions is absurd." Franklin retorted indignantly: "Does this justify any and every Imperfection that can be invented or added to our Constitution?"[33]

This attitude differs from the belief in moral progress and perfectibility. There are, however, some passages in Franklin's later writings, better known than the preceding ones, which seem to suggest his agreement with the creed of moral progress and perfectibility. Two years before his death, looking with considerable satisfaction upon the achievements of his country and his own life, he explained to a Boston clergyman his belief in "the growing felicity of mankind, from the improvements in philosophy, morals,

32. Jared Sparks, ed., *The Works of Benjamin Franklin,* 10 vols. (Boston, 1836–1840), II, 554.
33. Franklin's marginal notes in [Matthew C. Wheelock], *Reflections Moral and Political on Great Britain and the Colonies* (London, 1770), p. 48. Franklin's copy in the Jefferson Collection of the Library of Congress.

politics"; he also stressed "the invention and acquisition of new and useful utensils and instruments" and concluded that "invention and improvement are prolific. . . . The present progress is rapid." However, he immediately added: "I see a little absurdity in what I have just written, but it is to a friend, who will wink and let it pass."[34]

There remains, then, a wide gulf between this qualified view of human progress and the exuberant joy over the progress of man's rational and moral faculties so perfectly expressed in the lines of a good friend of Franklin's, the British nonconformist clergyman and philosopher, Joseph Priestley:

Whatever was the beginning of this world, the end will be glorious and paradisiacal beyond what our imaginations can now conceive. Extravagant as some people may suppose these views to be, I think I could show them to be fairly suggested by the true theory of human nature and to arise from the natural course of human affairs.[35]

Franklin himself was well aware of this gulf. He distinguished sharply between man's intellectual progress and the steadily increasing power of man over matter, on the one hand, and the permanency of moral imperfection, on the other. He wrote to Priestley in 1782:

I should rejoice much, if I could once more recover the Leisure to search with you into the works of Nature; I mean the *inanimate,* not the *animate* or moral part of them, the more I discover'd of the former, the more I admir'd them; the more I know of the latter, the more I am disgusted with them. Men I find to be a Sort of Beings very badly constructed, as they are generally more easily provok'd than reconcil'd, more disposed to do Mischief to each other than to make Reparation, much more easily deceiv'd than undeceiv'd, and having more Pride and even Pleasure in killing than in begetting one another.

He had begun to doubt, he continued, whether "the Species were really worth producing or preserving. . . . I know, you have no such Doubts because, in your zeal for their welfare, you are taking

34. *Writings,* IX, 651. See also IX, 489, 530; I, 226.
35. Quoted by Bury, pp. 221–222.

a great deal of pains to save their Souls. Perhaps, as you grow older, you may look upon this as a hopeless Project."[36]

One is struck by the remarkable constancy of Franklin's views on human nature. In 1787 he tried to dissuade the author of a work on natural religion from publishing it. In this famous letter, we may find the quintessence of Franklin's concept of human nature. There is little of the trust in human reason which is so generally supposed to be a mark of his moral teachings:

You yourself may find it easy to live a virtuous Life, without the Assistance afforded by Religion; you having a clear perception of the Advantages of Virtue, and the Disadvantages of Vice, and possessing a Strength of Resolution sufficient to enable you to resist common Temptations. But think how great a Proportion of Mankind consists of weak and ignorant Men and Women, and of inexperienc'd, and inconsiderate Youth of both Sexes, who have need of the Motives of Religion to restrain them from Vice, and support their Virtue, and retain them in the Practice of it till it becomes *habitual*, which is the Great Point for its Security. . . . If men are so wicked as we now see them *with religion*, what would they be *if without it?*[37]

One is reminded of Gibbon's approval of conditions in the Rome of the Antonines, where all religions were considered equally false by the wise, equally true by the people, and equally useful by the magistrates.

THE BELIEF IN "REASON"

Reason as a temper in the conduct of human affairs counted much with Franklin, as we shall see later. However, reason as a faculty of the human mind, stronger than our desires or passions, counted far less. Often Franklin candidly and smilingly referred to the weakness of reason. In his *Autobiography,* he tells us of his struggle "between principle and inclination" when, on his first voyage to Philadelphia, his vegetarian principles came into conflict with his love of eating fish. Remembering that greater fish ate the

36. *Writings*, VIII, 451–452.
37. *Writings*, IX, 521–522. See also II, 203, 393, and IX, 600–601.

smaller ones, he did not see any reason why he should not eat fish: "So convenient a thing it is to be a *reasonable creature,* since it enables one to find or make a reason for every thing one has a mind to do."[38]

Reason as a guide to human happiness was recognized by Franklin only to a limited degree.

Our Reason would still be of more Use to us, if it could enable us to *prevent* the Evils it can hardly enable us to *bear.*—But in that it is so deficient, and in other things so often misleads us, that I have sometimes been almost tempted to wish we had been furnished with a good sensible Instinct instead of it.[39]

Trial and error appeared to him more useful to this end than abstract reasoning. "We are, I think, in the right Road of Improvement, for we are making Experiments. I do not oppose all that seem wrong, for the Multitude are more effectually set right by Experience, than kept from going wrong by Reasoning with them." Another time he put it even more bluntly: "What assurance of the *Future* can be better founded than that which is built on Experience of the *Past?*"[40] His skepticism about the efficacy of "reason" also appears in his opinion that "happiness in this life rather depends on internals than externals; and that, besides the natural effects of wisdom and virtue, vice and folly, there is such a thing as a happy or an unhappy constitution."[41]

There remains one problem with regard to Franklin's rather modest view of the power of human reason in moral matters: his

38. *Writings,* I, 267. See also V, 225, and IX, 512.

39. Carl Van Doren, ed., *The Letters of Benjamin Franklin & Jane Mecom* (Princeton, 1950), p. 112.

40. *Writings,* IX, 489, and IV, 250. On another occasion Franklin acknowledged the weakness of reason by the use of a pungent folk saying: "An Answer now occurs to me, for that Question of Robinson Crusoe's Man Friday, which I once thought unanswerable, *Why God no kill the Devil?* It is to be found in the Scottish Proverb, '*Ye'd do little for God an the Dell' were dead.*'" To John Whitehurst, New York, June 27, 1763 (unpublished letter in the Mason-Franklin Collection of the Yale University Library). Cf. also III, 16–17; IV, 120; VI, 424.

41. *Writings,* III, 457. See also IX, 548.

serenity—some might call it complacency—in spite of his awareness of the disorder and imperfection of human life. Sometimes, it is true, he was uneasy:

I rather suspect, from certain circumstances, that though the general government of the universe is well administered, our particular little affairs are perhaps below notice, and left to take the chance of human prudence or imprudence, as either may happen to be uppermost. It is, however, an uncomfortable thought, and I leave it.[42]

But on another occasion Franklin felt obliged to quiet the anxieties of his sister, who had been upset by his remark that men "are devils to one another":

I meant no more by saying Mankind were Devils to one another, than that being in general superior to the Malice of the other Creatures, they were not so much tormented by them as by themselves. Upon the whole I am much disposed to like the World as I find it, & to doubt my own Judgment as to what would mend it. I see so much Wisdom in what I understand of its Creation and Government, that I suspect equal Wisdom may be in what I do not understand: And thence have perhaps as much Trust in God as the most pious Christian.[43]

Indeed, Franklin's pessimism does not contain that quality of the tragic sense of life which inevitably presents itself wherever a recognition of the discrepancy between man's actual depravity and the loftiness of his aspirations exists.

We suggest a threefold explanation for this phenomenon: first of all, as we have pointed out, the complex of ideas associated with the concept of the Great Chain of Being, predominant at the time of Franklin's youth, worked in favor of bridging this gulf by lowering the goals of human endeavor. Secondly, the success story of his own life taught him that certain valuable things in human life can be achieved. Thirdly, we cannot help thinking that Franklin himself was endowed with that "happy constitution" which he deemed a requisite for true happiness in this life.

42. Rev. L. Tyerman, *Life of the Rev. George Whitefield*, 2 vols. (London, 1876), II, 540–541, quoted in Mott and Jorgenson, p. cxxxvi.
43. Van Doren, pp. 124, 125–126. See also *Writings*, II, 61; IV, 388; IX, 247.

THE PASSION OF PRIDE

Having discovered that Franklin acknowledged the imperfection of human reason and consequently the existence and importance of the passions to a greater degree than one might have supposed, let us specify in greater detail his insight into the nature of the two outstanding passions of social life, the desire for wealth and the desire for power—avarice and ambition. "That I may avoid Avarice and Ambition . . . —Help me, O Father," was Franklin's prayer in the "Articles of Belief" of 1728.[44]

The universal fame of Poor Richard and the description of Franklin's own "way to wealth" in his *Autobiography* (Franklin's account of his life ends with his arrival in London in 1757 for the first of his three great public missions in Europe) have led many people to see in Franklin only the ingenious businessman pursuing thrift for thrift's sake and money for money's sake. Nothing could be further from the truth than this conception. To be sure, he recognized the existence and the nature of avarice in unequivocal terms: "The Love of Money is not a Thing of certain Measure, so as that it may be easily filled and satisfied. Avarice is infinite; and where there is not good Oeconomy, no Salary, however large, will prevent Necessity."[45] He denied, however, that desire for more wealth actuated his work. His early retirement from business (1748) to devote himself to the higher things of life—chiefly to public service and scientific research—seems to prove this point.

Franklin considered wealth essentially as means to an end. He knew that it was not easy "for an empty sack to stand upright." He looked upon his fortune as an essential factor in his not having succumbed to corruption.[46] In a famous and often quoted letter to his mother, Franklin said that at the end of his life he "would rather have it said, *He lived usefully* than *He died Rich.*" At about the same time (two years after his retirement) he wrote to his printer

44. *Writings,* II, 99.
45. *Writings,* V, 325.
46. Van Doren, p. 123.

friend William Strahan in England: "London citizens, they say, are ambitious of what they call *dying worth* a great sum. The very notion seems to me absurd."[47]

On the other hand, the motive of power and prestige found much earlier recognition in Franklin's writings; he even confessed candidly that he himself was not free from this desire and from the feeling of being superior to his fellow men. At the age of sixteen, in his first secret contributions to his brother's *New-England Courant* (he wrote under the pseudonym of Mrs. Dogood), he gave a satisfactory definition of what we nowadays would call lust for power, and what was in the eighteenth century called Pride:

Among the many reigning Vices of the Town which may at any Time come under my Consideration and Reprehension, there is none which I am more inclin'd to expose than that of *Pride*. It is acknowledged by all to be a Vice the most hateful to God and Man. Even those who nourish it themselves, hate to see it in others. The proud Man aspires after Nothing less than an unlimited Superiority over his Fellow-Creatures.[48]

As Arthur O. Lovejoy has pointed out, the idea of pride was frequently contemplated during the earlier half of the eighteenth century.[49] There are two different, though not unrelated, conceptions of pride. First of all, it means "the most powerful and pervasive of all passions," which manifests itself in two forms: self-esteem and desire for the admiration of others. The second conception is closely connected with the idea of the Scale of Being; it means the generic pride of man as such, the sin against the laws of order, of gradation, the revolt of man against the station which has been allotted to him by the Creator.

These different conceptions of pride are indeed inseparable. In Franklin's own writings, the accent is on the first rather than on the

47. *Writings*, III, 5, 6. Cf. Benjamin Rush to John Adams: "The Doctor was a rigid economist, but he was in every stage of his life charitable, hospitable, and generous." August 19, 1811, in Rush, II, 1093.
48. *Writings*, II, 18–19.
49. Lovejoy, pp. 62–68.

second meaning. This topic runs through his work like a red thread. In 1729, at the age of twenty-three, he wrote that "almost every Man has a strong natural Desire of being valu'd and esteem'd by the rest of his Species."[50] Observations in a letter written in 1751 testify to his keen psychological insight:

What you mention concerning the love of praise is indeed very true; it reigns more or less in every heart, though we are generally hypocrites, in that respect, and pretend to disregard praise. . . . Being forbid to praise themselves, they learn instead of it to censure others; which is only a roundabout way of praising themselves. . . . This fondness for ourselves, rather than malevolence to others, I take to be the general source of censure. . . .[51]

Quite revealing with regard to our discussion is Franklin's well-known account of his project of an "Art of Virtue." His list of virtues to be practiced contained at first only twelve: "But a Quaker friend having kindly informed me that I was generally thought proud . . . I added *Humility* to my list. . . . I cannot boast of much success in acquiring the *reality* of this virtue, but I had a good deal with regard to the *appearance* of it."[52] His account of his rise in Pennsylvania's public life and politics reflects his joy and pride about his career. In 1737 he was appointed Postmaster of Philadelphia and Justice of the Peace; in 1744 he established the American Philosophical Society; in 1748 he was chosen a member of the Council of Philadelphia; in 1749 he was appointed Provincial Grandmaster of the Colonial Masons; in 1750 he was appointed one of the commissioners to treat with the Indians in Carlisle; and in 1751 he became a member of the Assembly of Pennsylvania. He was particularly pleased with this last appointment, and he admitted candidly that his ambition was "flatter'd by all these promotions; it certainly was; for, considering my low beginning, they were great things to me."[53]

50. *Writings*, II, 108.
51. *Writings*, III, 54–55.
52. *Writings*, I, 337.
53. *Writings*, I, 374. For Franklin's acknowledgment of his own political ambition, see *Writings*, V, 148, 206, 357; IX, 488, 621.

There is no change of emphasis with respect to pride during his long life. The old man of seventy-eight denounces the evil of pride with no less fervor, though with more self-knowledge, than the boy of sixteen:

In reality, there is, perhaps, no one of our natural passions so hard to subdue as *pride*. Disguise it, struggle with it, beat it down, stifle it, mortify it as much as one pleases, it is still alive, and will every now and then peep out and show itself; you will see it, perhaps, often in this history; for even if I could conceive that I had compleatly overcome it, I should probably be proud of my humility.[54]

Furthermore, the experience of English political life which he acquired during his two protracted stays in England (from 1757 to 1762, and from 1765 to 1775) made an indelible impression on his mind. The corruption and venality in English politics and the disastrous blunders of English politicians which Franklin traced back to this cause[55] probably were the main reasons why he advocated at the federal Convention of 1787 what he himself said some might regard as a "Utopian Idea": the abolition of salaries for the chief executive. The reason he gave for advocating such a step has hitherto not been appreciated as being of crucial importance for an understanding of his political thought:

There are two Passions which have a powerful Influence in the Affairs of Men. These are *Ambition* and *Avarice;* the Love of Power and the Love of Money. Separately, each of these has great Force in prompting Men to Action; but when united in View of the same Object, they have in many minds the most violent Effects. Place before the Eyes of such Men a Post of *Honour,* that shall at the same time be a Place of *Profit,* and they will move Heaven and Earth to obtain it.[56]

It has never been pointed out that this scheme of what might be called the "separation of passions" had been ripening in Franklin's

54. *Autobiography* (end of the part written in Passy, France, 1784), *Writings,* I, 339.

55. *Writings,* X, 62. See also V, 100, 112, 117, 133. See also Verner W. Crane, ed., *Benjamin Franklin's Letters to the Press, 1758–1775* (Chapel Hill, 1950), pp. 59, 164, 232.

56. *Writings,* IX, 591.

mind for several years. The first expression of it is to be found early in 1783.[57] In 1784 he mentioned it several times, and it is in these statements that we find one of the few allusions to the concept of checks and balances in Franklin's thought. He recommended: "Make every place of *honour* a place of *burthen*. By that means the effect of one of the passions above-mentioned would be taken away and something would be added to counteract the other."[58]

THE NATURE OF POLITICS

Franklin's frequent praise of the general welfare did not blind him to the fact that most other people had a much narrower vision than his own. "Men will always be powerfully influenced in their Opinions and Actions by what appears to be their particular Interest," he wrote in his first tract on political economy, at the age of twenty-three.[59] Fortunately, one of the very few memoranda and notes dealing with the studies and discussions of young Franklin which have come to our knowledge directly concerns this problem. Franklin himself, in his *Autobiography,* gives us the text of *"Observations* on my reading history, in Library, May 19th, 1731," which, in his words, had been "accidentally preserv'd":

That the great affairs of the world, the wars, revolutions, etc., are carried on and affected by parties.

That the view of these parties is their present general interest, or what they take to be such.

That the different views of these different parties occasion all confusion.

That while a party is carrying on a general design, each man has his particular private interest in view.

That as soon as a party has gain'd its general point, each member becomes intent upon his particular interest; which, thwarting others, breaks that party into divisions, and occasions more confusion.

That few in public affairs act from a mere view of the good of their

57. *Writings,* IX, 23.
58. *Writings,* IX, 170; see also 172 and 260.
59. *Writings,* II, 139.

country, whatever they may pretend; and, tho' their actings bring real good to their country, yet men primarily considered that their own and their country's interest was united, and did not act from a principle of benevolence.

That fewer still, in public affairs, act with a view for the good of mankind. . . .[60]

These lines do not mirror Shaftesbury's benevolent altruism; Franklin's contention that men act primarily from their own interest "and . . . not . . . from a principle of benevolence," "tho' their actings bring real good to their country," strongly suggests the general theme of Mandeville's work: "Private vices, public benefits."

Many decades after the foregoing observations, the contrast between Franklin's views on politics and those of the enlightened rationalism of contemporary France is clearly expressed in a discussion with the French Physiocrat Dupont de Nemours. Dupont had suggested that the federal Convention be delayed until the separate constitutions of the member states were corrected— according to Physiocratic principles, of course. Franklin mildly observed that "we must not expect that a new government may be formed, as a game of chess may be played." He stressed that in the game of politics there were so many players with so many strong and various prejudices, "and their particular interests, independent of the general, seeming so opposite," that "the play is more like *tric-trac* with a box of dice."[61] In public, and when he was propagandizing for America in Europe, Franklin played down the evils of party strife: after the end of the War of Independence he conceded somewhat apologetically that "it is true, in some of the States there are Parties and Discords." He contended now that parties "are the common lot of Humanity," and that they exist wherever there is liberty; they even, perhaps, help to preserve it. "By the Collision of different Sentiments, Sparks of Truth are struck out, and Political Light is obtained."[62]

60. *Writings,* I, 339–340. Cf. also II, 196, and IV, 322.
61. *Writings,* IX, 659; see also 241.
62. *Writings,* X, 120–121. See also IV, 35.

In private, Franklin did not conceal his suspicion that "unity out of discord" was not as easily achieved as his just-quoted method of obtaining "political light" might suggest. But he certainly did not believe that passions and prejudices always, or even usually, over-rule enlightened self-interest. He held that "there is a vast variety of good and ill Events, that are in some degree the Effects of Prudence or the want of it."[63] He believed that "reasonable sensible Men, can always make a reasonable scheme appear such to other reasonable Men, if they take Pains, and have Time and Opportunity for it. . . ." However, this dictum is severely limited by the conclusion: ". . . unless from some Circumstance their Honesty and Good Intentions are suspected."[64] That Franklin thought those circumstances to exist frequently, we learn from a famous message to George Washington, written in France in 1780. He told Washington how much the latter would enjoy his reputation in France, "pure and free from those little Shades that the Jealousy and Envy of a Man's Countrymen and Cotemporaries are ever endeavouring to cast over living Merit."[65]

Although Franklin himself talked so much about "Common Interests," he could be impatient when others built their arguments on this point. He observed that "it is an Insult on common sense to affect an Appearance of Generosity in a Matter of obvious Interest."[66] This belief in self-interest as a moving force of politics appears with rare clarity in marginal notes in a pamphlet whose author argued that "if the Interests of Great Britain evidently raise and fall with those of the Colonies, then the Parliament of Great Britain will have the same regard for the Colonists as for her own People." Franklin retorted:

All this Argument of the Interest of Britain and the Colonies being the *same* is fallacious and unsatisfactory. Partners in Trade have a *common* Interest, which is the same, the Flourishing of the Partnership Business:

63. *Writings,* VII, 358.
64. *Writings,* III, 41–42.
65. *Writings,* VIII, 28. Cf. the expression of the same idea thirty-six years earlier in *Writings,* II, 242.
66. Crane, p. 183.

But they may moreover have each a *separate* Interest; and in pursuit of that *separate* Interest, one of them may endeavour to impose on the other, may cheat him in the Accounts, may draw to himself more than his Share of the Profits, may put upon the other more than an equal Share of the Burthen. Their having a common Interest is no Security against such Injustice. . . .[67]

DEMOCRACY

It is fair to ask how Franklin's views on the above matters square with his avowal of radically democratic notions after 1775. In view of the foregoing, Franklin would not, it seems, agree with the underlying assumptions of Jeffersonian democracy, stated by Jefferson himself: "Nature hath implanted in our breasts a love of others, a sense of duty to them, a moral instinct, in short, which prompts us irresistibly to feel and to succor their distresses. . . ." It was also Jefferson who believed "that man was a rational animal, endowed by nature with rights, and with an innate sense of justice."[68] On this faith in the rationality and goodness of man, the theory of Jeffersonian democracy has been erected. Vernon L. Parrington said of Franklin that "he was a forerunner of Jefferson, like him firm in the conviction that government was good in the measure that it remained close to the people."[69] Charles A. Beard, discussing the members of the federal Convention, tells us that Benjamin Franklin "seems to have entertained a more hopeful view of democracy than any other member of that famous group."[70] All this must seem rather strange in view of the none too optimistic conception of

67. Marginal comments in *Good Humour, or, A Way with the Colonies* (London, 1766), pp. 26–27. Franklin's copy is in the library of the Historical Society of Pennsylvania, Philadelphia. This comment is reprinted in Jared Sparks, ed., *A Collection of the Familiar Letters and Miscellaneous Papers of Benjamin Franklin* (Boston, 1833), p. 229.

68. Jefferson to Thomas Law, June 13, 1814, and to Judge William Johnson, June 12, 1823, quoted by Adrienne Koch, *The Philosophy of Thomas Jefferson* (New York, 1943), pp. 19, 139.

69. Vernon L. Parrington, *The Main Currents of American Thought,* 3 vols. (New York, 1930), I, 176–177.

70. Charles A. Beard, *An Economic Interpretation of the Constitution* (New York, 1913), p. 197.

human nature which we have found in Franklin. His radically democratic views after 1775—before that time his outlook seemed essentially conservative—baffled contemporary observers as they have later students.

There is, as a matter of fact, plenty of evidence of Franklin's sincere devotion to monarchy during the greater part of his life. It was the most natural thing for him to assure his friend, the famous Methodist preacher George Whitefield, that a settlement of colonies on the Ohio would be blessed with success "if we undertook it with sincere Regard to . . . the Service of our gracious King, and (which is the same thing) the Publick Good."[71] Franklin loved to contrast the corruption of Parliament and the virtues of George III. To an American friend, he said that he could "scarcely conceive a King of better Dispositions, of more exemplary virtues, or more truly desirous of promoting the Welfare of all his Subjects."[72]

Another "conservative" aspect of Franklin which cannot be glossed over lightly is his acceptance of the Puritan and mercantilistic attitude towards the economic problems of the working class. Throughout his life he was critical of the English poor laws. He deplored "the proneness of human nature to a life of ease, of freedom from care and labour," and he considered that laws which *"compel the rich to maintain the poor"* might possibly be "fighting against the order of God and Nature, which perhaps has appointed want and misery as the proper punishments for, and cautions against, as well as necessary consequences of, idleness and extravagance."[73] This was written in 1753. But as late as 1789, long after he had come out for the political equity of the poor and for a radical theory of property, he still confirmed to an English correspondent that "I have long been of your opinion, that your legal provision for

71. *Writings*, III, 339. See also II, 377–378; IV, 94, 213.

72. *Writings*, V, 204; see also 261. Another sign of Franklin's antiradical attitude during his stay in England is his disgust with the Wilkes case. See *Writings*, V, 121, 133, 134, and 150. Also Carl Van Doren, ed., *Letters and Papers of Benjamin Franklin and Richard Jackson, 1753–1785* (Philadelphia, 1947), p. 139.

73. *Letters and Papers of Benjamin Franklin and Richard Jackson,* pp. 34, 35.

the poor is a very great evil, operating as it does to the encouragement of idleness."[74]

Franklin's endorsement of democracy is most emphatically revealed in his advocacy of a unicameral legislature for the Common-
wealth of Pennsylvania, as well as for the federal government. The
issue of unicameral versus bicameral legislative bodies—an issue
much discussed in the latter decades of the eighteenth century—
reflected faithfully, as a rule, the clash of views of two different
theories of human nature and of politics. The bicameral system was
based on the principle of checks and balances; a pessimistic view
of human nature naturally would try to forestall the abuse of power
in a single and all-powerful assembly. On the other hand, most of
those who trusted in the faculties of human reason did not see the
necessity for a second chamber to check and harass the activities
of a body of reasonable men.

In the case of Franklin, however, this correspondence of political
convictions with views on human nature is lacking. He was the
president of the Pennsylvania Convention of 1776 which—almost
uniquely among the American states—set up a unicameral system.
This, of course, filled many of the French *philosophes* with great
joy. Franklin, they supposed, had secured a triumph of enlightened
principles in the New World. Condorcet, in his "Éloge de Franklin,"
had this to say:

Franklin's voice alone decided this last provision. He thought that as
enlightenment would naturally make rapid progress, above all in a
country to which the revolution had given a new system, one ought to
encourage the devices of perfecting legislation, and not to surround
them with extrinsic obstacles. . . . The opinion contrary to his stands
for that discouraging philosophy which considers error and corruption
as the habitual state of societies and the development of virtue and
reason as a kind of miracle which one must not expect to make enduring. It was high time that a philosophy both nobler and truer should

74. *Writings,* X, 64. See for an elaboration of his arguments "On the
Labouring Poor," *Writings,* V, 122–127, and "On the Price of Corn, and
Management of the Poor," *Writings,* V, 534–539.

direct the destiny of mankind, and Franklin was worthy to give the
first example of it.[75]

As a matter of fact, it has since been shown that Franklin, who
at the time of the Pennsylvania Convention also served in the Continental Congress, played a minor role in the adoption of the unicameral system. The unicameral legislature was rooted in the historical structure of Pennsylvania's proprietary government.[76] This,
however, is irrelevant from our point of view, since Franklin endorsed and defended the unicameral system in his "Queries and
Remarks respecting Alterations in the Constitution of Pennsylvania," written in November, 1789.[77]

In the opposition to checks and balances and a second chamber,
Franklin's most famous companion was Thomas Paine, author of
The Age of Reason. This similarity of views between Franklin and
one of the most vocal spokesmen of the creed of reason and the
perfectibility of man perhaps contributes to the misinterpretation of
Franklin's position among the eighteenth-century philosophers.
Paine's arguments against the system of checks and balances and
for a single house were characteristic of the later Enlightenment:

Freedom is the associate of innocence, not the companion of suspicion.
She only requires to be cherished, not to be caged, and to be beloved is,
to her, to be protected. Her residence is in the undistinguished multitude of rich and poor, and a partisan to neither is the patroness of all.[78]

This argument, of course, presupposes the rationality and goodness
of human nature. We might perhaps agree with Paine that "no man
was a better judge of human nature than Franklin,"[79] but Paine
certainly did not have Franklin's conception of human nature.

75. O'Connor and Arago, III, 401–402.
76. See J. Paul Selsam, *The Pennsylvania Constitution of 1776* (Philadelphia, 1926), and Charles M. Andrews, *The Colonial Period of American
History,* 4 vols. (New Haven, 1934–1938), III, 320.
77. *Writings,* X, 54–60.
78. "A Serious Address to the People of Pennsylvania on the Present
Situation of their Affairs" (December 1778), in Philip S. Foner, ed., *The
Complete Writings of Thomas Paine,* 2 vols. (New York, 1945), II, 284.
79. "Constitutional Reform" (1805), *ibid.,* pp. 998–999.

The reasons for Franklin's almost radical attitude in 1776 and 1787 appear in his own writings. One thing seems certain: belief in the goodness and the wisdom of the people is *not* at the root of his democratic faith. This idea is quite foreign to Franklin. Discussing the Albany Plan of Union in 1754, he thought that "it is very possible, that this general government might be as well and faithfully administered without the people, as with them."[80] Nor did he fundamentally change his view in the last years of his life. "Popular favour is very precarious, being sometimes *lost* as well as *gained* by good actions." In 1788, he wrote publicly that "popular Opposition to a public Measure is no Proof of its Impropriety."[81] What a strange democrat it was who told the federal Convention that "there is a natural Inclination in Mankind to kingly Government."[82] The most plausible and popular reason for belief in democracy, then, is eliminated.

On the other hand, Franklin did not believe in the intrinsic goodness of the wealthy or the wisdom of the powerful; he had no liking for aristocratic government, be it by an aristocracy of wealth or an aristocracy of birth. He was scornful of the House of Lords and thought "Hereditary Professors of Mathematicks" preferable to hereditary legislators because they could do less mischief.[83]

It is noteworthy that in the whole of Franklin's work only one reference to Montesquieu can be found; and that concerns his ideas on criminal law. Separation of powers, the role of the aristocracy in a healthy society—these are doctrines which never took possession of Franklin's mind.

The antithesis between Adams, under the influence of Harring-

80. *Writings,* III, 231; see also 309.

81. *Writings,* IX, 564, 702. In 1788, Franklin repeatedly said that there was at present the "danger of too little obedience in the *governed,*" although in general the opposite evil of "giving too much power to our *governors*" was more dreaded. *Writings,* IX, 638; and X, 7.

82. *Writings,* IX, 593.

83. *Writings,* VI, 370–371. For other attacks on the principle of hereditary honors and privileges, in connection with the Order of the Cincinnati, see *Writings,* IX, 162, 336.

ton, and Franklin, chiefly influenced by his own experience, is re-markably complete. Adams wrote:

It must be remembered that the rich are *people* as well as the poor; that they have rights as well as others; they have as clear and as *sacred* a right to their large property as others have to theirs which is smaller; that oppression to them is as possible and wicked as to others. . . .[84]

Franklin mounts a formidable counterattack:

And why should the upper House, chosen by a Minority, have equal Power with the lower chosen by a majority? Is it supposed that Wisdom is the necessary concomitant of Riches . . . and why is Property to be represented at all? . . . The Combinations of Civil Society are not like those of a Set of Merchants, who club their Property in different Proportions for Building and Freighting a Ship, and may therefore have some Right to Vote in the Disposition of the Voyage in a greater or less Degree according to their respective Contributions; but the important ends of Civil Society, and the personal Securities of Life and Liberty, these remain the same in every member of the Society; and the poorest continues to have an equal Claim to them with the most opu-lent. . . .[85]

It is this strong objection against the attempt to use—openly or covertly—a second chamber as a tool of class rule which seems to underlie Franklin's disapproval of the bicameral system. Franklin, it should be pointed out, was aware of the necessity and inevitability of poises and counterpoises. This is shown by his attempt, referred to above, to create a sort of balance of passions, checking avarice

84. Quoted by Zoltán Haraszti, *John Adams and the Prophets of Progress* (Cambridge, Mass., 1952), p. 36.
85. "Queries and Remarks . . . ," *Writings*, X, 58–61. For Franklin's dis-agreement with the bicameral system of the United States Constitution, see *Writings*, IX, 645, 674. The paradox of Franklin's attitude is thrown into relief if one considers that even Jefferson, in his *Notes on Virginia*, raised his voice against the dangers of an "elective despotism," and exalted "those benefits" which a "proper complication of principles" would produce. Paul Leicester Ford, ed., *The Works of Thomas Jefferson* (New York and London, 1904–1905), IV, 19.

with ambition. There exist some, though quite rare, allusions to a balance-of-power concept in his utterances on imperial and international relations. The most pointed and direct reference to the idea of checks and balances, however, may be found in an unpublished letter to a well-known figure of Pennsylvania politics, Joseph Galloway, in 1767. Franklin discussed and welcomed a new circuit bill for the judges of Pennsylvania. He suggested and encouraged an increase in the salaries to be granted by the Assembly for the judges to offset the nominating and recalling powers of the Proprietor: "From you they should therefore receive a Salary equal in Influence upon their Minds, to be held during your Pleasure. For where the Beam *is moveable,* it is only by equal Weights in opposite scales that it can possibly be kept even."[86]

Consequently, the arguments of Thomas Paine or the French *philosophes,* which derive their validity from assumptions about the goodness or rationality of human nature, do not hold in the case of Franklin. In a brilliant recent essay it has been suggested that "despite the European flavor of a Jefferson or a Franklin, the Americans refused to join in the great Enlightenment enterprise of shattering the Christian concept of sin, replacing it with an unlimited humanism, and then emerging with an early enterprise as glittering as the heavenly one that had been destroyed."[87] As far as Franklin is concerned, however, the alternatives of Calvinist pessimism and the "unlimited humanism" of the European Enlightenment do not really clarify the essential quality of his political thought. His thought is rooted in a climate of opinion which combined the rejection of the doctrine of Original Sin with a rather modest view of human nature.

It seems, then, that the desire for equality, rather than any rationalistic concepts, offers the clue to an adequate understanding of those elements in Franklin's political thought which at first sight appear inconsistent with his not too cheerful view of human good-

86. April 14, 1767 (William L. Clements Library, Ann Arbor, Michigan).
87. Louis Hartz, "American Political Thought and the American Revolution," *The American Political Science Review,* XLVI (June 1952), 324.

ness. His striving for equality also suggests a solution to the thorny problem of reconciling his democratic views after he had decided for American independence with his faithful loyalty to the Crown before that date. The American interest obliged him to fight against Parliament—an aristocratic body in those days—while remaining loyal to the King; in recognizing the King's sovereignty while denying the Parliament's rights over the colonies, Franklin by necessity was driven into a position which—historically speaking—seemed to contradict his Whig principles. The complaining Americans spoke, as Lord North rightly said, the "language of Toryism."[88] During the decade before 1775 Franklin fought for the equal rights of England and the colonies under the Crown. But his desire for equality went deeper than that. In his "Some good Whig Principles," while conceding that the government of Great Britain ought to be lodged "in the hands of King, Lords of Parliament, and Representatives of *the whole body* of the freemen of this realm," he took care to affirm that *"every man* of the commonalty (excepting infants, insane persons, and criminals) is, of common right, and by the laws of God, *a freeman"* and that "the poor man has an *equal* right, but *more* need, to have representatives in the legislature than the rich one."[89] It has not been widely known that Franklin, in a conversation with Benjamin Vaughan, his friend and at the same time emissary of the British Prime Minister Lord Shelburne during the peace negotiations of 1782, has confirmed this view. Vaughan reported to Shelburne that "Dr. Franklin's opinions about *parliaments* are, that people should not be rejected as electors because they are at *present* ignorant"; Franklin thought that "a statesman should meliorate his people," and Vaughan supposed that Franklin "would put this, among other reasons for extending the privilege of election, that it *would* meliorate them." It was Franklin's opinion, Vaughan thought, "that the lower people are as we see them, because oppressed; & then their situation in point of

88. Quoted by G. H. Guttridge, *English Whiggism and the American Revolution* (Berkeley, 1942), p. 62.
89. *Writings*, X, 130.

manners, becomes the reason for oppressing them."[90] The fact is that Franklin's overriding concern for equality foreshadows the attacks of the socialism of later generations on the absolute sanctity of private property:

All the Property that is necessary to a Man, for the Conservation of the Individual and the Propagation of the Species, is his natural Right, which none can justly deprive him of: But all Property superfluous to such purposes is the Property of the Publick, who, by their Laws, have created it, and who may therefore by other Laws dispose of it, whenever the Welfare of the Publick shall demand such Disposition.[91]

Franklin's previously quoted speech in the federal Convention provides us with an essential insight: he expressed belief in "a natural Inclination in Mankind to kingly Government." His reasons are revealing: "It sometimes relieves them from Aristocratic Domination. They had rather one Tyrant than 500. It gives more of the Appearance of Equality among Citizens; and that they like."[92] Equality, then, is not incompatible with monarchy.

From all this a significant conclusion may be drawn. It is an oversimplification to speak of Franklin's "conservatism" before 1775 and of his "radicalism" after 1775. Professor MacIver illustrates the conservative character of the first stage of American political thought preceding the appeal to natural rights by reference to Franklin, who, in spite of his later attacks on the Order of the Cincinnati, "nevertheless clung to the principle of a hereditary, though constitutional monarchy, until the tide of revolution rendered it untenable."[93] The term "conservative" does not do justice to the possibility of paying faithful allegiance to a monarchy and still disliking aristocracies of heredity or wealth. Because of his

90. Benjamin Vaughan to Lord Shelburne, November 24, 1782 (Benjamin Vaughan Papers in the American Philosophical Society, Philadelphia. Photostat in the Benjamin Vaughan Collection in the William L. Clements Library, Ann Arbor, Michigan).

91. *Writings*, IX, 138 (written in 1783). See also X, 59.

92. *Writings*, IX, 539.

93. R. M. MacIver, "European Doctrines and the Constitution," in Read, p. 55.

innate desire for equality, as well as his defense of the American cause against the encroachments of Parliament, Franklin found it much easier to be a monarchist. Monarchy, rather than aristocracy, was compatible with those elements of his thought which after 1775 made him a democrat.

Another of the factors which, while not incompatible with monarchical feelings, contributed greatly to Franklin's acceptance of democracy, is the belief which he shared with Hume that power, in the last analysis, is founded on opinion. "I wish some good Angel would forever whisper in the Ears of your great Men, that Dominion is founded in Opinion, and that if you would preserve your Authority among us, you must preserve the Opinion we us'd to have of your Justice."[94] He thought that "Government must depend for it's Efficiency either on Force or Opinion." Force, however, is not as efficient as Opinion: "Alexander and Caesar . . . received more faithful service, and performed greater actions, by means of the love their soldiers bore them, than they could possibly have done, if, instead of being beloved and respected, they had been hated and feared by those they commanded." Efficiency, then, became an argument for democracy. "Popular elections have their inconvenience in some cases; but in establishing new forms of government, we cannot always obtain what we may think the best; for the prejudices of those concerned, if they cannot be removed, must be in some degree complied with."[95]

It has rarely been noticed how detached Franklin, the greatest champion of democracy in the federal Convention, was from the problem of the best government. His speech at the conclusion of the deliberations of the Constitutional Convention may give us a clue to the perplexing problem of why he gave comparatively little attention to the theoretical questions of political philosophy and devoted almost all his time to the solution of concrete issues. He stated his disagreement with several points of the Constitution,

94. Van Doren, ed., *Letters and Papers of Benjamin Franklin and Richard Jackson*, p. 145 (written in 1764). See also *Writings*, VI, 129; IX, 608.
95. Crane, p. 193; *Writings*, II, 56; III, 228. See also III, 231; V, 79.

nevertheless urging general allegiance and loyalty to its principles. Asking his colleagues to doubt a little their feeling of infallibility, Franklin summed up the experience of his life: "I think a general Government necessary for us, and there is no *form* of government but what may be a blessing to the people, if well administered."[96] Perhaps in speaking these words he was thinking of one of the favorite writers of his younger days, Alexander Pope:

> For Forms of Government let fools contest;
> Whate'er is best administer'd is best.[97]

THE DUALITY OF FRANKLIN'S POLITICAL THOUGHT

There are two outstanding and sometimes contradictory factors in Franklin's political thought. On the one hand, we find an acute comprehension of the power factor in human nature, and, consequently, in politics. On the other hand, Franklin always during his long life revolted in the name of equality against the imperfections of the existing order. He himself stated the basic antithesis of his political thought: Power versus Equality.

Fortunately, Franklin's notes on the problem at hand have been preserved; they are to be found in his marginal comments to Allen Ramsay's pamphlet, *Thoughts on the Origin and Nature of Government,* which presents the straight view of power politics. Franklin rebelled against the rationalization and justification of the power factor. "The natural weakness of man in a solitary State," Ramsay proclaimed, "prompts him to fly for protection to whoever is able to afford it, that is to some one more powerful, than himself; while the more powerful standing equally in need of his service, readily receives it in return for the protection he gives." Franklin's answer is unequivocal: *"May not Equals unite with Equals for common Purposes?"*[98]

96. *Writings,* IX, 607.
97. Pope, "Essay on Man," Epistle 3, *Selected Works,* p. 124.
98. [Allen Ramsay], *Thoughts on the Origin and Nature of Government* (London, 1769), p. 10. Franklin's copy in the Jefferson Collection of the Library of Congress. (My italics.)

In the last analysis, Franklin looked upon government as the trustee of the people. He had stated this Whig principle in his very first publication as a sixteen-year-old boy[99] and he never deviated from it. So in opposition to Ramsay's doctrine, according to which the governed have no right of control whatsoever, once they have agreed to submit themselves to the sovereign, Franklin declared the accountability of the rulers:

If I appoint a Representative for the express purpose of doing a business for me that is for *my Service* and that of others, & to consider what I am to pay as my Proportion of the Expense necessary for accomplishing that Business, I am then tax'd by my own Consent.—A Number of Persons unite to form a Company for Trade, Expences are necessary, Directors are chosen to do the Business & proportion those Expences. They are paid a Reasonable Consideration for their Trouble. Here is nothing of weak & Strong. Protection on one hand, & Service on the other. The Directors are the Servants, not the Masters; their Duty is prescrib'd, the Powers they have is from the members & returns to them. The Directors are also accountable.[100]

Franklin refused to recognize that power alone could create right. When Ramsay declared that according to nature's laws every man "in Society shall rank himself amongst the Ruling or the Ruled, . . . all Equality and Independence being by the Law of Nature strictly forbidden . . . ," Franklin rejoined indignantly, "I do not find this Strange Law among those of Nature. I doubt it is forged. . . ." He summarized Ramsay's doctrine as meaning that "He that is strongest may do what he pleases with those that are weaker," and commented angrily: "A most Equitable Law of Nature indeed."[101]

On the other hand, Franklin's grasp of the realities of power inevitably involved him in moral and logical ambiguities of political decision. At times he expressed the tragic conflict of ethics and politics. Characteristic of the peculiar contradiction within his political thought was this statement three years before the Declara-

99. "Dogood Papers," *Writings,* II, 26. Cf. Crane, p. 140.
100. Marginal notes to Ramsay, *op. cit.,* pp. 33–34.
101. *Ibid.,* pp. 12, 13.

tion of Independence on England's prospects in the Anglo-American conflict: *"Power* does not infer *Right;* and, as the *Right* is nothing, and the *Power* (by our Increase) continually diminishing, the one will soon be as insignificant as the *other."*[102] In this instance, obviously, he was trying to make the best of both worlds. But there were times when he was only too well aware of the conflict of these two worlds. In a passage which seems to have escaped the notice of most students of his political thought, Franklin observed that *"moral and political Rights sometimes differ, and sometimes are both subdu'd by Might."*[103]

The measured terms of Franklin's political thinking present a striking contrast to the optimism and rationalism which we usually associate with the Age of Enlightenment. Franklin's insight into the passions of pride and power prevented him from applying the expectation of man's scientific and intellectual progress to the realm of moral matters. To be sure, he would not deny the influence of scientific insights upon politics, and he thought that a great deal of good would result from introducing the enlightened doctrines of free trade and Physiocracy into international politics. But Franklin, unlike many of his friends in France, was never inclined to consider these and other ideas as panaceas. The mutual adjustment of interests would always remain the chief remedy of political evils. It was in this domain that reason, as a temper in the conduct of human affairs, made its greatest contribution to his political thought. Moderation and equity, so he had been taught by his experience (rather than by abstract reasoning), were true political wisdom. His belief that the rulers ought to be accountable, together with his more pragmatic conviction that force alone, in the long run, could not solve the great problems of politics, brought forth his declaration of faith that "Government is not establish'd merely by *Power;* there must be maintain'd a general Opinion of its *Wisdom* and *Justice* to make it firm and durable."[104]

102. *Writings,* VI, 87.
103. *Writings,* VIII, 304. (My italics.)
104. Carl Van Doren, ed., *Benjamin Franklin's Autobiographical Writings* (New York, 1945), pp. 184–185. Cf. *Writings,* IV, 269; VII, 390.

Bibliographical Note

Franklin's life has been frequently chronicled, but the definitive story cannot be told until the complete Yale edition of his papers is published. Thus far thirteen volumes have appeared, containing all the correspondence that Franklin wrote and much that he received up to 1766; some further thirty volumes are planned to cover the rest of his long life. Superbly edited by Leonard W. Labaree and his associates, ton, 1954); and Esmond Wright, *Benjamin Franklin and American* Philosophical Society, are among the finest products of contemporary American historical scholarship. They are infinitely fuller and more accurate than previous editions of Franklin's *Works* by his grandson, Temple Franklin (6 vols., 1818), by Jared Sparks (10 vols., 1836–1840), by John Bigelow (10 vols., 1887–1888), and by A. H. Smyth (10 vols., 1905–1907). Franklin's *Autobiography* has been issued in many editions, the best being *Benjamin Franklin's Memoirs,* the Parallel Text Edition, edited by Max Farrand (University of California, 1949). It recounts Franklin's life only until 1757.

There are a number of single-volume biographies of Franklin. Among them are Carl Van Doren, *Benjamin Franklin* (New York, 1938); Verner W. Crane, *Benjamin Franklin and a Rising People* (Boston, 1954); and Esmond Wright, *Benjamin Franklin and American Independence* (London, 1966). Carl Becker's sketch of Franklin in *The Dictionary of American Biography* (New York, 1931) is still excellent reading. Some useful essays are collected in J. H. Smythe, ed., *The Amazing Benjamin Franklin* (New York, 1929), and Verner W. Crane has edited *Benjamin Franklin's Letters to the Press 1758–1775* (Chapel Hill, N.C., 1950). Gerald Stourzh has written a thoughtful essay on Franklin's ideas in *Benjamin Franklin and American Foreign Policy* (Chicago, 1954). There are three excellent collections of the correspondence of Franklin with particular individuals: Carl Van Doren, ed., *Letters and Papers of Benjamin Franklin and Richard Jackson 1753–1785* (Philadelphia, 1947); William Greene Roelker, ed., *Benjamin Franklin and Catharine Ray Greene* (Philadelphia, 1949); and Carl Van Doren, ed., *The Letters of Benjamin Franklin and Jane Mecom* (Princeton, 1950). There are some admirable background studies; especially noteworthy are Carl and Jessica Bridenbaugh, *Rebels and Gentlemen, Philadelphia in the Age of Franklin* (New York, 1942), reprinted in paperback (New York: Oxford University Press, 1962), a picture of a "mature, urbane and democratic culture"; Carl Bridenbaugh's *Cities in Revolt: Urban Life in America 1743–1776* (New York, 1955); Frederick B. Tolles, *Meeting House and Counting House: The Quaker Merchants of Colonial Philadelphia* (Chapel Hill, 1948), and his *Quakers and the Atlantic Culture* (New York, 1960). The volumes of *The Pennsylvania Magazine of History and Biography* are also invaluable. For a hostile view, D. H. Lawrence's essay in *Studies in Classic American Literature* (New York, 1923) and William Carlos Williams, *In the American Grain* (New York, 1956) are pungent and vigorous. So is William Cobbett, *Porcupine's Works* (London, 1801), IV, 32–33.

Contributors

I. BERNARD COHEN is Professor of the History of Science at Harvard University. He has received Guggenheim and National Science Foundation fellowships and is the author of *Benjamin Franklin, His Contribution to the Making of the American Tradition* (1953).

PAUL W. CONNER received his doctorate in political science from Princeton University, where he was also on the teaching staff. He is now an associate professor at Pace College in New York City. He is the author of *Poor Richard's Politicks: Benjamin Franklin and His New American Order* (1965).

VERNER W. CRANE retired as Professor of History at the University of Michigan in 1959, after a long and distinguished career. He published *Southern Frontier, 1670–1732* (1928), *Benjamin Franklin, Englishman and American* (1936), and *Benjamin Franklin and a Rising People* (1954).

WHITNEY GRISWOLD (1906–1963) was the President of Yale University and, prior to that, was a member of Yale's History Department for many years. He published *The Far Eastern Policy of the United States* (1938).

DAVID LEVIN is Professor of English at Stanford University. He is the author of *History as Romantic Art* (1959) and *In Defense of Historical Literature* (1967). Mr. Levin is also editor of *The*

Puritan in the Enlightenment: Franklin and Edwards (1963), *Bonifacius: An Essay upon the Good* by Cotton Mather, and *Jonathan Edwards* (1968), a companion volume in this series.

RICHARD B. MORRIS is Gouverneur Morris Professor of History at Columbia University. He has taught at the College of the City of New York and Princeton University, and was Fulbright research scholar at the University of Paris. Among his books are *Alexander Hamilton and the Founding of the Nation* (1957), *The Peacemakers* (1965), and *John Jay, the Nation and the Court* (1967).

CLINTON ROSSITER is John L. Senior Professor of American Institutions at Cornell University. Among his published works are *Seedtime of the Republic* (1953), *The American Presidency* (1956), and *Seventeen Eighty-Seven: The Grand Convention* (1966).

GERALD STOURZH is Professor of American History at the Free University of Berlin. His article included in this volume appeared in the *American Political Science Review* and subsequently became the first chapter in his *Benjamin Franklin and American Foreign Policy* (1954), published by the University of Chicago Press under the auspices of the Center for the Study of American Foreign Policy at the University of Chicago.

FREDERICK B. TOLLES is Professor of Quaker History and Research and director of the Friends Historical Library at Swarthmore College in Pennsylvania. He is the author of *Meeting House and Counting House: The Quaker Merchants of Colonial Philadelphia* (1948), *James Logan and the Culture of Provincial America* (1957), and *Quakers and the Atlantic Culture* (1960).

CARL VAN DOREN (1885–1950) was Benjamin Franklin's great biographer and one of America's great men of letters. He was headmaster of the Brearley School, lecturer at Columbia University, editor of *Cambridge History of American Literature,* and author of a number of distinguished biographies. His biography of Franklin won the Pulitzer Prize in 1938.

ESMOND WRIGHT has been a Member of Parliament since March, 1967, when he won a by-election in Glasgow. He has been a member of the House of Commons Committee investigating student problems in British universities and is joint author of the seven-volume report on this. Until his election, he was Professor of Modern History at the University of Glasgow and Chairman of the British Association for American Studies. With degrees from the universities of Durham in England and Virginia in the United States, Professor Wright is transatlantic in his interests. Among his books are *Fabric of Freedom: 1763–1800* (1961), biographies of Washington (1957) and Franklin (1966), and *Causes and Consequences of the American Revolution* (1966), which he edited. He has also edited *Illustrated World History* (1964) and the twenty-volume *History of the World in Colour* (1970).

✪

AïDA DIPACE DONALD holds degrees from Barnard and Columbia and a Ph.D. from the University of Rochester. A former member of the History Department at Columbia, Mrs. Donald has been a Fulbright Fellow at Oxford and the recipient of an A.A.U.W. fellowship. She has published *John F. Kennedy and the New Frontier* and *Diary of Charles Francis Adams*.

DATE DUE